THE HEALING

PARTNERSHIP

THE HEALING PARTNERSHIP

The Patient as Colleague
in Psychotherapy

Bernard Steinzor, Ph.D.

HARPER & ROW, PUBLISHERS

New York, Evanston, and London

FIRST EDITION

LIBRARY OF CONGRESS CATALOG CARD NUMBER: 67-11344

A-R

CONTENTS

PREFACE

I am a psychotherapist, a professional healer. I am sought out by people who have been led to believe that I can give them something special—a way to a meaningful life and a measure of happiness. Those who come to my office are often willing to make a considerable sacrifice in time and money in return for this something.

As a psychotherapist, a man systematically educated to be a healer, I am usually believed to have a conceptual base from which I work, an operative philosophy to guide me, and even perhaps a systematic blueprint by which to chart the way to success with my patients. Of course, I do have a philosophy, but it is part of my philosophy not to believe in blueprints where people, in their infinite variety, are concerned.

A therapist stands a bit apart from his philosophy as he confronts his patient person to person—which should give him pause before he relies wholeheartedly on any particular school. He stands apart from his "system" because he can never separate himself from his own humanity, from his own experiences of grief and joy and searching which create a bond with his patient much firmer than intellectual loyalty to a concept could ever be. In short, the voices of his experience are more compelling than the tenets of his system.

My voices have compelled me to set forth in this book what my years as a psychotherapist have taught me about the healing relation, not as it rests upon a systematic foundation, but as it thrives in the strength-giving medium of personal interaction and response.

For most patients seeking help in clinics, family agencies and the like—and we should remind ourselves that such patients far outnumber those who come to the private practitioner—the theories the therapist proclaims or the school to which he professes his allegiance are irrelevant. They seek someone with whom they can talk things over, from whom they can get advice or at least another point of view to help with their problems.

It is only the educated individual who shows some curiosity about the therapist's philosophy of the healing relation. I think it would be a good idea and quite useful for every patient to obtain from the therapist a concrete description—perhaps even in writing—of just what philosophy he is "selling." The patient does have the right to know what kind of person he is choosing and what he is "buying." And since we therapists prize honesty, we should warn the patient that it does make sense to hesitate before entering psychotherapy. A democratic society is based on the making of choices which grow out of the voter's consideration of as much information as can be obtained. Throwing in one's lot with a therapist is one of the most crucial votes a person can cast.

This volume is thus addressed to persons who are considering therapy, to persons who are and have been patients, and to all my colleagues who call themselves healers. Rather than bemoan diversity, we should articulate it, because, as I will try to demonstrate, the therapeutic relation is as simple and at the same time as complex, as obvious and as mysterious, as any relation informed by love, equality and justice. This view is, I think, a consequence of the social character of men. It is justified by the present knowledge we have about therapeutic relationships, and it is consistent with the ideals of our democratic culture. And, I believe, it is required by the latest ideas regarding science as a method of gaining knowledge of the various worlds in which we live.

One title I could have given this book is *Healing Is Meeting.* Whenever we meet a person, there is psychotherapy. It is present in the concrete reality of relationships in which we experience change. The word "psychotherapy" itself suggests that only in a professional relation can there be healing of the mind. I shall try to alter this prevailing impression in the first chapter. Here, for example, is a patient saying to me that it is the contact which heals, in a letter she wrote after a session during which we clarified a series of misunderstandings between us:

You speak about the rapid pace at which our sessions have progressed. It strikes me the same way, but I think for different reasons. You speak of it in terms of changes that have taken place, the big example of that being the correspondence with my father. I, however, am not so impressed with the changes, apparent as they are to me, but rather by the fact of our relationship. It absolutely amazes me—in fact, I find it nothing short of a miracle—that you and I have anything remotely resembling a rapport. I have never in my whole entire life talked with an "adult" the way I talk to you. Every time I think about it, I am amazed.

I am grateful to her and to all the people who have opened their doors to me, whether our engagement was as patient with doctor or as friends or as colleagues. In the anecdotes I tell, I hope the persons will recognize themselves. I have tried to keep each person's confidence through eliminating identifiable facts and giving him or her a pseudonymous first name. Yet I hope this effort to maintain confidentiality and to make a point of which the incident is an illustration have not led me to distort the events so that participants do not remember them as I do. In fact, to those patients, the degree to which I am successful in not distorting an event is a measure of my appreciation of them. There are many other patients whom I remember but who never directly enter these pages. To them I can only say that I do believe they have also affected me.

In writing the first draft of this book, I became aware that my "voices of experience" had the habit of turning out to be academic and abstract voices. I was, I believe, rather well educated and trained for my profession, and the strongest emphasis in academic work is on so-called basic ideas and the description of theoretical orientations. This has left me with built-in commands to rationalize basic issues and to cite relevant authorities—who, of course, are chosen because they agree with me—before I get down to cases. And since my professional colleagues rather expect this of me, I become a little anxious unless I reveal how studious I am and how well I know "the literature."

So, following the advice I often give to patients, I will go against my grain. I will discuss in the last four chapters some of the issues which provide a "scientific" rationale for my ways of meeting a person. Along the way to these closing chapters I will try to convey something of the ambiguities of the healing relation, including the relation between what goes on in the inner sanctum and what is happening in the world at large. I will discuss the ambiguous problems inherent in the patient's payment of a fee and my making a living out of being human. I will articulate my approach to the interpretation of the images that possess us at night, our dreams. Since everyone must have a vision of what makes for a joyful life and what causes suffering, I will present my "wisdom" on the nature of celebration and tragedy. And running through the entire volume, as well as being presented in a special chapter, will be the values which infuse the healing relation with meaning. Here I will give a central place to the value of equality: that the core of what makes for change is the recognition that the patient and I have equal power for good and for evil.

We also have the power to change, and it is in the context of the necessity for constant renewal and development that my ideas should be considered. For example, what I offer now I believe in fully, but I look forward to a time when I will look back on these words from a different perspective and will review my ages of man in a different spirit. I hope that I will then have changed enough to want to amend what I now hold to be true.

Among those to whom I am indebted I wish to mention one colleague in particular. Dr. Daniel D. Williams of Union Theological Seminary invited me to join him in a seminar on religion and psychiatry. It was during the sessions of the seminar that I found a new voice, so that the spring of 1964 will always be remembered by me as a time when I experienced a sense of breaking out of the systems of thought I had been following, of creating something new. Too often, my anxiety that my colleagues respect my ideas, and the requirement that I justify my right to be a scientific psychologist, had hampered my saying what I sensed. Not so with Dan, whose books brought to me a deeper appreciation of other ways to grasp the redeeming spirit of life.

The quotations which appear in this book are themselves acknowledgments that we live during a time of great change in our concepts of therapy. I do not see myself as being far out in front, but rather as somewhere in that group comprising the vanguard of a movement reaffirming a faith in the power of life in action. And I am sure that there are many other authors in this vanguard whose work

I have not met. I am grateful to all those who have influenced my thoughts, wittingly and unwittingly.

Learning to reveal my office lives in writing has been therapeutic for me. Mr. Richard McAdoo and Mr. Norbert Slepyan are the doctors of writing, called editors at Harper & Row, who helped me describe my thinking more clearly than I thought was possible.

Most important of all is the luck of meeting Luciana, who helped me become a more open person than I had been. She and I have made marriage the healing relation—bar none—that it is supposed to be. This has then encouraged me to participate more in self-revelation with others and given me an unshakable belief in the possibilities of love.

THE HEALING

PARTNERSHIP

I

ON SCHOOLS AND SYSTEMS

The currents of change presently transforming our concepts of healing are many. Psychotherapy continues to proliferate and expand into more and more "schools"—which may seem to the interested observer and especially to the interested patient to be a sorry state of affairs. For instance, a recent book on contemporary psychotherapies lists on its jacket the following types of therapy, each one of which is represented in its pages by one of the school's outstanding leaders or disciples: Adlerian, client-centered, group, interpersonal, transactional, family, interactional and family, existential, reparation-adaptational and psychoanalytic.[1]* This is far from all. Without effort I can think of a half-dozen glaring omissions—Jungian, Rosenian, Wolpian, Salterian, Kleinian and Gestalt—and I am sure there are another six or more which can be added by anyone inclined to do so, since, according to still another writer, there are three dozen systems from which the patient can choose.[2]

Should someone ask me, "To what school do you belong?" I usually answer, "Steinzorian." I hasten to add that I'm not about to establish still another organization, but that it is my whole being, in all my lived and dreamed-of lives—my "voices of experience" —which infuses my interpretations, advice, actions, hopes and confrontations. If pressed far enough, I could add that my allegiance is American; my values are to some extent an amalgam of my working-class background and my present economic level; my idea of progress is affected by the Judaeo-Christian spirit of Western cul-

* Superior numbers refer to Notes, beginning on page 249.

ture; my choice as the most significant person in modern psychotherapy is Freud; the teacher who has inspired me most is Carl
Rogers; my latest enthusiasm and applause for authors in my field
are directed at Jerome Frank and Thomas Szasz—and so on. And
with hardly any provocation I will quote an entry Dag Hammarskjöld made in his *Markings* which articulates my theory as well or
better than any other few lines I know:

False-furtive. When shut out of the room, you must not peep through
the keyhole. Either break down the door or go away.

False-furtive. Only among people to whom the truth would have
seemed a denial of your choice. Nevertheless, whatsoever your reasons
for concealment, so long as you feel ashamed it may, in spite of everything, turn out for the good.[3]

In sum, I can review and list all the social systems and relations
which have shaped my thoughts, directed my passions and still left
me with an invaluable sense of freedom to recognize a new creation.

In the future, descriptions of psychotherapeutic theories may be
largely autobiographical, for much of what goes on in the office is a
telling of stories. The patient's story, so everyone agrees, should be
directly disclosed. He should drop his disguises and be his real self.
The doctor's story, so most of us agree, should have been revealed
to his own doctor, filtered and purified through his own education,
and then organized into a set of techniques. The paradoxical quality
of this view of the doctor's story is discernible in the very keystone
of the arch that modern psychology has dedicated to the nature of
man. We have been taught, quite correctly, that the ideas we use to
describe other relations are inextricably and deeply rooted in the
experience of our own lives, just as novelists relive and reweave their
memories through characters who are fictional only in the narrowest
sense. And if we agree with Freud's central idea that in our intimate
relationships our actions are overdetermined by forces not in our
consciousness, it follows that in the intimacy of the consulting room
the therapist is also acting out of his entire being.

FAITH AND DOUBT

The most significant fact which should give a therapist pause
before he invests his faith in his own approach or in the theory he

espouses is the very existence of the multitudinous types or schools of psychotherapy. Though he must have faith and hope in himself and his ideas as being potentially useful to many and actually helpful to some, he must also preserve a measure of doubt in his particular creed. That there are many schools of treatment brings to mind the large number of religious denominations and sects, and generally the large number of approaches—both sacred and secular—which have been made to the problems of suffering people.

Faith and doubt have always been experiences central to sacred orientations. As a continuing and hopeful quest for the meaning of life, faith brings people into relation with others and ultimately into confrontation of the mystery embodied in the coexistence in life of immeasurable possibilities and the certainty of death. At the core of the mystery is the person's solitary involvement with the universal, with his God, which at any moment may be heart-rendingly felt as a state of forsakenness. For the Christian, the depths of faith and doubt are most profoundly expressed in the last moments of Jesus on the Cross, between his crying out at his sense of abandonment and his utterance of love in the assertion that his tormentors knew not what they did. Similarly, Moses grasped the tablets in the blinding presence of Jehovah and Job transformed his tribulations into affirmations of his faith. Though bound, Prometheus could still shake his fist in affirmation. In solitary meditation, the Buddha sensed his contact with the cosmos, as did Mohammed simmering in the desert.

The differences among philosophies, sects and religions therefore lie in the variations of the beliefs, values and rituals by which each expresses the *universal* experience of the ambiguity of existence. Although we realize that particular beliefs arise within the limits of particular cultures at particular times in history, sadly enough we find it difficult to maintain a sense of the relativity of our own time and place. History is a woeful story of how differences in the expression of faith have become "heretical" conflicts which have in turn degenerated into wars to determine the "right" versions of the commandment to love. In a wink, any one of the myriad of ideas used to conceptualize hope and fate may become like a cherished child, to be defended as a matter of principle. Even institutions and systems established to liberate men from the abuses of power may develop such inertia that they themselves are perpetuated by ideologies and rituals which interfere with the humanization of life.

Yet values, ideologies and a common concern for those very problems which occupy religious people lie at the heart of the therapeutic relationship. The therapist, be he psychiatrist, psychologist, social worker, marriage counselor, pastoral counselor or other, is a descendant of the shaman, the medicine man, the faith healer and the witch doctor. There is an element of truth in the popular image of the psychotherapist as a "headshrinker."

The patient and the doctor must, therefore, share a common belief in the *good sense* of their meetings and have a common faith that there are meanings to be revealed in the patient's suffering. The patient must aspire to change; he must believe he can change, and hope that the differences in him will be lovingly affirmed by those who matter to him. At its best the therapeutic relation is a means to inspiration, for it is an actualization of the possibility of a true meeting between persons in honesty, warmth and respect.

The person who enters patienthood is, of course, intensely preoccupied with faith, doubt, suffering and joy. The person who enters doctorhood, though he should be more self-possessed than the patient, also becomes quite as concerned with clarifying his own beliefs, self-criticism and the sources of his love and anguish. Otherwise, why, as he trains for his profession, should he need to undergo analysis or need to become aware of his own prejudices?

The Quality of Information

However sensible the foregoing ideas may be, the fact is that we therapists have been taught otherwise. We have been trained to take what a patient tells us as information which is brought in for our objective attention, very much like the data presented to a physician by an ailing person or to a pathologist by a cadaver at an autopsy. Clearly, I don't believe this can be, as my relations to cherished friends and to my family tell me it can't. In a relation concerned with the gamut of life, what information emerges depends largely on the passions, convictions, interests, prejudices, attitudes and even gestures of the two people. Should the data from a relationship appear similar to those arising from another, seeming thus to warrant a generalization applicable to others, it is mainly because we share our culture, our language and our assumptions about the nature of reality. And if we observe continuities in a person's behavior —and call them facts—it is only because the person is geared by the social and biological systems in which he is behaving to run in the same, repetitive way.

Because of this, practitioners in different therapeutic schools do get different information, or at least they report what they get according to the theory toward which they are disposed. It has become commonplace to say that Freudians get Freudian dreams, Adlerians get Adlerian dreams and Jungians, Jungian dreams. As in the case of a teacher dealing with students who desire only to "pull down" good grades, the doctor is often fed back just what he feeds—and the patient "improves" in much the same way as the parroting student "learns."

"Convergence of beliefs" may be as useful a phrase to define successful therapy as any other. Yet could such a thing be brainwashing? Could it be faith healing? Maybe some of both. Each therapeutic system so far developed has tended to perpetuate itself to the point where these systems are impoverished out of a lack of concepts which might stimulate change. Revisions proceed, though rather slowly, sometimes under the impact of a patient who just won't fit into the conceptual mold, but usually under the duress of a disciple who becomes a heretic and a leader of a new school. Even if the therapist doesn't write a new dogma for others, he will continue to change through meeting his patients in the unfolding complexity of their lives.

Finally, the rationalization of faith into a set of articulate ideas about the self and reality is a value in itself, though not necessarily an ultimate truth. In our Judaeo-Christian tradition self-awareness has a highly significant value. Certainly it appeals to well-educated, sensitive and refined people. The concepts of modern psychotherapy are loaded with abstract signs and ideas based on the verbalizations of highly articulate people—that is, except for a few who write about children and the mute cries of the totally estranged whom we call psychotics. And even the observers of children too often proceed into their work on the basis of their sophisticated communion with adults. It might be a good idea for all therapists to begin training with children or psychotics and stay with them until they can look a mute child straight in the eye and wrestle on the floor or stand in silence with a deluded man. For all we know, it is the distended nostril, the wandering eye and the impact of gesture and stance which make the difference. To the sophisticate this may appear as plain quackery, but healing does occur on the basis of such magic and guileless faith.

Faith in the potency of the relation between two people, in the power of meaningful communication outside the limits of systems and schools, in the healing quality of educated but nonsystematic psychotherapy and in what my experiences as a person and therapist tell me in terms of abstract ideas and concrete happenings—this essential faith and the lessons uttered by these voices are the foundation of my confidence as a doctor, and they form the substance of this book.

2

OUT OF THE INNER SANCTUM

The cloister has undergone a metamorphosis from sanctuary to museum. On Sundays or holidays we stroll through the enclosures, admiring the lofty tower and glancing at the chancel. Yet where do we moderns, a people who have included the pursuit of happiness within a trinity also sanctifying life and liberty, go to find the way to peace of the spirit?

When God is dead, with whom do we lament our trembling faith? Those who falter before the need to relate with humanity, who sense their solitary core and cannot reach out to some part of mankind in affection, who in the midst of the crowd momentarily awaken to their being neither better nor worse than their fellow strangers, but who, still in boredom, turn away from them—where can they go?

When you cannot work well and love well and even pray well, you are told to seek help in an office before an asylum or some frantic activity hardens your heart. Thus the therapeutic chamber has become the sanctuary, and it is a powerful sanctum. So intense may be the patient's longing for a close relationship that the center of gravity of his interests can—and often does—shift toward concern only for the sessions with the therapist. He may live for the appointed time of the session, and consequently neglect the hours of living called for beyond the session. Understandably, the relationship to the therapist must be different enough from all the patient's other relations if it is to enable him in time to use therapy to alter his contacts with others. The patient and the therapist are there so they may in time get out of there, but it may easily happen that when action with others is under scrutiny, the therapeutic situation can become an end in itself rather than the means of liberation.

The aim of psychotherapy could be defined as the development of a relationship which, in its openhearted readiness to consider the ambiguities and uncertainties of hope, faith, love and indignation, makes it desirable and feasible for the patient to act in the world with others. In an open, expanding society, tasks, responsibilities and opportunities challenge each person. New roads open before us— sometimes quite suddenly—by design to provide us with pleasure or adventure or by accident to demand of us courage and sacrifice. Such opportunities do—and should—compete for the patient's interest and therefore can—and should—cause the therapeutic pair to be humble in their endeavors.

Take the word "psychotherapy." It calls for both the counselor and the client to believe in a very special providence that is more important than any other in effecting a cure. Who would not sacrifice much for mental health in a land where medical miracles prolong the body's existence beyond all previous expectation? The Greek ideal of a healthy mind in a healthy body is one of the first things we are taught. Everyone is told, "Your health comes first." The doctor (how often I am called "Doctor" and nothing else) is believed to be a far more powerful adversary against suffering because he is half-facetiously called a headshrinker. All too often we "headshrinkers" ourselves tag such a label as a "negative reaction" to therapy. Such mockery actually reflects more the familiarity of a teasing friend than an expression of doubt.

Give a relationship a scientific name, such as psychotherapy, and there is set in motion the tendency to forget that in science nothing is sacred. Psychologists cannot agree on a commonly accepted definition of the psyche which distinguishes "it" from the mystic soul. Whether it be called ego, self or mind, the words defining the limits of these structures have been more graciously and stirringly used by poets and prophets. Yet psychotherapy has its highly special aura because American practitioners tend to believe that rational research into the causes of psychopathology is the major, if not the only, way to improve its administration. Freud reminded us of the limits of science, but he said, too, that what science cannot give us no other approach to the interpretation of existence can.[1]

Nevertheless, always before the two in the office should be the question: "Why are we discussing this complaint and why are you not describing your feelings to your friend, your lover, your supervisor? Why do you choose to tell me this?" If the therapist does not raise this question, the implication conveyed to the patient is that only through the therapist will true revelation appear, like a miracle vision in the desert. The patient must be confronted with his choice in bringing any thought or feeling before the doctor rather than elsewhere. When he says, "I cannot speak to my boss," he assumes responsibility for his inhibition. Once he has done so, possible explanations for his inability become the center of attention, and the person turns his sensibilities to the reality of the relationship in which he claims he cannot act.

For me it has become a proven hypothesis that the patient really knows his feelings about those people with whom he says he is anguished and exasperated. He knows somewhere why he avoids a confrontation with another. This hypothesis can be demonstrated with any particular patient. "Do you have any diaries you kept as an adolescent? Have you, perchance, written down any dreams before you came for help? Do you have any old photographs or letters which show you in contact with your parents? Read and look at them. You'll see how wise you were before you came to me for wisdom."

When I ask the patient why he is telling me instead of speaking with his parents, I affirm the value of openness. In effect, I say to him, "Look them in the eyes; you will find revealed your truths and know why you are frightened. You long for a close friendship with your father, yet you do not act with him. Yes, you have been repeatedly rebuffed. The fact that you came to speak with me says you have not given up, that you do care for those who you believe have hurt you and who have not listened enough. But we are here to make it possible for you to become as clear as you can at this time in your life, to find out how thick is the door, how much you must knock and whether it will open. Only you through your participation in living with others outside the office will justify our being together."

Patients are not the only ones who object to speaking their mind. I have practiced within the belief that I am best able to judge whether the patient will act fairly or "act out" to hurt himself and dominate others. There are occasions when I still become frightened that the patient will get himself into a mess and only make trouble for others, that he will lose his job, commit an offense against the law or say something which will break again a fragile but treasured friendship. A comment such as "I think your anger is exaggerated" means that in my empathy with the person's images of life I would not feel as intensely as he does. This is a personal judgment, and if other professionals should agree with it, that is because we all have assimilated a common code which shapes our passions. Response is judgment and evaluation, and thus I try to assess the impact of my values on the person. Among those whom I remember as the most tormented are the people who were constantly asking, "What is *appropriate* behavior?" Whenever I have tried to define this, the patient has become even more confused.

When I have become afraid that something drastic might occur, I have learned to confess my anxiety rather than interpret his fantasies of revenge only as sado-masochistic impulses. I admit to the patient my momentary intolerance for his intense feelings toward others and my anxiety, which, though it may be motivated by affectionate protectiveness, may also have welled up because I have in my life failed to assess possibilities and dangers, and have run away or behaved badly. "I am your doctor, I am involved in what happens in your life, and I want you to know not only those of my opinions which may point to a way, but also where my doubts and my own mistakes may close the clearing you have been making."

But a confession of my anxiety is not enough. I also think of another reason why we therapists often are conformists to a dominant value of our social class. When we tell the patient to think before he acts, to know himself before he engages himself with another, we are judging that he and his intended partner are weaklings in danger of collapse at the first display of intense feelings, be they of pleasure or anger. I have come to see that even the most disturbed person can take an honest expression of thought and that his disturbances or withdrawal are often consequences of being treated like a coward and driven into isolation.

Sharing Responsibility

To develop such a partnership based on openness must be our goal from the outset. How, then, do I meet with the person for the first time so that if we do agree to go on, we will have begun by placing our "official" relationship properly among all the others which could be therapeutic for him, and thus start on the way out of our sanctum? As I will set forth in greater detail in the chapter "The Defacement of Persons," I hope to convey to the prospective patient that the relationship he and I are considering is one for which we are equally responsible.

The patient requests help. He asks me whether I think he needs it and may wonder if I think I can help him. In this way he plays the proper role. When you go to a doctor, it is for him to look you over, to diagnose and to prognosticate. For him to do so effectively, you must answer all his questions honestly. How lopsided this is becomes readily apparent as soon as we remember that whenever we go to a helper, such as a physician or a lawyer, we actually are as occupied in looking him over as he is in surveying us and our problems. As clients we usually do not inquire about him directly, but we do get our impressions some way, by observing his manner, by noting the nature of his questions, by studying his reactions, or perhaps by comparing him with others of his profession we may already have consulted. We may even compare him with an image we carry with us as to what a doctor or lawyer should be like. At any rate, though we may never voice them to the man himself, we form our judgments of him.

Extending this to psychotherapy, we run against a peculiar paradox. Psychotherapists impress upon the public the great significance of unspoken impressions and unconscious communications and yet rarely ask their patients, "What is your diagnosis of me, and why?" And yet our patients' ideas about us will directly influence our ability to help them. I try to cut through this paradox by speaking to each patient in some such terms as these: "You probably expect me to interview you, to ask you why you are here and to determine whether I think I can help you or whether I think you need help. If that is necessary in your case, you would be a usual 'case.' But as I'm here to discover something about you, you are here to discover me, too. I'll be glad to answer any questions you have about me as clearly as I can. If I don't know the answer, I'll of course say so."

Since my experience has taught me that I should never try to help someone whom I immediately dislike, I listen to my responses to his person, and if my first impression is negative, I refer him elsewhere. In this spirit of equality, I ask the patient what his first impression is of me. If it is negative, I indicate that this could be sufficient reason for him to go to someone else. So accustomed are people coming to psychotherapists to think that it is they who have to prove their right to be "taken on" that they neglect to ask the therapist to reveal enough of himself so they can choose. Some patients have been given my name and it is the only one they have. They accept me because otherwise they would have to start shopping around. I encourage "shopping." The patient should not select a suit of clothing if it doesn't fit, let alone a therapist in whom he will entrust his secrets, if the therapist isn't the right person to receive them.

The patient is too often inhibited by the community of psychotherapists from recognizing his right to choose. I know of no book or paper which counsels the person to choose and which makes this a critical issue of the first session. When I have discussed it with colleagues, the argument has been raised that the patient may feel rejected if I tell him that I need to choose him on the basis of my positive feelings for him as a person and that he may feel unable to say what he feels toward me because he is confused. That may be so, and I do say to the patient, "You have a choice which you cannot avoid, but which is difficult since you are here presumably because you cannot trust your judgment of people. But I'll try to help you make it."

Sometimes a patient may come to a clear decision about continuing to see me before I do. If I am not yet sure, I say so. I told one such patient, Barbara, this when she exclaimed, "I have made up my mind about you." In the following session I realized why I had hesitated when she had not. "Barbara, I'm about the fourth doctor you've come to see and you also have said how dependent you get. I hesitated because at the first meeting I had been feeling overworked and just wasn't sure I was ready to take on your kind of burdens." She was visibly appreciative, and remarked that she usually would feel rejected. I added that she and I had begun through frankness so that if I became impatient with her demands she could be sure I would say so.

As a way of emphasizing the significance of personal choice and of liking one another, I refuse to discuss my fee before the patient and I have agreed to work together. The majority of patients want to know what I "charge," and some even request the "price" on the phone. I answer, "After we are sure we want to continue meeting, we can discuss the fee. If we don't agree on the financial part of our contract, it is better we part on that basis. Otherwise the necessity of personal choice is obscured by issues of money." This attitude is generally quickly understood, though I think it is also accepted because the patient already has a fairly good idea as to the fee before he even comes to the doctor's office.

If, from the very beginning, the doctor and the patient emphasize the mutuality of their meeting, the artificiality of psychotherapy is reduced. The uniqueness of therapy is then more a matter of the uniqueness of two people involved rather than of the procedures and structures assumed to be necessary for the practice of the profession.

Therapy: Terminable and Interminable

I have borrowed this heading from one of Freud's papers in which he considered criteria for determining when an analysis was completed. Affirming that at times the idea of termination is meaningless, he wrote: "So not only the patient's analysis but that of the analyst himself ceased to be a terminable and became an interminable task."[2]

Though Freud was thinking of analysis as that which occurs only with an analyst, his idea that self-examination and self-revelation are lifetime pursuits was very much in line with the direction of social evolution in the nineteenth century. Self-consciousness had then become, and is even more so today, the dominant value of educated people. With this in mind, the official therapeutic relation can be seen as one among many which concretize this value. When a patient asks, "How long will therapy take?" I can answer, "For the rest of your life—and I wish you a very long one." And I add, "But our meetings will cease as quickly as we can possibly help you become involved in relations which aren't dull and in which you can act spontaneously."

Many therapists speak with each other and with their patients about interrupting psychotherapy, or about being in the beginning, middle or closing phase of the therapeutic process. We do this as if we had reliable criteria by which we could determine a cure has occurred. Actually the word "cure" is no longer in good standing among therapists because it implies the elimination of disease. The term smacks too much of antibiotic bullets aimed at specific infectious organisms, as if a good shot eradicated the noxious agent and restored the person to good health. The problems of life which bring the person to a professional are not of this order, and many psychotherapists do not wish to be thought of as curing anything.

The Rogerian approach has dealt with this question in the simplest way: "You come as long as you wish."[3] This take-when-needed approach has much to recommend it, but I think the rationale given by Rogers and his students for this practice is inadequate. The Rogerian attitude says in effect: "I'll teach you to take full responsibility by denying that I have any for what takes place." The moral imperative is overbearingly recited: "You should take responsibility." The incompleteness of the Rogerian approach has been revealed by applying it to the person who considers not returning for further sessions because of the onset of suicidal thoughts. Though the expression of the counselor's understanding of the client's torment can help, the necessity for a more active intervention or engagement with the client may be required because the client's experience that the therapist cares needs to be demonstrated at times by other means than verbal empathy.

I am suggesting that the ambiguities of the criteria involved in any statements referring to cessation of psychotherapy should be clarified directly with the patient to help him place the therapeutic relationship in balance. My attitude regarding the desirable way to stop coming is: "Whenever you wish to stop, I want you to bring it up and we can consider it as a real possibility. I do not believe in termination of therapy, except in the sense that you and I no longer meet regularly. I do not think it is correct, either, to think of therapy as being interrupted, during vacation times or whenever you stop coming. I think of healing as a continuous process which is felt as centering on one or another relationship. Our relation as doctor and patient is being transformed all the time. When you stop coming regularly, that is only one obvious marker of the transformation of our relation. Another occurs when you wish to see me again after we haven't met regularly for some time. I hope you could feel it possible to stop and return at will. I am even ready to see you on a P.R.N., take-when-needed basis."

Leslie, a bright eighteen-year-old, was considering therapy. She told me she was afraid of beginning because she had reason to believe that it would drive her into being overly dependent, and that it was this quality which troubled her most. Her mother had been under psychiatric care for many years, but wasn't helped by it at all, and Leslie had met other people who could not make a decision without first squaring it with their analysts. Apparently she had accepted the idea that psychotherapy required some procedures which limit the individual's freedom. After I discussed with her what she meant by independence—being able to live alone in her apartment rather than not needing someone to talk with—I affirmed my P.R.N. approach. Looking a little startled, she responded, "But I thought that was to happen *after* therapy!" "Of course," I teased, "as a reward for your good behavior you will be permitted to come and go as you please." In like manner, other patients have been indoctrinated before they have seen me to believe, for instance, that the frequency of sessions is related to success. It is my responsibility to clarify with the person what his notions are about the proper procedures in therapy and to criticize such views through marshaling the best kinds of evidence we have.

I go on to say to the prospective patient, "Whatever we decide, or whatever you decide with or without my 'blessing,' we cannot put an end to our relation. It may be an end to formal sessions, in the same way the schedule we adopted marked the beginning of formal therapy. But neither you nor I can cut out any relation which has had significance for us. Certainly my thoughts will turn to you after we stop, though *perhaps* with less frequency than yours will turn to me. I accent the 'perhaps.' Once you and I became engaged for better or worse, parts of our beings were linked—probably more of your selves with me than mine with you, since you came to me and you revealed more than I did. Sometimes I have felt that I was more involved with a patient than he with me, but this is relatively less frequent. This fact is in itself a motivation to stop coming. It is frustrating and inequitable and will help you get out of here. You will feel like leaving when you enter into other relations which are more satisfying and less frustrating than ours, when you no longer feel the need for 'purchasing friendship,'[4] but give and take with people as an equal. That is why I try to remember my limits in being with you and emphasize the many ways we are equal. This should help you wish to stop paying—that is, to stop coming. I look forward as an occasion for celebration when you can say, 'Why pay for a relation in which revelation, constant revelation, is defined as the process of living?' "

Schools of psychotherapy employ their particular jargon for describing the criteria used in assessing the patient's improvement. The specific languages speak of such matters as the reduction of anxiety, the diminution of symptoms, increased ego strength, increased self-awareness, more appropriate use of defenses, increase of positive self-regard, increase of self-criticalness, increase in the tolerance of others, increase in the direct expression of feelings toward others and so on. Research psychologists have devised highly elaborate and sophisticated tools for measuring these variables. They have had success in demonstrating that patients do change and benefit from a period of formal treatment or counseling in terms of these admittedly ambiguous but still measurable dimensions.[5]

I find that if I continually observe the patient in terms of any of these criteria I am encouraging him to go about with a thermometer in his mouth and his fingers on his pulse. This is an uncomfortable position at best, and one in which many patients have been going about before they sought professional help. The patient is usually plagued with the ailment of self-watchfulness and self-consciousness. Rather than increase his grip on his pulse, I act with him to encourage a fuller experience of our relationship. I do this by letting go of my watchfulness over his strengths or weaknesses and, instead, emphasizing that he will stop coming when our relationship makes less of a difference than do all the others in which he is involved.

Related to this is the question of how often we should meet. Often the frequency of meeting is determined by the fee and the patient's resources. Yet under the influence of the psychoanalytic tradition of four or five sessions per week as the best and most intensive therapy, patients still ask how often it is desirable to come. I used to say that I preferred twice a week, giving as my reason that twice a week provided continuity while at the same time stimulating the patient to act in his other relations. I believed then that meeting every day tended to induce an attitude of putting matters off until the next visit. More recently I have simplified my answer to "How often would you like to come?" For I don't know of any evidence that frequency of sessions is positively correlated with success—whatever we mean by that. In fact, the available research suggests that the *duration* of formal therapy may be of some importance.[6] One study has even indicated that a time-limited relationship of a certain kind was, for a group of patients, as good as, if not better than, an open-ended one.[7] In another study it was found that, while therapists emphasized the length of treatment as a criterion of successful outcome (of course, the longer, the better), the patients who were satisfied with their experience in therapy hardly mentioned the length of time. For the patients, the important factor was the way they remembered the therapist as a person of understanding and one who cared.[8]

So I say to the patient, "Let us induce you to trust your feelings by beginning with your decision as to how often you wish to come. If, as we go along, either one of us wants to meet more or less often, we can always discuss it, and we can stop at any time."

"Deep" Versus "Not So Deep" Therapy

Some patients tell me that they do not need deep therapy, that is, psychoanalysis. Others ask me if they need an analyst rather than a therapist or a marriage counselor. Whenever I inquire what the patient means by these statements, I hear the essential arguments made by eminent authorities for differentiating types of therapy. The patient tells me, in a less sophisticated and therefore more comprehensible language, that deep therapy means coming three or more times a week and delving into the past, especially the sordid effects of childhood conceits. Superficial therapy has to do with the reality of here and now and ignores the essence of existence.

Curt, a very bright nineteen-year-old sophomore, had been struggling for years with homosexual impulses. He knew quite a lot about psychoanalysis, having read in the field and discussed his therapy with friends who were in analysis. Apparently he became restless with my approach to him, which emphasized acting with others. He complained, half jokingly, that this approach wasn't deep enough. "I'm acting more firmly with my friends and feel much better about not being a coward, but when do we get to the essentials of why I am changing?" Gordon Allport, in effect, answered Curt when he wrote: "The individual's conscious report and the contemporary thrust of his motives are rejected as untrustworthy in favor of a backward tracing of his conduct to earlier formative stages."[9]

I usually do not pursue the matter further. The patients have as much right to bother themselves with these differences as do the experts. But I do occasionally suggest that the attempt to distinguish depth therapy from others is as fruitful as the attempt to determine whether learning how to read is more or less significant than learning the most profound philosophies or the most difficult of sciences. Actually this analogy is deficient. It doesn't take into account the extent to which a complex of values extraneous to the core of values generally considered to be therapeutic enters into the designation of depth versus superficial therapy. I think that social status, economic resources, intellectual and aesthetic preferences and the like are the significant criteria determining whether a person is administered to by a psychoanalyst or a counselor. Our common experience tells us that deep relations are those in which we believe we have met a person significantly different from others and that superficial relations are those in which the person is a type and not an individual. Such common sense applies to therapy no matter what theoretical and technical paraphernalia may be bandied about by the doctor to impress the client. Once a patient asked me, after I had carefully sweated out what I thought was a useful and probing interpretation, "Why not stop your calisthenics and save them for your conventions?" I'll always be thankful to him.

I have come more and more to inquire with prospective patients what relationships they want changed and in which ones they believe they could make a change without undertaking the expense of psychotherapy. When Joyce, a young college student living with her parents, told me that she knew she was too dependent on her mother, I asked her why she didn't try discussing this with her so as to alter her dependency. She looked surprised since she had been in therapy some time previously. She presented me with a review of symptoms, which my training had taught me were likely indices of chronic disturbances. When we agreed that she try "therapy" with her mother before she do so with me, she was "delighted," and added, "I was sure you would take me just because I came." Between the two visits she and I had, she had applied for a job. How this experiment turned out I did not know for some time. I wrote to Joyce twice and was, met with silence. Eighteen months later she came to see me and claimed she was in very good spirits. She now wanted me to affirm that I didn't think it was necessary for her to be in therapy just because she had defied her father and quit school.

Encouraging Action

Another rule which converts the therapeutic room into an inner sanctum is the classical psychoanalytic dictum: no major decision while in therapy. This rule pertains to such major decisions as marriage and divorce and might also include a change in occupation if not in job. I'm not sure the rule has been strictly enforced in recent years. After all, modifications are made by analysts in the face of the practical dilemmas of their patients. But it is usually labeled a modification of standard procedure or an extension of the parameters of treatment, as if the doctor must apologize and explain himself to his own mentors.

The reason that had been given for establishing this rule was consistent with the view that psychoanalysis was akin to the disassembling of an apparatus which had a peculiar though erroneous proclivity to run out of the assembly shop before the parts were properly put together. Taking a major step while in therapy would only obscure the analytic work. It would be an acting out and a discharge of tension. Though the way I have described the reason for the traditional rule reveals my feeling about it, I think my image is apt. And I think that any limitation on the person's right to act with others outside the session is akin to the vow of chastity, poverty and obedience which a novitiate in a religious order is required to make. Any requirement to postpone decisions until the end of analysis is contrary to the value of respect for the patient's autonomy. It inhibits him in discovering the healing possibilities in other relations.

I do adhere to the letter of the rule regarding marriage, though the spirit with which I invoke it is different. When a patient is contemplating marriage, I tell him that as soon as he is married we shall stop our formal meetings. "I want to be as far away from your honeymoon bed as possible. Since I believe that a marriage can be the best of therapies, I would rather you try it without confounding the experiment by continuing with me. If at a later date you wish to return, we can discuss it then. After all, if you and your spouse make a real go of it, then the two of you can take all the credit for yourselves." I realize that this position contradicts the one I have on the patient's freedom to say when and how often he wants to meet with me. But when it comes to marriage, which again I believe is the most powerful relation for bringing out the best and the worst in us, I draw the line. I have no other way with which to deal with my experience that social pressure on the educated patient can push him and the therapist into an interminable inner sanctum.

Different Therapists for Married People?

As is true about any issue, the question of different therapists or the same doctor for a married couple is a debatable one. I do not have a set position on the matter. When it arises, the patients and I discuss it with the understanding that the decision must involve an experimental attitude, akin to flying by the seat of one's pants. At this point, however, I want to illustrate my thesis that some doctors teach their patients to guard their private relation against intrusions from the outside world, with a case involving a husband and a wife seeing different therapists.

Caspar came to see me about six months after his wife, Alicia, entered therapy. He told me that he wished to have his own doctor and didn't even want to go to the agency through which his wife had found a therapist. I accepted this as his right and didn't inquire further about his feelings, since the conflicts he described were so aggravated that I turned my attention immediately to these.

Within four months after we began, Caspar's self-destructive fantasies, which I later learned had directly plagued him ever since the age of nine and marked his earliest memory dating to the age of two and a half, erupted in a frightful manner. Because of this event, in which he went to the brink, and which also proved to be the hinge on which he turned toward more honest relations, he could no longer conceal that he had repeatedly committed adultery.

Alicia was shocked out of her ostrich-like "innocence" and became overtly disturbed. She discussed the events with her therapist and asked him for his prognosis for her husband, whom he had never met. She then reported that her therapist told her that his chances for recovery were rather poor. I think most therapists would agree that if Alicia's report of her discussion with her therapist was correct, he had violated an important principle: no diagnosis without actual contact with the patient. Other questions could be raised about this event, which I learned about from Caspar. Alicia could be distorting the discussion with her therapist and using it to hit at her husband. Perhaps her therapist, for his own reasons, was siding with Alicia. And it was evident to me from my past experience with Caspar that the road ahead would be very rocky. I was not that confident about our relation that I could just dismiss the reported poor prognosis as factually untrue.

I also found it interesting that her therapist did not suggest that Caspar could come to see him or encourage Alicia to see me. And it was this issue which I chose to discuss with Caspar. I indicated my readiness to discuss my feelings and opinions about the situation with both of them. I spoke to Caspar about my concept of prognosis (which I will take up at another point) and reflected on my disagreement with Alicia's therapist. As matters developed, Caspar and Alicia did draw further apart and were divorced. In retrospect, I think this would have occurred even if both had been in treatment with the same person. Caspar came to speak more openly about his negative feelings toward Alicia before they were married and the fact that he had tried to call the wedding arrangements to a halt but was dissuaded from doing so by Alicia and her mother. There were thus many signs from the past which could explain the very poor marriage. However, this experience and similar ones notwithstanding, the notion that each patient should maintain a hands-off policy regarding the therapeutic relation of his or her spouse is a dominant idea in many psychotherapeutic systems. The marital relation becomes a second fiddle to the solo virtuosity of the therapeutic pair.

Even when I have worked with a husband and wife, I have caught myself talking with each one as if their marital relation were a threat to the recovery of noxious memories. When I think of marriage as only a screen and a ghostly shadow of some yet undiscovered real self which therapeutic work will uncover, I am bound to come between the husband and wife. Now, when I am the therapist to a husband and wife, I counsel them to talk as much as they will about me. I say to them, "Why not take a chance and discover that both of you have something to learn from and teach to the other about a person presumably important to each of you? Maybe this could make a difference." I think it is worth considering for any member of a family to turn the usual attitude of privacy on its head and encourage an open and active interest in the therapy of the other. The members of a family have the most to lose or gain from the therapeutic relation of any one of them.[10] It is through active interaction rather than a distant and presumably respectful politeness toward the right of privacy of the other person that each person can learn whether involvement is a sign of domination or a sign of affectionate concern. Of course, I do not push a patient to report his discussions with me as soon as he gets home. If he hesitates to speak with his mother or his wife, I believe he has some good reasons for doing so. I ask him, "How come?" and consider his hesitancy as an issue before us rather than as a "given" which is not to be touched.

Certainly a great deal of noise can occur when patients and doctors open their office door. Therapists themselves can become competitive, and patients may, for a time at least, take this as an occasion to beat down their friends and relatives with the authority and magic of "My doctor said so and so." The virtue of this noise is that it brings into the open obscurities and rivalries and sometimes deep affection which can be then inspected by all concerned. As I did with Caspar and Alicia, I try to meet the emergence of differences as an occasion for clarifying the opinions I hold. I try to use any differences as a basis for the revelation of my own values as well as the interpretation of what uses the patient makes of the differences. I think that Caspar, at least, came to know a little better with whom he was contending.

From the very start of our first meeting, in the office or on the telephone, I try to place the relationship between the patient and me in the context of all possibly significant relations. As much as the patient or I would like to believe, in our vanity, that psychotherapy is the keystone to his change for the better, we should know better. Luck, among other unknown forces affecting our existence, requires us to maintain an open door and open-minded policy. So let us continue in the following chapter to keep the door open, for our exiting from the inner sanctum as well as for our entering into a different experience.

3

KEEPING THE DOOR OPEN

There are many issues that arise in the course of our talks which call on me to clarify the place of psychotherapy in regard to other possible healing relations. Among these questions we must deal with are: What are the limits of confidentiality between doctor and patient and what is the meaning of privacy? The importance of the values of privacy and the confidentiality of the patient's confessions and revelations to the doctor has been emphasized by our democratic tradition and in the law.[1] Violations of privacy are strongly resisted by almost every citizen. Yet, as I hope to show, an uncritical acceptance of these values without an appraisal of their relevance to the particular circumstances of the patient and the doctor can interfere with the achievement of the goals the person and I aim for together.

It is a common experience to meet a stranger on a journey and, after sharing memories, to leave him without even learning his name. Some days or months later, he surprises us and appears in a dream or reverie. It seemed that it was easy to leave him because he was a stranger but impossible to neglect or forget him because we had been intimate with each other. An hour of trivial exchange incurs forgetfulness while a moment in which we confess and expose a laugh or a sob intrudes itself into our consciousness and arouses our passions. This is the stuff of existence and of our nature, which impels the child to become a person seeking intimacy and tolerating superfi-

ciality only for the sake of getting by. This is the stuff of our allegiance and faithfulness to those with whom we can call a trick a
trick and nothing more than that. This is the stuff of any healing in
any relation. The talking cure of professionals is the laying on together of tongues to soothe our blistered memories.

The patient and the doctor sit together one or two hours a week.
The patient is encouraged to talk about his most intimate feelings,
and the therapist is required to reveal himself as the finest person the
patient has ever met. And then, when the patient's yearning for his
therapist becomes intense, a development which in every other situation is normally expected, the relationship is evaluated as a repetition of childhood events and childhood fantasies.

Marsha is twenty-six, unmarried and, I think, unusually intelligent. She called me on a Saturday afternoon and said, "I am just
about to leave, but I want to tell you how much I wanted to talk
with you." She wrote to me very often, and in one letter declared,
"Bernie, sometimes I want to talk and talk and talk to you. Something's wrong and I don't know what. But I am restless." Marsha
frequently expressed her intense longing to embrace me, to touch me
and to walk with me. I told her, "I like to be with you, too, so your
expression of your wish is the hearing of my affection. I hope, too,
that you will soon find someone with whom you can talk and embrace
and not have to return to another place." Her craving is life in its
essence in the very present, and it need not be any more intense
because in the past an affectionate relation with her parents was
repeatedly thwarted. Her need to love and be loved was not intensified by its absence at home; rather, she learned to ask for affection
from those who couldn't requite her.

When we add to this power of revealed memories the requirement
that the exchanges between patient and the therapist remain completely confidential, the office becomes a solarium. The patient's
right to expect that the therapist will not go behind his back should
never be knowingly violated by the therapist unless he is prepared to
accept the patient's right to leave therapy. I would take this position
even when treating a very young child whose permission to speak to
his parents cannot be sought from him. With such a youngster, I
would conduct any conference with his parents in his presence. The
earlier the lesson in "nothing to hide" (because you cannot hide

anything from the child anyway) is learned, the quicker the child will develop his capacity for facing a person rather than defacing a figure. The first time a patient's parent calls or writes to me, I inform him of my policy and ask him if he wishes that this time I keep confidential the fact that he called. Any further communications behind the patient's back are mentioned to the patient.

The privacy in which the relation takes place is not an absolute condition for therapy and indeed can interfere with the achievement of greater self-reliance. In psychoanalytic therapy the analyst encouraged the individual to isolate himself from continuous involvements with others so that his interpsychic processes, his real nature, could be discovered.[2] The patient was discouraged from sharing his experience on the couch with others. The therapist, in turn, refused to communicate with the patient's family, colleagues, teachers or anyone having an influence on the patient's life. Strict privacy and secrecy were demanded.

However, when one believes that the healing relationship shares many qualities found in all growing relationships, when one believes that the differences in a psychotherapeutic relationship can be greater than the differences in an involvement between two friends, then the therapist can respect the wish to keep the discussions confidential and yet encourage the elimination of privacy. Though I do not wish to go behind the patient's back, I do not have to discourage him from involving other interested people. If he wants to keep them out, it may be for defensive as well as expressive purposes. A parent who is helping pay for a child's treatment does not have the absolute right to see me. But whether he helps his child financially or not, the child, no matter how old, can be confronted with the contradictions inherent in his refusal to have his parent come. Interested and concerned relatives have been so well trained to stay out of explicit involvement that they may appear either indifferent to the patient or underhandedly try to sabotage his relation to the therapist. My question to a patient about a friend's or relative's concern can better be phrased as "Why not?" rather than the prohibitive-sounding "Why?"

During recent years I have directly indicated to a patient who was engaged or married and occasionally even just going steady that I was ready to meet his close friend, if the patient and friend wished this. I justify this suggestion simply on the basis of the friend's understandable curiosity. How can he be a friend and not be curious about the doctor? I indicate that I will not enter into any discussion about any ongoing fracas or pleasures between them unless they ask. I say I am ready to be "looked over," so that when fantasies arise about what goes on in the inner sanctum, the friend has some basis —a very small basis, to be sure—for making his own judgments about me, the therapist. Whenever parents consult with me about problems they are having with children, I always indicate that I am willing to have their children come and meet me. "If they can have a concrete image of the real person and office where you go to tell about them, they will begin to feel your readiness to be open with them. This is therapeutic itself. I happen to think we all have the basic need for at least one relationship in which we can believe we are naked and still know there is another garment to take off, not necessarily from the past but one we have put on unwittingly to protect ourselves from the inevitable blast of coolness we often get."

There is no way to demonstrate that this "technique" is more effective. I use it only to reveal my attitude that it is in a sense more important to live actively and honestly in the world outside the office than with me since the hours in the office are only a small proportion of the hours in the week. Living for the session is a deadening of life before and after the session and heats up the session itself to a suffocating degree.

I encourage patients to speak with others about what goes on between us. I only hope he quotes me correctly when he is using my name.[3] If he doesn't and he misrepresents my position, perhaps even hurting my reputation, then that is a price I'm ready to pay for the growth of his freedom. Rather than begin with the prohibition not to speak with others because he may or will distort what I have said and thus "drain off tension" from therapy, I say to him, "You can say anything to anyone about me."

Do I also reserve the right to speak about him to anyone I please? Of course, and whether we therapists say so or not, we actually do. We speak about "interesting cases," write papers and books, use our experiences with patients as illustrations in lectures we give and go to our own therapists and supervisors to help us with our confused reactions to patients. The patient need only be assured that his identity will not be revealed when I am talking about him.

Even this assurance is not absolute. There are situations which hopefully do not occur often, but which do expose the relativity of privacy and confidentiality.

The right to confidentiality is not absolute in the event that the patient gives evidence that he may become homicidal against himself or another. I hope that I will be able to tell the patient first my wish to introduce a community agency, such as the police or a hospital, before I betray him. But when I am fearful for the person's welfare, I will consider breaking the confidentiality of the therapeutic contract. The only absolute position I take is that neither the patient nor I has the right to determine whether he or anyone else should live or die. Murder or suicide is one action about which no therapist has the right to say to the patient, implicitly or explicitly, "That is your choice." I am therefore appalled by Ludwig Binswanger's attitude regarding the suicide of Ellen West, a patient whom he did not know personally but whose case he discussed from an existentialist point of view. He wrote regarding the antinomy of the dread of death and the dread of life: "The suicide, however, is the willful breaking through this antinomy by a 'resolute' [Dr. Binswanger's quotes] deed of practical action, in which freedom finally and necessarily triumphs over unfreedom. So deeply founded is the essence of freedom as a necessity in existence that it can also dispose of existence itself."[4] This is not my kind of existentialism. Dr. Binswanger makes his pronouncement like a god. Did Ellen West have the opportunity to answer his opinion?[5]

FREE ASSOCIATION, OR TELLING IT ALL

The notion that the patient must tell all to the therapist is embodied in the analytic rule about free association. This rule was established to circumvent the patient's defensive maneuvers and to get at repressed material. As a rule it is impossible to follow since, among other reasons, no train of thought is free of the relation in which it appears. Though I may at any moment feel disappointed that the person hasn't told me something before, an untempered demand for full disclosure always leaves the patient with guilty feelings that he has betrayed the analyst and gone against his own best interests. "Dr. Steinzor," Margie said when I asked her why she had not previously mentioned an important matter she had just disclosed, "I better tell you now something I had promised myself I would divulge only during the very last session. I have a very strong dislike for lavender toilet paper." This image has lots of grist for the analyst's mill. I laughed with her mockery of my attitude. It would have been better to wonder why she needed to tell me what she did at all, and to accept her timing as an expression of her right to reveal or not to reveal. Not only should I remind the patient to feel free to speak about anything he wishes, but also to feel free not to do so. The First and Fifth Amendments apply to every citizen.

Certain common human experiences whose moral is courage and fidelity are embodied as principles in formal as well as common law, and apply also to the therapeutic situation. Historical accounts of men who have not betrayed a secret under the threat of excommunication or death call us to admiration of their heroic principle. Moving to a much less dramatic observation, psychologists have affirmed that the child saying no to the adult is saying yes to his own being in the relationship. A child will say to his father, "Don't look in my face," and though he may not yet understand that he can hide his face from his parents, he is demanding the right not to be seen through. From the heroic to the simple, everyday happenings between ordinary people, the value of voluntary revelation is an honored one. The patient as well as the therapist expects honesty and openness, but a willful act of mistrust is also a part of a full relation.

When the therapist has a double standard regarding communication, that is, when the patient is expected to tell his secrets to the doctor but not to others, the therapeutic relation becomes a hothouse. It reduces the person's investment in other relations and often encourages the patient, in the name of his therapy, to avoid taking responsibility for his relations with friends, colleagues or spouse. As necessary as privacy is in therapy, it can interfere with an important goal of treatment: the practicing of honest confrontations with those who matter to the patient.

Hobart Mowrer, in a paper on the expiatory meaning of the fee in private practice (he calls it blood money), is extremely critical of privacy in psychotherapeutic practice. I quote him because, though I think he goes too far, he does stress the danger of the inner sanctum: "Here I wish to suggest that perhaps its greatest weakness and defect lies precisely in the fact that it offers as treatment what, in reality, is the very essence of the disease itself, namely *continued* privacy and personal withdrawal."[6]

Dr. Mowrer asks for a radical openness between the patient and others, suggesting that therapists urge and even insist that the patient confess his real guilt. He thinks that an oppressive conscience arises not so much because of fantasied guilt over crimes and offenses not committed as out of real guilt for dishonest avoidance in expressing one's responsibility and loyalty toward others. He appears to be speaking of what Paul Tillich[7] and others have called existential guilt, that burden unavoidable in being human and that responsibility which Dostoyevsky spoke of in this way: "Each of us is responsible for everything and to every human being."

However, I think that Dr. Mowrer goes too far in his criticism of psychoanalytically oriented therapy. People do withdraw because they have been frequently punished, rejected and ignored. Children are crippled by guilt over "naughty" impulses which, when confessed, were met with a demand for expiation. Their guilt is real and excessive because they have fantasied they deserved the punishment they received. The therapist can help reduce automatic inhibitions which developed because others punished the patient when he was open. I also disagree with Dr. Mowrer in that I not only affirm the patient's right not to speak but must and do accept the patient's sense of timing and readiness to speak with others.

A person can become more inhibited if pushed into a situation when he is excessively anxious. The other person will smell the fright and may in turn become frightened and hit back. I recall Maxine, who at the time was twenty-two and living at home after she dropped out of college. She was struggling to clarify her values and construct a sense of self-respecting independence. Maxine grieved over her mother's coldness but was terribly frightened of her father. Trembling, she once told him that she did not want to go to church. Her father began to yell, Maxine ran into the bathroom and her father almost broke the bathroom door.

We do withdraw when we are frightened. It is not possible just to confess one's attitude toward another by willing to do so. But the patient and the therapist also need to say to each other that what is shared can also be tried with others. The possibilities and limits of any relation can be reassessed only through direct action in that relation.

John, studying to become a minister, opened a session with: "I feel protective in discussing with you my relationship to the relationship between Susan and me." Though this statement sounded a little stiff, I first noted with approval the existential language, which John as a seminarian may have absorbed from Kierkegaard. Then I asked him whether the hesitation to talk about some experiences with Susan was because he felt I would disturb his growing love for her by analyzing it. "Are you asking me to 'handle this with care,' because you care very much or are you afraid that some unpleasant feeling you may have toward Susan will emerge and thus I am a threat to you?"

John had become engaged to Susan shortly after we had made a contract to see each other. During the consultation, when he spoke of his feelings toward her and the possibility that they would become engaged, I told him about my general policy regarding marriage while in therapy. "When a patient marries, we stop our formal sessions. I don't want to be in your marriage bed." Often John would discuss his feelings toward Susan, and with my direct encouragement he talked with her about some of our exchanges. She had recently become upset with him because, as John quoted her, "You are getting too analytical, everything is open to question!" John had affirmed his good feeling about our relationship, saying to Susan that the talks we had were enriching his appreciation of many things in life. Apparently, after having assured her that she should express her feelings toward our relationship but could not disturb it, he was able to share with her what he had never shared with me.

Since the last session they had shared with each other the fact that each one masturbated and how each felt about the forbidden pleasure. Susan said she thought of him and then spoke of how she had never felt her father recognized her as a woman. She had the urge to become pregnant soon after marriage so that her father would notice her. On reflection, Susan had thought this was a factor in her having intercourse with another man at the time John had begun courting her. John noted that he had later realized that when Susan had said she had something to confess, he had not for one moment anxiously thought she was about to inform him of another affair. Without minimizing the focus in therapy that we had given John's jealousy as it markedly affected his sense of being a man, and its contribution to the increasing freedom of mutual sharing of shameful thoughts between them, I strongly approved of this turn. "As long as you and Susan can talk to one another this way, whatever I think of any particular interpretation each of you gives to your past is quite irrelevant. This is your therapy, and I am glad you spoke about masturbation first with Susan before you had mentioned it with me. I hope you convey my opinion to Susan since friends and relatives of patients so frequently get the idea that I approve the patient's running first to me with his trouble."

"Gossiping" About the Therapist

My approach can be criticized from the psychoanalytic point of view as encouraging both the patient's resistance to therapy and the acting out of impulses with friends and strangers alike. The patient, it is believed, is less able to judge what he should not reveal and it is thus better if he leaves that evaluation for the therapist. Delaying an action until the patient and the therapist can review it is thought to be a procedure which increases the chance that a crucial memory will arise because tension has not been discharged. This model of the mind reflects the basic concept of psychoanalysis that it is the repressed experience which returns as a symptom. Psychoanalytically oriented therapists uncritically have accepted this idea, which is basically a medical one. The underlying infectious parasite exudes its poison into the brain and behavior. The image is one of actions and thoughts as static things, relatively fixed and encapsulated and removable by the probing surgery of analysis.

This model of the mind lies behind the advice to the patient not to censor anything in the session but to watch what he says and does outside the office. This is in itself quite a feat! The therapist himself does the reverse, of course, since he is supposed to be spontaneous when he is not working. If the patient is discovered to be telling others details about his therapy or discussing with friends his feeling about his therapist, he is often advised to stop because the tension and anxiety which should be built up in therapy are being drained off into other relationships. The patient's psyche is treated like a leaking hydraulic jack or pump, which, when the pressure is applied, does not exert the proper amount of elevating force. With such advice, the privacy of the relationship takes on the additional aura of a secret one. The patient has come to learn to be freer with others, when at some point he is suddenly told that his freedom regarding the discussion of therapy and his other problems is antitherapeutic.

A person I know told me that her analyst, who is quite prominent, suggested she not even telephone him in front of her husband after she had reported that her husband had become anxious about what was transpiring between the analyst and herself. Rather than given help to confront her husband with her perception of his anxiety, she was told to become even more secretive about any activity with her analyst. The result of this advice, as could have been foreseen, was that the husband became even more anxious. From my own acquaintance with her husband, I think an element in his reaction was his unresolved envy. However, one must also consider the possibility that the analytic relation itself can make matters between a husband and wife worse than they have been. In this particular instance, the wife's description of her analyst as a person contrasted sharply in many ways with her husband's temperament. There was hardly a trait which the two had in common beyond the fact they were both men and both psychologists. This contrast may have been the basis for the wife's choice of a doctor. Whether her choice was a wise one, in the final analysis, time, as always, will tell. However, the realities of their differences as people and the analyst's suggestion that she save her confessions for him had resulted in an increase of the tension between the patient and her husband, and also, as must happen, in an intensified mistrust between the patient and her therapist.

I always affirm the patient's right to talk things over with others. I would rather he discuss his therapy with people who are antagonistic toward the whole psychotherapeutic system than to carry on his secret pact of silence with others and his confessions solely with me. Some other schools of therapy do not discourage the patient from sharing his counseling experience with friends, but do not encourage him to do so either. Clients or patients or whatever they are to be called should be told to speak out with others and to open the doors of the inner sanctum.

The Therapeutic Relation Embattled with Others

Here is another example, this one from my practice, which illustrates how a sharp contrast between the office relation and the patient's other affairs can become dangerous for all concerned if it is not dealt with as a realistic dilemma.

Patience, whose name belied the symptoms for which she sought help, had been referred by her pediatrician for the diagnostic testing of her daughter. After I discussed the results with her, she accepted my recommendation that she enter therapy and asked me to help. About a year before this she had left her husband, taking their three children to live with a brother. Her husband's violent threats coupled with pleas for her to return brought them together, though in the course of therapy she realized that other feelings had motivated the reconciliation. Matters had not improved, even though her husband had been seeing a psychiatrist. He had stopped his visits to the doctor a short time before Patience came to see me. Frequently, she thought about divorce. She reported that her husband often threatened to strike her and occasionally did, once so severely that she had to seek first aid. He had opposed her coming to see me, though he did not actually interfere with her visits.

Patience finally decided to seek a separation and informed her husband of her intention. This she did in no uncertain terms. Though she knew he would refuse to consider it, she agreed that making a clear statement of her wishes, divested as much as possible of threats, would be a very important step for the entire family, including herself. When I asked what his response had been, she said, "Oh, the same old blather, that he would do a thing or two."

Fantasies of being assaulted already had assailed me. Though a rare occurrence, the newspapers occasionally carry stories of a husband or wife attacking a therapist or his family. A recent TV program had dramatized just such an instance. I wanted to head off any such possibility and immediately told Patience, "I am also a little scared of your husband. You may provoke him to attack me as well as yourself with just such an attitude that his feelings are blather. He undoubtedly knows I am directly involved in your plans for separation."

I reviewed her own stories of his style of revealing intense feelings, and though it seemed clear from these and other reports that he could become quite disorganized, she could not respect him enough to think he might mean just what he said. Obviously his children and the preservation of his family meant a great deal to him, even if her decision to separate made a lot of sense to her. She had to recognize his style as well as her provocative way of playing off one person against another. This trait had been discussed by us as a characteristic tendency developed quite early in childhood. This time she saw the danger of this tactic, which blinded her to her husband's deep affection for his children. She wanted to do something about it because it could endanger what she was trying to achieve and might result in people for whom she cared getting hurt.

She had told me she liked me, and I had accepted this on its own terms. I had told her I liked her, partly because I admired her courage and the way she behaved with her children. During a session shortly following the one I am recounting, she told me that for the first time in her memory she realized that liking someone meant and demanded an attitude of protecting that person from foreseeable danger. The more we discussed her life situation and my part in it, the fact that I was responsible as well as she for the future of her family, the less anxious I became about a possible assault by her husband on either his wife or myself. When she realized that our relation could make not only a positive difference but a negative one too, she could then act more respectfully with her husband.

Again it is the entire web of relations in which the person is involved which affects his being in any one of them. The happiness and satisfaction I find in my marriage are more important to my relationship with a patient than is my knowledge of his character. My wife is with me in the office, as is my colleague in a course I am giving, or my mother, whose telephone conversation with me the night before had aroused old aggravations.

MORE THAN ONE THERAPIST AT A TIME?

The patient's wish to get help from another therapist may be frowned upon or encouraged by his doctor, but if such a consultation is arranged it is believed that it is best for them to part company. This notion has been adopted from medicine, where only one doctor is in charge of the case even if others are brought in as consultants. If a minister, let us say, is also counseling the patient-parishioner, this help is considered to be an adjunct, at best. If a patient consults a lawyer, we think of it as legal advice even though such guidance often markedly affects the person's life and thus his emotional integration. It seems to me that in principle one should always consider that all professional people concerned with the patient, his physician, his surgeon, his minister, his dean and his attorney are colleagues, whether they are actively collaborating or, as is usually the case, are not.

Actually the attitude I am advocating is often implemented without the patient's knowledge. I'm not referring to such occasions as a therapist telephoning a patient's internist but to the very common event of a patient's therapist being supervised by another professional in training institutes and the like. Isn't this a form of multiple therapy? Dr. Whittaker and his colleagues in Atlanta have brought this approach into the open and have made it a practice for two doctors simultaneously to treat one patient and confer with each other.[8]

In some training institutes the candidate is informed in advance that he will change therapists after a given period of time. This training procedure acknowledges that no one relation alone can bring out the "real" self. And, of the many therapists who have been in treatment with more than one doctor, how many have informed their patients of their multiple experiences? So why not more than one therapist at a time?

I know colleagues who see the parent of a child they are treating while the parent is himself in analysis. I try to help patients who are in a therapy group led by another person, and I know this arrangement is not uncommon. Who is to decide which professional is helping the patient more at any particular time? So why not extend this somewhat atypical practice and encourage a patient to discuss his problems with any professional healer he wishes to consult?

For example, in her twenty-fourth year Bettina is having a very hard time completing college. She repeatedly assails me because I do not comfort her enough. "You don't understand why I don't wish to graduate," she angrily cries through tears. She suffers through such symptoms as crying and nausea before examinations. I was her fourth or fifth official therapist, and the pastor of the church she joined was one of numerous ministers to whom she turned for that kind of ministering clinicians usually characterized providing a crutch. It was easy to think that the church symbolized her ideal mother. Often she would tell me that after leaving a session with me she would go to Pastor Sillman's home and spend a few hours in his study. On weekends she constantly sought him out. Bettina mused, softly and provocatively, whether I thought she was taking advantage of him. "I hope that Sillman will express whatever feelings he has toward your request to be with him."

I continued to interpret the rebelliousness implicit in much of her behavior toward me and to indicate what I was able to take without feeling imposed upon. When she complained about being unable to study or about her physical aches or about having to take one of the numerous pills she had in her medicine cabinet, I refused to listen. "Talk to me about your feelings in concrete relations and then I may be able to understand, but these messages we call symptoms make no sense to me."

The reports of her visits with Pastor Sillman gradually took on a different character. Bettina let me know that he was not only holding her hand and assuring her that his being with her was a manifestation of his calling as a pastor. He also was confronting her with the possibilities of caring for others. In a session with me following one during which she wept in anger over my refusal to "console her," she told me of an exchange with Pastor Sillman. Apparently she spoke to him of her need to hurt herself. He then took out his cigarette lighter and challenged her to place her finger in the flame. At that moment she thought, "I'm not so self-destructive as I've been pretending." I told Bettina that they must have a very active and creative relation. "You don't have to go to the fires of hell to prove your right to your place here on earth. He may have been making a theological point, but he certainly helped you realize something which you and I are also trying to agree on."

Later Bettina told me that Pastor Sillman had assured her he was not practicing therapy, for which he was not trained. His disclaimer was conventional, and though it may have had the effect of encouraging Bettina to continue her visits with me, it also suggested to her the limits of Pastor Sillman's tolerance for certain kinds of experiences. I would guess that if Bettina hadn't been seeing an "official" psychotherapist, he would have referred her to one. Of course, if her pastor was opposed to the whole idea of psychotherapy, he would have tried to discourage her from seeking such help. In that event, Bettina would have stopped seeing me or her pastor. As it turned out some months later, she left both of us for another minister and therapist. At this moment I do not know how she is faring.

Was Pastor Sillman's help to Bettina secondary to mine? I don't know. But if the prevailing opinion changed about what is psychotherapy, then it might not be necessary to decide who is chief change agent. Then a person would feel that it was his right to see as many therapists as he believed could help him. The objections to this idea are well known. The patient would play one doctor off against the other. Bettina tried to do this as children do with parents who are out of touch with each other. The patient presumably would avoid becoming deeply involved in the analysis of her difficulties since she could always claim to be taking up the problem with the other doctor. The patient might also object on the grounds that one deep relation at a time is enough, that different opinions are confusing and so on.

The reasons for encouraging the patient's freedom in this regard help clarify our assumptions about the nature of psychotherapy. One advantage to the patient would be the discovery that the therapists' views are often matters of opinion arising from their own characters. This would then help the patient realize that he had a real choice between perspectives on living. His choice could then be more responsible and reasonable and less freighted with unacknowledged bias. The patient would less likely become wholly dependent on one therapist, with all the consequences of any clinging attachment. The patient would be told, from the beginning, that the relation has its limits. This would help him revise his expectations of the "miracles" a doctor can perform. The patient would soon understand that therapy is comparable to education and that, as everyone knows, we can't learn everything from one teacher. The patient's right to leave or change to another therapist without feeling that he is running away would be affirmed from the outset.

When Therapy Is Going Badly

Patients are trained through the communications media and through their talks with the doctor to believe that if their relationship with the therapist is going badly, then everything else must be disturbed. I think this notion pervades every system of psychotherapy from the left to the right, from Rogerian, nondirective orientation to the client to the Wolpian, conditioning form of treatment directed at getting rid of symptoms. Obviously the patient is the sick one, and thus it follows that his feelings toward the doctor are his problems. The average patient will readily admit that most of his complaints against his therapist are the same as those which appear in his other relations. This understanding of the patient's relation to the therapist is called transference by the psychoanalytically persuaded. But other schools also partake of the assumption that the patient's contrariness toward his helper is a sign of his condition and a manifestation of his resistance to treatment.

This is a useful notion, insofar as it helps the person recognize the blind repetitions in his responses which disregard the person he is addressing. But must a disturbance between doctor and patient generally mean that the patient is revealing his illness?

I once said to a patient, Jack, that I didn't conclude from the fact that we were repeatedly misunderstanding each other that he must be having a difficult time with others. Revealing a capacity for humor too often concealed from others, Jack replied, "For a long time I thought I was the only one who was sick here." And if the patient is better in the session than in his other relations, it is said that he must be so because under the benign influence of his therapist he has become more open and honest than ever before. During a period when Jack, a twenty-five-year-old seminarian, was talking about his homosexual temptations, I bore down on the analysis by inquiring for details of his feelings toward others and me. When he recalled his intense but frustrated longing for his father and the smothering possessiveness of his mother, which had almost snuffed out his ability to grieve for her when she died, he left our meetings pale of face.

Jack, however, could leave his "sickness" at the door. His relation with Sal continued to grow, as did his ability to concentrate in his studies. We would say that Jack had a good ego and that he could tolerate frustrations. Therapy proceeded according to the text. But I also believe it was useful for Jack to know that the ups and downs of our relationship were hardly the measure by which to assess the health of his other relationships. If we take the therapeutic relation as the yardstick, how can we account for the changes a patient experiences despite an abrupt and ambivalent cessation of contacts with the therapist? We know this happens, though less often from our own patients than from our friends who are patients.

I also know that patients change for the better when I go on vacation. After my return, many tell me that things have improved since "you went away." I have learned to anticipate this and to tell those who are anxious about the forthcoming separation that, though we can make special arrangements for being in touch or for their visiting with someone else, the interruption of scheduled meetings can be a real advantage. I may cite as evidence a number of instances where both men and women, shy and fearful of becoming intimate with the opposite sex, have initiated their first significant involvement during the period when I was on a holiday.

When we speak to the public about the usefulness of therapy and do not remind our audience that any therapeutic relation can also make trouble for the patient, we are culpable of increasing the unrealistic expectations patients have of us. Psychotherapy should be described as a real relationship in which other relationships are discussed and differentiated from one another. But always it is a relationship with its own potential for good and evil.

It is quite a commonly held belief that the more the patient suffers in therapy, the better the result. Superficial therapy, we are told, covers up wounds which people with weak egos cannot face, while deep therapy uncovers old hurts. Patients are usually very ready to accept this formula. Most of them have heavily guilt-ridden consciences. When we therapists hear a woman imply that suffering is punishment, we object, and rightly so, to the turning of the screws of conscience. Yet what are we doing when we say, "Treatment must be painful"? What are we saying when we tell a patient who leaves a session more upset than when he entered, "The increase in anxiety must show we are coming close to something meaningful"? Though this explanation may be true, it is also possible that the patient leaves sourly because we have not caught what he has been telling us. Anxiety accompanies unclarity in a relationship. Unable to express his disappointment over having to part in an unclear frame of mind, he may tell us this in the next best way, by speaking of his anxiety. A therapist is not bound to try to make the patient happy or to please the customer. Yet we can affirm to the patient that enduring suffering is not a necessary mark of coming to a creative breakthrough.

Creation also occurs in a context of recreation and diversion. Mildred is freer to tell me something she had been ashamed of revealing because she took her behavior to mean that she was running away from therapy and not facing the causes of her disturbance. "Back in January when I was first able to tell you about my abortion, I used to leave the session feeling depressed. I would visit John, and though he didn't listen to me very much, our talking was diverting and I felt better." Why not? Why should we not encourage Mildred to be diverted, to escape, as we do when we go home, go to the theater, read a good book or have a cocktail with a friend? How often have I heard patients express the belief that joy in other situations must be partly an escape since "my deepest feelings are confused and I haven't discovered what they are." At best, they think they have only gained a respite from the true search for the real self. These people make the very same point some authorities make in more elegant language.

The Devaluation of Other Deep Involvements

In every session I need to be alert to my tendency to devalue the healing possibilities of other relations, past and present, into which the person has plunged. I must counter the thought that, because our relation is called therapy and because the patient was in trouble in other relations, it must follow that he did not grow in other situations which were disturbed. When a married person arrives complaining of marital difficulties, I am expected to lend a sympathetic ear and help him see what is disturbed in his marriage. Yet do I listen also to the possibility that the person could and did perceive the marriage, as bad as it is, as a therapeutic situation? When I do, I hear such people tell me that the deep involvement has made them aware of some difficulties in themselves which otherwise might have been innocently dismissed. I support such comments and add: "That is just what happens in therapy, too. The engagement between the patient and doctor leads each of them to become more aware of his 'peculiarities.' You have already saved yourself years in analysis by having a troubled affair and listening to the noise."

Here is one final illustration of the basic point of view under discussion in these chapters on getting out of the inner sanctum. Will, a married engineer in his mid-twenties, had become quite alert to his insensitivities in his actions with women. His wife Judy was still in confinement, a few days after she delivered their first child, whom they had christened Cora. Judy's mother had arrived to help out even before the baby was born. In the session following Cora's birth, Will directly asked for my help. "Judy asked me to tell her mother to leave her alone. But before I did, I wanted to ask you about it. I don't care much for my mother-in-law, and I agreed with Judy. But you know the trouble I have with mother figures, and I did not want to make a mistake. So I didn't say anything until I could talk it over with you." Will had interpreted the arrival of his mother-in-law in the same way he viewed the entire relation between Judy and her mother. It was another instance of his wife being dominated and spoiled by her mother.

He and Judy had often quarreled about this, but he had begun to understand his own relation to his mother as being of critical significance in the anxieties which had brought him to consult with me. In this particular session he said he had been surprised by Judy's request since he had never seen her stand up to her mother. Here she was, only three days after delivery, asking him to help her stand up to her mother. Yet Will, an overtly cautious man, was not ready to take any chances before he understood his own motives more adequately.

I have no doubt that even this brief partial and partisan account of a meeting between Will and me lends itself to a number of other approaches and interpretations. I could have reflected on the meanings of Will's anxiousness regarding his wife's request, and perhaps linked it with his oft-expressed indictment of her as spoiled and demanding, or questioned him about his passive negation of Judy's feelings. Why, for example, did he not object in advance to the coming of Judy's mother? Could it be that he was repeating his experience with his own mother, whom he described as deaf to his opinions even when she had solicited his advice? Will, it seemed clear, was referring to this when he gave as his reason for postponing action "my trouble with mother figures."

My reply reflected on his concept of what is a mistake in a relationship, or, as therapeutic jargon would put it, "acting out." I suggested that the postponement of action also could be considered a mistake. My accent on his conception of healing as occurring first in the office and then elsewhere, rather than the interplay among all the relations in which he was implicated, was answered a few sessions later. "Now that I have taken the lead with Judy and Cora at home, I feel much less trapped there and can speak with you more directly. I can say better what I think here." This may be labeled indoctrination, I realize, as well as acting on his own and his wife's behalf. However, I think Will confirmed my surmise by reporting that he had not mentioned to Judy his wish to delay speaking to his mother because he first wanted to talk with me. "It was only a couple of days, and she was just three days out of labor," he explained to me. When I suggested that not telling Judy why he would not speak with her mother was itself an instance of avoiding both open action and the statement of his position, Will seemed to understand. However, in the following months I was also sure that he often nodded in agreement when he actually wanted to tell me to stop reminding him of a failure of nerve.

But that is in good measure why many patients come to my office for help: their nerve has failed them. They believe they cannot live things through with those who matter to them and would rather see it through with me. I am ready to help them do so, but must also remind them that the test of courage is in the world immediately at hand and in the world at large.

4

INTO THE WORLD AT LARGE

I feel lucky when I leave my apartment overlooking the Hudson River. I walk around the corner to my office in the early morning after looking out the window at the inbound commuters in their automobiles and think what a madness surrounds our lives. These people driving to work have fled with their families from the crush of New York into the suburban sprawl. They also must believe in the good fortune which permitted them to get out of the city noise and smells. The story of the rise of cities is the story of civilization, but the city lights look lovely only at a distance and city life lacks both urbanity and civility. Urbanization, as sociologists call it, has almost destroyed our meaningful participation and involvement with others in the development of a good life. *The Eclipse of Community*, Maurice Stein's title for his book which reviews and interprets the outstanding sociological studies from 1920 to the present, is an apt description of the fragmentation of our sense of belonging and acting with others.[1] The eclipse has been accompanied by individual anxiety and isolation.

Sociologically speaking, psychotherapy is one modern institution which has been developed to help the isolated man in his search for meaning in a world in which traditional institutions no longer make much sense. In the past a person developed his individuality through participation in rituals and forms of life approved by the whole community; today he is required to forge his own style of living with a very small number of people. Even if he is successful with a friend or a lover or his club, he still cannot know whether others will

[44]

support or reject him or, what is worse, be indifferent to him.

I used to think the patient's comments about the weather, the traffic he had to move through to get to my office or subway dirt were only chitchat preceding our getting down to the real business of our meetings. Now I wonder whether the patient and I do not become more preoccupied with our sixth sense because the five nature has given us have been so violated by our own nature. We concentrate on our yearly vacation and, when we get a little money together, purchase a weekend country place. And who knows where we'll be in the next five years, so why get worried about the immolation of the physical environment? And since the problem of city planning is not within our discipline, why concern ourselves with the effect the physical environment has on the moods of people and on the development of their character? We leave these matters to the poets and novelists who speak of mountain folk, river people and the plains mentality.

We also leave the newspaper at home. I have no systematic data to support my contention that therapists almost completely ignore the events which make the news columns of the *New York Times* or even the *Daily News*. From publications as well as from discussions in meetings at conventions, one gets the impression that such events are ignored or, at the most, accepted in the same spirit as are comments about the weather. The patient's concern about the action of a congressman is listened to with the interpretation, "What is he saying about his father?" The world turns and the headlines announce the movements of men and the evolution of ideas which could have a more profound effect on the well-being of patient and doctor alike than all their hours of discussions. Fateful events may overtake us all, but the business before the doctor and the patient is circumscribed to such parental and other authority figures as the analyst, the boss and the chairman of the department.

Here are two exhibits in evidence of my contention that the conduct of therapy tends to be isolated from the social and cultural forces affecting all of us.

The first exhibit is a study done by Thomas Szasz and Robert Nemiroff.[2] A questionnaire distributed to members of the American, British and Canadian Psychoanalytic Association in the fall and winter of 1959-60, inquiring about a number of practices and opinions, included the following two questions: "Do you believe that psychoanalysis (as theory or practice) is neutral with respect to religious beliefs?" and "Do you believe that psychoanalysis (as theory or practice) is politically neutral?" Of 392 American analysts, 59 and 61 percent, respectively, answered yes to the above question. Notwithstanding the likelihood that each analyst had a somewhat different definition of the key terms of religion, politics and neutrality, the critical point is that they believed that when they were with their analysands they did not convey their private political and religious opinions.

We can assume that these analysts would not maintain they had no definite views on political and social problems. It is just that they believed such attitudes were irrelevant in the conduct of treatment. It should be pointed out that the minority of analysts who believed that psychoanalysis was not neutral on religion or politics did not necessarily mean, in answering these two questions, that they discussed their personal views or directly used what they thought were the religious and political values of psychoanalysis in analyzing the patient's own attitudes. It is only from those who answered yes that we can directly infer a belief that on the couch the patient was not being subtly or actively indoctrinated with any political or religious point of view. For them, the analytic chamber had an aseptic existence.

The large number of analysts holding this point of view is puzzling. The notion that the analyst's communications can be aseptically given, much like the application of a surgeon's knife, is in stark contradiction to key concepts of psychoanalysis. One key idea is that social ideology is in a significant way affected by identifications with parents which are formed as ways to cope with sexual and aggressive impulses toward them. Sociopolitical views, even as sublimations, are connected with the primary complexes to which psychoanalytic therapy is directed. Another and related key idea is that the development of social ideology occurs largely through unconscious communications between the child and his parents.

Are we then asked to believe that in the analytic situation the patient no longer responds unconsciously to the analyst? Or are we to believe that the analyst's only significant communications to the patient are verbalized interpretations and questions which are in turn so neutrally devoid of vocal and facial inflections that they do not

betray the real attitudes of the analyst?[3] The very concepts of transference and countertransference include the notion that communication is basically outside the awareness of each person and must be
brought into consciousness through an expenditure of considerable
energy. Yet, when asked by Drs. Szasz and Nemiroff whether in
theory and practice analysis can be neutral on questions that normally move intelligent men to complex and warm debate, a majority
of these analysts blithely answered yes. The requirement that contradictions in ideational productions be clarified apparently applied
only to patients.

It would be useful to repeat this study. I suspect the results would
reveal a change toward the view I am proposing. Among the evidence of this prediction is the increasing frequency with which professional people are taking public stands on vital issues such as
disarmament, Vietnam and civil rights. When patients see their therapists' names listed in published open letters and when therapists
become activitists in politics, it hardly seems possible to maintain
the belief that a doctor can be neutral on problems of social, political and religious values.

The second exhibit is the well-received volume by Dr. Walter
Bonime, *The Clinical Use of Dreams*.[4] I have chosen this "testimony on my behalf" because the interpretation of dreams is a hallmark of modern therapy and because Dr. Bonime identifies himself
with the cultural school of psychoanalysis. He is explicitly critical of
the lack of sensitivity of classical psychoanalysis to the social forces
which have shaped the person's character. Throughout the volume
he frequently refers to the competitive spirit in our society which
distorts the development of cooperative and affectionate relationships deemed by authorities to be necessary for sound mental health.

Dr. Bonime labels 115 dreams in the index. I have counted about
eight which could be classified through their names as referring to
socially significant events, such as "Atomic Reactor," "Rabbi's
Curse," "Old Negro Prostitute" and "Oil Well." Calvin Hall's research has shown that dreams reflecting historical events are relatively rare, so we need not be surprised by the small number in Dr.
Bonime's list whose manifest content is not clearly related to "current events."[5] But we should also bear in mind that since Freud's
work on dreams almost every therapist has distinguished between

the manifest face of a dream and its latent meanings. A therapist does have to provoke his patient to associate to the dream, and thus he does contribute to the "final" interpretations given to it. Dr. Bonime makes this explicit. He thinks of dream interpretation as a collaborative enterprise and himself contributes his own association to the patient's dream. It follows that the paucity of socially significant dreams may then be caused, in part, by Dr. Bonime's "insensitivity" to the social values implicit in the patient's dream.

As far as I could discern, none of these dreams was used to question the patient about his association to the possibilities of atomic war, his religious beliefs, his racial prejudice, his feelings about the use of money for social purposes or his sensitivity to the torture and degradation of millions of people in war, poverty and persecution. I am not saying that Dr. Bonime's patients did not get better because he did not attend to social issues. I am only claiming that the lack of attention to the social aspects of the patient's difficulties reinforce in him a narrowness of perspective and heart.

Since my own "awakening" to the mystification of the inner sanctum, I have realized how often I must have turned patients away from revealing their social, political and religious consciences. Now I wonder out loud with them why they have not mentioned the events marked by such headlines as "Kennedy Declares Blockade of Cuba" or "Johnson Resumes Bombing" or "Civil Rights Bill Is Passed." And though it rarely happens, events do occur which produce such a strong reaction in me that I declare my inability to go on as usual. During the days following the assassination of President Kennedy I told those patients who wished to come that I could not do anything but discuss with them their reactions and the contents of my grief. Perhaps I was avoiding some anxiety about my own parents, but I could not consider any intense reaction to the President's death as a sign of unresolved complexes or infantile helplessness. Rather, I wondered later if, in the final analysis, healing is not essentially the sharing of grief, anxiety and rage when events beyond our doing overtake us.

One of Dr. Bonime's patients dreams of finding himself in bed with an aged Negro prostitute. He is revolted by her eagerness to make love with him. Dr. Bonime wrote that the "Old Negro Prostitute" was really the analyst. Ignoring the possibility of what most leaders in the civil rights movement insist is a fact—namely, the virulent and latent racial prejudices in even liberal whites—Dr. Bonime discouraged the patient from considering relations beyond his own viewpoint. Discussion of possible ethnic prejudices in the patient is, of course, believed to be less therapeutic than interpreting them as disguises for attitudes held toward the analyst. But why did this patient select a Negro? At least he was bothered enough by something to choose a figure with another cultural background, but the therapist's attitude suppressed any such thoughts.

Another illustration is the interpretation of a dream presented to Dr. Bonime by an affluent suburban housewife. In it she imagined an oil well had been drilled in her flowerbed. One of her associations to this was the fact that her husband had recently arranged, without consulting her, to put in a swimming pool costing between five and six thousand dollars. She was annoyed about this. The patient reported, too, "As I looked at this oil in the dream I felt a great dismay." Dr. Bonime then noted: "Since this was her first expression of emotion in the dream . . . I therefore said, 'Concentrate on the feeling of dismay.'" The patient's associations and the therapist's interpretations were then summarized by Dr. Bonime: "Pursuit of the dismay in the dream brought *the meaning* [my italics] of the dream into awareness. It furthermore brought into focus this wife's practice of seeking, with cleverness and dexterity, to solve her marital difficulties by herself as though they were a tricky mathematical problem. It was then possible to see more clearly her role in perpetrating the difficulties with her husband."[6] Is that all the patient was dismayed about? What did she feel about her affluence and the use made of it besides the payment of her analytic fee and the purchase of an unwanted swimming pool?

I think the essential reason given for excluding an exchange of points of view about social events is not only that everyone has the right to his opinion, but that all of us are prone to project our own wishes into the social scene. Undoubtedly a crucial, if not the essential, concept of psychoanalytic theory, accepted now as a commonplace, is the mind's very strong proclivity to project desires and perspectives onto the world and in turn to consider these projections as the reality with which one must contend. This concept of unconscious projections has served reasonable men well as an antidote to self-centeredness, to smug complacency and to self-righteousness. The irony of any position could be exposed when a self-critical intelligence entertained the likelihood that his values were relative to his history. The self-critical mind recognizes the universal tendency to endow one's enemies with the evil in one's own soul and to grant one's friends the glory of one's own aspirations.

Freud discussed ideologies, with particular attention to religious beliefs, and showed how a person might project his particular feelings about his parents onto his religious concepts. The fact that others later criticized Freud and suggested that his own views of religion as an illusion could be a projection of his childhood experiences with a religious people was itself a demonstration of the usefulness of Freud's concept of projection.[7] Harold Lasswell, in the 1930's, was among the first of many to apply the new psychology to politics, in his classic study of political leaders, *Psychopathology and Politics.*[8]

The moral to be drawn seemed obvious: therapists must beware of their own tendency to impose their position on others. They must be prudent in discussing ideologies, and only therapeutic strategy could require the direct analysis of a particular value. But by and large the therapist was to remain neutral. His involvement in discussions with the patient about national and international events would only be participating in the patient's avoidance of his emotional difficulties. It might also lead to arguments which could disrupt rapport or lead to false agreements which could encourage the patient to believe that the therapist is on his side of an ideological dispute the patient had with his spouse. In short, the injunction has been: "Stay out of it."

No one can prescribe for the operation and application of the good sense which can leaven any particular point of view and keep it from disturbing the very issues it is supposed to clarify. Yet the notion that intrapersonal exploration in depth will by itself help a person become a more just individual and a more active person is questionable. Psychotherapy can lend itself to encouraging the patient to be self-centered and concerned only with what he sees before his nose.

But the rebuttal can be legitimately made: "Should the therapist be responsible for all aspects of the patient's life? He is after all only an 'expert' on the psychological, interfamilial relation and would actually arrogate to himself the mantle of the all-wise priest if he were to consider it his duty to educate the patient in responsible citizenship. This would really make psychotherapy the center of the patient's life, a matter which you are deploring. The patient has come to the therapist not with an obsession about joining a civil rights movement. More often than not the patient is disenchanted with social movements, and the therapist, knowing full well how social groups of all kinds can and do exploit and manipulate individuals, should be the last person even to imply that the patient be concerned with and act in his church or in an organization to reduce the threat of nuclear war. Should the therapist suggest social action as a way out of a personal impasse?"

These arguments must be weighed in any particular case as well as in one's orientation to all patients. The fact is that there has been a general and traditional neglect of the possibility that action with others toward a goal promising to enhance the freedom and dignity of the person can be therapeutic for a patient. Given the facts that no one therapeutic school produces better results than others and that it appears that the increasing consensus between patient and doctor is the essential factor in a satisfactory therapeutic outcome, psychotherapists should reconsider their traditional assumptions.

For some patients, as for example ministers, whose calling requires them to take a position on social questions, joining in concerted actions with others may, during a particular period of their lives, be more therapeutic than an analysis of heterosexual anxiety. Erik Erikson in *Young Man Luther* recounted the psychotherapeutic attitude of Dr. Staupitz, who not only listened to the young Luther but put him to work.[9] Interpretations of the radical questioning of institutions and social rebelliousness as inevitably a sign of illness may tell us as much about the values of the therapist as they do about the condition of the patient. In sociopolitical terminology, there is a very strong strain of middle-class conservatism and individualism underpinning the techniques of modern psychotherapy. Concerted group action has been considered for the poorer, less fortunate members of society who suffer from what Durkheim called "anomie." Such social-action approaches have been useful in helping the dispirited reorient themselves to family and neighbors. But again, this is believed to be therapy for the lower class.[10]

I have encouraged patients with aspirations to act in political organizations to do so, even if this meant leaving therapy. I told Geoffrey, a young minister, who had been offered the opportunity to direct a new civil rights section of his church in the South, that his evident commitment to and passion about the action of his church was itself a significant change. Some years before, when he had come to see me, he said during the first session, a little flatly I thought, that he needed help because he couldn't love. Throughout the time we had met, he repeatedly brought in evidence of the fearful dryness of his heterosexual relations. A summary of his complexes would not suggest anything different from what psychologists are trained to recognize as a rather severe type of obsessional person who dilutes any strong feeling.

Here, now, he had become engaged in a task inspiring, though belatedly, the just passions of many. Was he running away from the still very noticeable trembling he felt whenever he talked with a woman he thought attractive? Had his negative stubbornness, a trait which followed any display of warmth toward me, become the ground for acting against the therapeutic process? These questions occurred to me in passing, and I dismissed them as the kind of inner sanctum twist a psychoanalytic orientation tends to give to any strong interest displayed by a patient who considers leaving therapy before he has, according to the doctor, thoroughly analyzed the complexes from which he sought relief.

However, I could not dismiss the possibility that I might be expiating my own guilt for not doing enough for the struggle for equality. I had daydreamed of being an attorney presenting a brief in a desegregation case. The figure of Martin Luther King had moved me to a renewal of my occasionally flagging confidence in American ideals. I discussed this possibility with Geoffrey. What effect this had on his final decision to go South, or whether my emphasis on the possibility that his efforts in the civil rights campaigns of his church could also release his capacity for intimacy, actually was a determining force in his choice, no one can say. I think, though, that this brief synopsis of a few sessions with Geoffrey exemplifies how I have tried to open the door of the office so that the patient and I can look outward without seeing the world as a projection of transference problems. After a year "on the firing line," during which we had corresponded and occasionally visited together, Geoffrey returned to formal therapy. But now his fearfulness of a close relation to a woman could be confronted within the context of the courage he had displayed in running the gantlet in various Southern communities.

Another example of the way I speak with patients regarding their political beliefs occurred during the turn of 1964 into 1965. This was the time when a majority of the case workers in the New York City Department of Welfare went out on strike in violation of the state law against government employees resorting to this form of protest. Two of my patients at that time were employees of the Department of Welfare. The intricacies of the issues and the particular sentiments of these people need not be discussed at this point. However, in both instances the conflicts aroused in them by their protest, and their thinking through the contrast between their own position and the one their parents took, helped each realize again how much of his own life he had abdicated to the authority of his parents.

When we were children, we witnessed our parents acting in the world. Did they go their own way or did they join with others in actions which today make us ashamed of their behavior? Or did our parents, no matter what their personal relation was to us, so act with courage and devotion for the ideals which stir us today that we will always admire them even if we cannot be friends with them?

Here are two illustrations of the positive impact that a father's social action for a humanitarian cause had on his child.

Among the reasons Cecile gave for seeking help was a "sense of anger" against her father. A very attractive woman, she had come to her teens at the end of the war in a small village in northern Italy. Her memories of her family included few in which she was directly involved with her father. In one or two he appeared as a tempestuous man, ready to strike her for disobedience. The only time she heard him praise her was when she happened to eavesdrop on a conversation he had with a neighbor who had dropped in and admired the Christmas decorations. "Cecile made them," he had said with a certain pride.

This recollection contained an element which was abundantly present in her description of her father as she saw him functioning in the village apart from her. He was the much admired postmaster whose cordiality to others appeared to Cecile as the opposite of his attitude to her. And during the Nazi occupation of Italy he became a leader of the Partisans while keeping his official job. In retrospect, she realized she had even been aware of his courage since she recalled frequent clandestine meetings and secretive words passed between parents and visitors to the home. And she certainly remembered how her parents had hidden a Jewish family fleeing the persecutions. It was only after the war, however, that she could know the risks her parents undertook in their living beyond the issues of immediate survival. Though her father was not an idealist, he was a libertarian in deeds. And with such a recollection of her father, I was fairly sure that reconciliation with him would occur, even though he had died a few years before she sought help.

I rarely encounter a story like Cecile's in my work, but the second illustration is one of many that I have heard from friends as well as patients. In fact, once I had given value to the patient's recollections of a parent's social involvements as providing his child with a focus for integration, I heard many more accounts of such events as Barry described. His father worked in a garment factory and was very active in the union. "The union came first, and I sometimes didn't believe my mother when she insisted I was not an orphan and that it was her husband who was in bed with her on Sunday morning. He'd come home late at night and leave even before I was awakened to get ready for school. Now, Doc, don't get me wrong. I did see him enough to be afraid of his cold way of calling me down if he didn't like what I said. My mother could hit me without reserve and I wouldn't cry, but if my father called me stupid, I'd break into tears."

Barry's ambivalence toward his father was known to him long before he walked into my office. I had nothing to do with arousing his animosity toward his father, whom he remembered as cold, indifferent to the feelings of his family and as unable to express appreciation as he was able to express his criticism. What Barry and I did learn together was the extent to which he had always admired his father's activities outside the home, which gave Barry a view of life as a struggle for equality in dimensions extending beyond the confines of the family triangle. Barry's rage at his father was ameliorated by his father's dedicated efforts to improve the dignity of the laboring man. He could love his father's values even if he could not feel the friendship he sought with him.

The majority of social scientists are politically liberal people. The theories they develop and the research they do to test their ideas always involve values. Psychotherapists cannot maintain that they can be neutral since every personal act with another reflects a choice and a judgment. The revelation of these values as they are provoked by important world events is a responsibility of the therapist, since, in effect, he says to the patient that they meet to criticize the cultural forces which have affected the well-being of the patient. A narrow, provincial definition of these forces, which implies that the only significant relations are the ties to one's immediate family, ironically perpetuates the dependency on fate which therapy is intended to alleviate. It intensifies the person's self-centeredness, which in the most troubled person is blatantly evident.

5

SUFFERING: REMEDIABLE AND NOT

It is a rare patient who, when asked, "Why are you here to consult with me?" answers directly and simply, "To increase the pleasure in my life and reduce suffering." Popular songs sloganize the accentuation of the positive and the elimination of the negative, but for the educated person this is supposed to be an oversimplification of the human situation and a romanticized faith healing worthy only of the low-brow consumer of soap operas. Patients have been educated by the texts of psychologists not to say, "I wish to be happier than I am," but to disguise their wishes and list a whole set of psychic complaints and somatic aches which they appraise with the knowing phrase, "Psychosomatic, I'm sure." I am supposed to be a serious professional, who equates a taste for pleasure with frivolity.

However, whatever the elaborated theories about the human condition used by the therapist to interpret the patient's "neuroses," they are there together because both think that psychotherapy can bring relief for chronic suffering and can brighten the person's total life. At the beginning, and too often for a long time to come, the patient and the therapist differ over what will increase pleasure in living and what is the nature of anguish. The therapeutic relation becomes successful when the patient and the therapist have learned to agree on what makes for celebration and what is reason enough for sorrow. Change occurs as they act together in compassion for the tragic and laugh together in mutual recognition of the comical.

Theories of personality development are metaphysical systems

[56]

and like any philosophy are concerned with truth and beauty, verity and happiness, joy and the wisdom in bearing suffering. Every therapist, being a practicing metaphysician, has his particular ways of teaching the patient the difference between expected heartache and unnecessary or, as most therapists say, "self-inflicted and masochistic" pain. This the therapist reveals concretely and I believe only through the way he relates to the patient.

Most often, a discussion of maladjustment or the treatment of "neurotic" conditions begins with the therapist's outline of what has made the patient "grow up absurd," as Paul Goodman might say,[1] with special emphasis on the disorders between himself and his parents. Rather than do this, I will convey my prescriptions for a better life by describing the impact made on me by the "model" patient. Ever since Freud's philosophy affected the thinking of psychotherapists, it has been understood that patients do things to the doctor. However, I think we have not given enough attention in public discussions to what we make of our personal feelings.

In describing my experiences of hurts and pleasures, I of course imply, as well as occasionally mention directly, conditions in my patients' histories which generate unrewarding contacts and symptoms. Present in every patient's background are qualities which have given rise to traits I experience as painful or pleasurable. It is my sensitivity, my taste really, which directs my attention to "causes" which need interpretation and change. And to sharpen my argument, I reiterate that the most unhappy therapeutic relation occurs when the two people never reconcile their respective senses of humor and their particular thresholds for wincing when it hurts.

FEAR OF CLOSENESS

Every patient tries me before he exposes his embarrassments, shame, guilt, awareness of his own meanness and his fear of loving. Each patient and I must traverse storms as the very medium through which he learns that I am willing, hopefully able and ready to be with him in his suffering. My critical failure occurs if he becomes convinced that I do not wish to hear and share his burdens.

Sometimes a person will remain silent for sessions on end to test whether I am listening and ready to hear him. The worst anguish anyone undergoes is to feel alone in a cry, to scream in silence and to be so full of hate that the very utterance of it is sensed as degradation. This is the stuff of suicide, be it impulsively wrought or planfully carried through or slowly lived out through dying innumerable times each day. The patient's burdens and cries are not pleasant to hear, and I try to make this clear to him. I do not wish him to go away with the idea that I enjoy hearing his difficulties. However, the exposure of his suffering is for me much easier to bear than his silent brooding, his churning stomach, his heavy-lidded eyes and immobile face. I find it very difficult to be with the person when he shuts me out or expresses himself in language I do not understand. When I find ourselves for a considerable length of time wandering in inclarity, with the patient persisting in disguising himself, I begin to doubt my ability and to question my readiness to reach him where it hurts the most. At such times I hope I also convey that my seeming impatience is not rejection.

During the consultation period, prior to making a contract, I emphasize the idea of my trying to help rather than offering any guarantee of success. I tell him that he is taking a considerable risk in agreeing to expose himself to me. However, as we proceed and live together face to face in the scheduled hours, voice to voice on the telephone whenever it is reached for, and in our thoughts about each other, my necessary hope of a change for the better and my faith that we can achieve it leave me vulnerable to being shut out. My experience with others and my knowledge of the so-called "defense mechanisms" do provide me with possible challenges to the patient's ways of concealing his soreness and possible ways not to take his impact on me personally. But the signals that something is seriously awry between us come to me most when I am in doubt about being in touch with him. My response to feeling shut out and to my doubts about being in touch depend on, among other factors, my sense of the immediate situation. But when I am best in touch with my feeling of being excluded, I can convey my critique with the compassion necessary to ameliorate his feeling humiliated by my criticism.

I try to achieve a close contact with each patient. I need to become involved with his life if I am to make a difference. I feel this need for a deep involvement in almost all my relations and often feel frustrated when it does not occur. That I can exploit my friend and my patient is certainly a risk we take, but I think the circumscription of exploitation begins with my acknowledgment of the expectation I have in meeting each person.

My personal disposition certainly affects the patient's responses. In later chapters I will discuss why I believe it is reasonable that I explicitly tell the patient what I am gaining from our relation. I am not only earning a living. And if my primary aim were to test hunches about the structure of the mental apparatus and refine my techniques of investigation, my office could be used as a laboratory. But I doubt that much change would occur in the patient's other relationships. I think that the concern with technique and the covert use of patients who have come for help as subjects in an experiment lead to therapeutic nihilism. My first hope and expectation is that I live the hour with the patient as meaningfully as possible, without boredom and with passion expressed when it is felt. The session is not the patient's alone; it is also mine because neither of us can retrieve the time we are together. My expectation, then, does sensitize me to the patient's avoidance of closeness and the fear of contact he shows when he communicates unclearly and treats me like an object rather than a person.

This is not altogether an outcome of the person's early experiences with parents who did not play with him and who sent him to his room to sulk alone. The individuals who come for help whose parents have shared with them their own histories are a small minority. Those who have been fortunate in this respect are usually easier to reach in their sense of isolation. Yet we doctors reinforce this view when we teach the person to keep the doctor at a distance. My conditions and my moods are supposed to be none of his business. He greets me with the conventional "How are you?" If I say, "Do you really want to know? Take a good look, as I do at you," or I answer, "Come in and find out," or "We'll both know better by the time you leave," he becomes embarrassed. It is his disorder we are there to cure.

It continues to surprise me how patients, apart from their inhibitions, have been indoctrinated by the literature on psychotherapy not to ask personal questions. Such gifts of interest have been often analyzed as voyeuristic curiosity. The doctor's questions are presumed to be technically pure and loving, while the patient's questions are avoidance of his problems. I don't spend much of any hour talking about myself, but I assume that there is much of the patient's interest in me as a person which he never allows to come out. Encouraged by the rituals of psychotherapy to stay away from my person, he also avoids my ministrations.

I think all my patients wonder what I feel about them, and yet I need to encourage them to ask questions which might be read, "Do you like me?" In part this stems from the prevailing notions that therapy is a relatively objective approach to suffering more analogous to the medical relationship than to others such as those of friends, parents and children, or man and wife. The patient suspects that if he asks me about myself I will in turn inquire, "Why do you ask?" and imply by this that I am interested only in what his questions reveal about him. If I do this, I tend to intensify his self-centered preoccupation by suggesting that an interest in me may be really displaced aggression.

And do not I deny to him that he has an interested right to know me and my moods? I often say to a person, "The state of my mood is of considerable importance to you, and your question is not a perfunctory one. I can be false because it is easy for me to put up a mask of attentive listening." After all, the patient has heard and learned that the initiative for a meaningful discussion is up to him. The silence of the therapist is by definition therapeutic. He is supposed to listen and the patient is supposed to do all the talking. I think this is a rather common distinction between the relation of friendship and the relation between patient and psychotherapist. The patient's silence is supposed to signify many different things while the therapist's silence should mean only an accepting attentiveness. Obviously, I think this is not so. Whenever the patient expresses his sense that I am not with him, I receive it as a gift. Almost every time the patient has asked me where I am he has helped me become aware of some thoughts which were keeping me from traveling lightly with him.

Interest in another person is the most natural attribute of human life, and closeness is naturally experienced in accompaniment to a mutual relationship. Furthermore, equity demands that if I am allowed to ask the patient to disclose his being, I should be prepared to do the same. It helps the patient check his fantasies about me against what I think is the truth and what he hears about me through my version of the truth. I encourage patients to read my papers so that they can spot inconsistencies and see me in my contradictions. The more he knows about me, the more he fulfills his right to know.

Contrary to what one would think, patients are not gossips and voyeurs who spend most of their time poking around in my other lives. The relatively few inquiries they do make, when met without embarrassment and with candor, become part of their awareness that I am available to them when needed. However, time and again when I would expect a personal question, I don't get it, even when the question would be conventionally appropriate to ask.

For example, after my return from the summer holiday, a patient thinks of asking me how I enjoyed my vacation but doesn't. Why? Because it is not called for in therapy and she has some difficulties she wants to discuss. Is she angry with me for leaving her alone? Is she denying her anxiety over separation? Whatever the particular reasons, the fear of closeness is manifest. This patient would rather relate to me as aseptically as possible. If I feel fumigated, I object. One morning, after some two years of meeting, without as much as a "good morning," Jane began the session with "I've had two dreams." When I called her attention to this automatic opening of her mouth, as if she'd come to a dentist, she soon admitted that her dreams embarrassed her and that she'd rather tell them to a total stranger. Interestingly enough, both dreams involved sexual feelings toward her father. In the second one, he was preparing to get into bed with her, as if he were preparing for surgery. In the dream she calmly refused to give in to temptation. She was wiser than she knew in her dreams: no contact when there was no feeling. But with me she still was not sure and tried to treat me like a surgeon.

Touching and Feelings

Fear of closeness is also a natural correlate of the therapeutic situation. June expressed this very clearly when she wrote to me, "The more I reveal myself to you, the more I want to be with you. I know you can't meet my wishes and sooner or later you will reject me for wanting to be with you." Feelings such as June's have been interpreted by psychotherapists as an aspect of transference neuroses and have been satirized by critics of psychotherapy as "the crush in the doctor's office."

I experienced June's expressions as also appropriate to the situation. I had asked her to reveal herself to me, and who hasn't known increased longing to be close to a person who drops his mannered façade and with whom we are more honest than ever before? June is a young unmarried woman in her late twenties, and whatever the reasons for her being single and calling on me for help, the fact is that she speaks to me more freely than with anyone else and does so only for two hours a week. That I am a man with whom she feels she can speak also contributes both to her learning to disclose herself to others and to the frustrations that arise in doing so.

Polly, thirty-four, married, with two children, began to dress better and move her body and arms in a less inhibited way. She wanted to touch and embrace me and said that her longing was also felt in her genitals. I appreciated her frankness since it helped me acknowledge more than I had previously done that she is attractive. Was this a manifestation of an Oedipal wish transferred onto me as a father figure? I interpreted it as an increasing awareness of her power. She had been so frightened of her sensual interests that, though she admired many of her husband's liberal values, she never found him physically or emotionally appealing.

Sam is eighteen. After many months, he dares ask me to embrace him as he lets himself speak with me of the physical ache in his limbs and bones for his father's friendship. Sam's father recently said to him, "I'd like to take you around," but didn't. Sam had stood there silently before his father and suppressed the words, "Why don't you?"

The desire to be physically close to me I expect will be awakened in every patient. Whether or not from the very beginning there is an immediate physical attraction, the longer the patient and I talk together, the more reason there is to expect an urge to touch. I do not see how it can be otherwise. Feelings and intimacies shared between any two people cannot be so contained that their expression can occur without at least an impulse to hold hands and to embrace affectionately.

Most patients are very much afraid of such feelings. They experience them with the kind of guilt therapists have been taught to consider a consequence of incestuous desires. This may be so for some or to some degree may be so for all of us, but I see the patient's wish to be physically close to me as a natural consequence of what the relation calls on him to be emotionally. I have been stirred to a desire to embrace a person crying out in pain or exulting in the pleasure of a release of pent-up memories never before recalled with anyone. At times, having noted the fire in a woman's eyes, I realize the glint in mine. Though this exchange of warmth through the "mirror of our souls" is pleasurable, I realize, too, how much my own needs for complete physical intimacy are cared for in the bosom of my family, where an embrace is not a medium of exchange but a way of reducing the loneliness that lies at the core of existence.

I will never embrace a patient for a technical reason or to assure him that I am not afraid of sensual contact. The fraudulence of such a meeting will be laid bare very soon by the patient's skin and muscles as they sense the manipulative turns of my arms. To use the patient for my own persistent need for physical and sexual embrace would be an exploitation. As a therapist I have been sought out because I promise more and mean more to her than a transient affair. The possible moments of pleasure would soon give way to embarrassment and hurt. That this may momentarily frustrate the patient is understandable, and his or her frustration will help him leave therapy. However, he and I should not so emphasize the physical limits of our relation that we adulterate the power of our intimate meetings by seeing sensual longings as reflections of parental attachments. This rejects the patient's need to be close to me.

I don't believe in routinizing into a technique any gesture or any approach that has helped one person, since it often turns out to be a deadly caricature of the patient's own lack of spontaneity. Yet the literature on therapy with hospitalized patients and with young children discusses much more often than do the presentations of therapy with adult outpatients the effectiveness, indeed the necessity, of physical contact. The therapist's faith that he can meet the person in his suffering must often be demonstrated to the patient in the concreteness of physical closeness. Patients who come to my office are usually wary of touching and being touched. They do not look at my face, and many hardly even let their eyes move about the pictures or furnishings. Months after we first met, a patient may allow himself to approach the bookshelves and survey the journals and volumes. I encourage them to look and take hold of things as well as to let go of their feelings.

I hope to convey this to the person from the beginning. Somehow this did happen with Larry, a twenty-five-year-old teacher. He told me in our first consultation of his homosexual urges, which he feared would get "out of hand" with his nine-year-old pupils. As the meeting came to a close he asked me if he could shake my hand. I was moved by his boyish warmth, extended my hand and took his responsive arm in my other. He then told me that his first therapist, with whom he had worked for two years, disavowed handshaking. For Larry our handclasp was a sign that touching need not be a prelude to sexual relations.

Larry's request was relatively clear, but most often the patient's wish that he and I meet physically is so garbled that I am also uncertain about my feelings. So I try to clarify what is wanted of me. Rose is a twenty-seven-year-old social worker who speaks in an almost inaudible whisper whenever she expresses the wish that I hold her in my lap. When she told me of her wish directly, it was easy for me to answer. "I really don't feel like doing so. This is the best reason for saying no. The fact that you can speak directly to me of your desire is itself to be celebrated. Of course, it is possible that I inhibit myself because I might be erotically moved and would become embarrassed, but I don't think so. The great effort to understand your unclear thoughts itself largely transforms my possible sensual feelings."

Rose did not respond. A few months later she recalled my comments when we were discussing a dream in which she had considered going to bed with me. In the dream she refused intercourse because she had another engagement, and in the session she said, "When you told me why you hesitated to take me in your lap, I felt you were taking me as a grown woman and not the little girl I asked you to be kind to." And a few months after that Rose recalled a story her mother had told her when she was an adolescent. "When you were a little girl you used to follow me around and cling to my skirts. When you were about fifteen months, I went away for two weeks and left you with an aunt. She wrote how clinging you were." Clinging at fifteen months! Rose, like many women in whom so-called Oedipal feelings arise, had been deprived of physical contact. Such women wish more to be held by their fathers than to go to bed with them. This, as well as the particular circumstances of the person's life history, has contributed to the confusion between the physical expression of closeness and erotic sensations.

It is from this perspective that I relate to patients with prominent disturbances in their expression of sexual feelings, whether the disturbances appear in the sexually inhibited or in the so-called perversions manifested in homosexual display or heterosexual promiscuity. Theories of and research on the developmental histories of sexual perversions usually emphasize previous hostile and sexual stimulation which has overwhelmed the child before he became a patient. Not only did the family fall victim to the conflicting values toward sex prevalent in our rapidly changing society, but the child frequently was a victim of the distorted sexual and aggressive feelings of his parents. Almost all studies of male homosexuality, for example, have revealed the common pattern of a weak, passive father, who may at times show his ineffectiveness by physical violence, and a dominating, possessive and quite often seductive mother.[2] In brief, there is no Oedipal complex in adulthood which does not reflect psychosexual anomalies in the parents.

Such findings as these are helpful in understanding the welling up of diffuse anxiety and other symptoms when the patient experiences an increasing closeness to me. Harriet, who had studied medicine for a few years, still could not bring herself to speak about the fact that she masturbated. A visit to a physician was difficult, and talking about her erotic sensations with any doctor was almost beyond her. Whenever she would block, she later told me, she would have the thought, "I will lose him if I tell him." This is, I think, typical of patients who equate sexual intimacy with emotional and physical intimacy because they are so ashamed and frightened of their erotic feelings toward me. Often enough, outside the office the patient caricatures this longing for affection by playing out his sexual feelings with persons who degrade him. With me, he is terribly afraid I will respond in kind to an erotic impulse, that I will take him at his face value and in an embrace cheapen his need to feel me with him. The erotic overtone, in whatever way it is shown, is signaled always by shame. Its occurrence tells me that my presence is felt, but it also says, "I am not ready to betray my depth of suffering."

The sexual instinct is very powerful, of course, and the definition of healthy norms of sexual intimacy, an extremely variable and debatable problem. Here I am saying that the craving for sexual intimacy is frequently a disguise for the anxiety that accompanies emotional intimacy, which must occur if the patient is to grow out of his feelings of inferiority to the doctor. To illustrate, when I discuss homosexual symptomatology, as it may appear in consciousness or disguised in a dream, I emphasize the tender longing to be close to one or the other parent. In men, at least those who come for help, homosexual feelings usually cover up a longing to be close to the father. I sense this often in the scattered thoughts of patients which follow an open give and take. Heterosexual bed jumping is more socially acceptable behavior in which longing for the parent of the same sex is revealed. Heterosexual promiscuity is less frowned on than homosexuality. Still, the common feature in all those suffering from sexual disturbances, whether displayed in excess or in inhibition, is that one or the other parent—and usually both—have been indifferent to the child, have not held or romped or tickled him enough. Seduced and dropped, yes, but not wrestled with or carried piggyback.

CLOSENESS AND INTIMACY: DO THEY FETTER ME?

A conventional interpretation with which many therapists badger their patients is: "You're passive-dependent; you're demanding too much but not taking responsibility." I have used this kind of confrontation, but more and more I have realized that I have retorted in this manner when I have felt cornered. If I want to convey to the person that he is asking too much, why not say explicitly that the kind of wish he is expressing has little probability of being satisfied, but that he has a right to cry out in protest. The so-called demanding individual who appears to complain about every frustration is always the very person who doesn't tell you what really hurts. Most patients have been explicitly taught not to be crybabies and have been punished for complaining. As in the case of severe pain, which the American credo urges them to suffer in silence or take a tranquilizer, but by all means not to bother anyone, they hide their deepest emotional hurts. Through their childhood years, they lose almost all their confidence and judgment as to when it makes sense to say they are in pain, so preoccupied are they with the idea that unless they are terribly and clearly injured they are considered malingerers if they wince. I try to help by interpreting this self-denial and by accepting their right to whimper as well as scream.

I must always be grateful if in an act of impatient interpretation of the patient's passive, demanding communication I do not reinforce his guilt over feeling injured and thus discourage him from telling me more. I do hear a great deal of noise which sounds irrelevant, but I try to keep in mind that becoming noisy is a necessary transition to coherence. Often, when I feel beset by the patient's clamor, the evaluation of tranquilizers made by an English friend comes to mind. Dr. Thomas Main told me, "Whenever I get the urge to prescribe a tranquilizer I take one myself." And perhaps I cannot unambiguously tell the patient that he is overly demanding because I feel a continuous sense of my unresolved demand on life. I constantly wish that we could choose to live forever. I don't think I am afraid of death, but Dylan Thomas expressed my view when he wrote:

Do not go gentle into that good night.
Rage, rage against the dying of the light.[3]*

Does an interpretation of the patient's thoughts which tells him he is passive, dependent and demanding mean that I think he is disguising his wishes to such an extent that he appears to me to be immobilized? Why not, then, say that the issue between ourselves is that his suffering is being stated in such an unclear way that his manifest behavior lacks vitality?

Much of the time, however, the concept of passivity is correlated with what I consider an unrealizable goal emphasized by our culture, that of independence. We have been taught that reliance on another person will lead to overdependence and loss of initiative with others. We are warned that love can be suffocating. What I have found in my years is just the opposite. The more I have been able to be together with another in mutual self-disclosure, the more vitality I have had and the less I have been an ax-grinder for any system. My experience has convinced me that creative thought and action follow from loving closeness. And I think this is the correct and major conclusion from the study of the person's growth.[4]

* Copyright 1952 by Dylan Thomas. Reprinted by permission of the publisher, New Directions Publishing Corporation.

The very gifted will do something often enough despite their loneliness and not because they suffer. Their creative acts are the saving remnants not burned in the fire of rejection. For most of us who are not geniuses, isolation freezes our voices. Mathilda, who came to see me because she was afraid she might kill herself, expressed gratefulness for my speaking of some of my hurts as well as of a particular happy event. She described the searing pain she felt accompanying the pursuit of her talent:

I look at a couple of pretty good drawings in front of me and I know there is something good. There is a power in my hands, but I don't know if it will ever get out and onto paper. And that tears me apart. It's there to do, but my God, how much faith it takes to draw. I despair of it.

One other thing. It's a very small, subtle thing, I guess. But I'm glad you said now you want to know how I feel, have felt, about my parents. I almost feel stupid in saying this, but it's a kind of liberation because most of the time I was hearing something like "Tell me about your parents," which I found very abstract. It meant almost nothing at all to me. I think maybe you will have to help me somehow, though, to know how to talk about it. I know the dominant impressions I used to have. . . . What hurt the most was not so much that something was done to me and I would be angry on account of it, which is bad enough, but the worst thing seemed to be the awful and terrifying bewilderment of fury, futility, blind uncomprehending anguish in my mother—from which I wanted out. I didn't want to understand, to try to heal, to assess blame and cause, etc., etc. I wanted out, to be cut off.

Mathilda is eloquent, more so than many patients, but she defines what I experience with all of them. They wish to run away because they were frightened out of their wish to console their parents as well as to be consoled. When I am there in the feelings I have conveyed in confidence, she can integrate the paralysis in her hand with the urge to flee. She can hear me as being genuinely concerned about her pain and not asking a technical and abstract question about her parents.

Self-disclosure and honesty are the grounds of morality. They will give rise to a disciplined and nonexploitative relation which will liberate the person in his other relations.

My Own Suffering

I have already referred to the fact that many patients are unable to grasp in a meaningful and appreciative way that I also have been in pain and still do cry. They do acknowledge the bold-faced fact that I am human, but they hardly act on it. I try to be as patient as I can, but often enough the person gets to me and hurts me. I usually get angry when I am kicked, but when I do the patient quite regularly will not believe the genuineness of my reaction. I may be accused of being overdramatic or of using a technique, or if he recognizes my annoyance as such, he will ask if I got out of bed on the wrong side. Now that is quite possible, and I also must try as I listen to my feelings to assess whether I'm displacing my irritation onto his innocent shoulders, or displaying my strong feelings in an openly direct way. I have been both commended for my directness and criticized for my temper. Whatever the case, it is relatively rare that a patient will stay with me and try to assess for his own satisfaction whether I'm being unfair. They usually retreat in self-pity or to a sulking silence in the face of my irascibility.

Penelope, thirty-four and married, was an exception and did stand her ground and ask again, "What is eating you?" after I brushed aside her first query with an interpretation that she was avoiding her involvement with—well, I hardly remember who it was. I dropped my posture as the doctor in charge and spoke of my vulnerability to the experience of being shut out which had been rearoused just a few hours before our meeting. She took care of me. However, Penelope and I had already some months earlier discussed the possibility of my getting hurt through our relationship since her own situation had some realistic dangers in it which could be aggravated by her being in therapy.

Many patients take much longer to comprehend that they have the power to hurt me and thus the power to help me overcome my reaction. My anger and the immediacy of its display with the patient are often enough a cue that his negative will is very potent and has brought me to express my exasperation. How difficult it is for the "innocent" person to claim the power to bring out the worst in me! He grants me the power to hurt him, which I certainly have and inevitably use, and he often believes I have hurt him when I do not

think so. But it takes quite a series of encounters before he accepts
his power to reach the mark with his usually indirectly expressed
anger. When the person realizes his power to hurt and exasperate
me, he has begun to change from the posture of innocent and
therefore isolating self-pity to an involvement with me in a concern
each for the other. I tell him that a loving relation must include
suffering in the awareness of being able to hurt the other. "Not guilt,
not anxiety, not self-loathing and not pride in the confession of sin,"
I say to him. "It is on a fine and narrow edge we stand together
when we mutually acknowledge that it can hurt to hurt another, even
a foe. And it does often give us pleasure."

Joan is twenty-seven and an aspiring actress. She had been in
treatment with someone else for about a year but felt dissatisfied because "all we did was talk about why I didn't talk." She wrote to me
after one session in which I became exasperated and expressed it less
in anger and more in a plea that she tell me what was on her mind.

You know I am very much aware that my ability to hurt your feelings
is a power that I have. That thought has very definitely crossed my mind,
and I tell you I don't like it. We have talked about my "not talking"
being a control, but there are times when I think it's a control designed
to hurt. Not always but sometimes. And my having to call you or write
to you is an attempt to alleviate my guilt for not only having hurt your
feelings, but for having done it deliberately. Does that makes sense? But
where I'm stumped is why.

Joan speaks directly and clearly to us and for both of us. The only
point at which she falls out of our relation into the system of thought
required of us by society of knowing men is when she asks why. Isn't
her recognition answer enough? But she needs to ask, and she draws
her own connections. She continued in the following paragraph:

I knew that with my father I made a conscious decision never to tell
him anything. I mean I knew how much he wanted to know what I was
thinking and doing (in fact, it drove me crazy because it wasn't simply
fatherly interest that prompted him to question me but a rather perverted
desire to see dirty pictures), and by making a decision to never tell him
anything I think I was punishing him by denying him the thing he
wanted most—my confidence. . . .
For God's sake . . .

At the very moment Joan affirms her control over her father she
recognizes his need for her love—"my confidence." And some six

months later, she was able to see the price she had paid for the way she dealt with her father. Joan began to realize that her silence was also a pretense, a way of appearing to the world as disengaged and disinterested. She was deeply shaken as she recognized the faking in her life.

When the patient believes I am vulnerable and he can reach me where it hurts, he usually drops all the defenses so adequately described in the books. When he is annoyed, he shows it very clearly and immediately. Of course, he may have a thin skin and flash his irritation at any comment which is even a little unfair. However, I much perfer this to that kind of expression of rage we call symptoms.

Gertrude and I have been through a period when her deep and chronic despair revealed itself in near-suicidal action. In the years following her first and only suicide attempt, I said that we could be thankful and feel lucky she was still alive. One repeated theme which she hurled at me in different ways was: "You are healthy. What can you know about what I have been through?" She was so afraid of feeling close to me that she had to persist in her claim that since I was a therapist I had to be a fully healthy person. Once when she said this to me I revealed to her something about my health which few people knew, doing so perhaps because I could no longer think of any other way to deal with her fantasy about my perfect health. I did not expect her to receive my story with compassion, partly because I had largely overcome my deep disturbance over the event I related to her and partly because I could account for her adamant denial of me as that of a suffering person.

She did not say much, but shortly afterward she became very angry with me over another matter. As much as I had encouraged Gertrude to express her anger directly, and as much as I know how much better she was because she could tell me off, it was still hard to take. I became angry in turn and tried to draw a connection between my self-revelation and her anger. This did not make much sense to her. After she left, I wrote to her, something I have done more and more with patients, and I quote from her answer:

DEAR BERNIE:

Thank you very much for your warm letter. And thank you for restating so clearly the problem. It did not occur to me last week that I was in such a tizzy because you showed yourself to me. But when you referred to a statement I made about your being so healthy, I felt a smug satisfaction that forces me to admit that I was trying very hard to hit at you. Unfortunately, I still don't want to admit that you can hurt. I don't know whether or not it is just that I want exclusive rights, but it has got something to do with being human. I asked myself why I waited until you showed me that you were like me, with problems and sorrows, and I thought that "like me" might be the point—with "weakness" in my mother's house. My mother always strikes when I show her I am weak. I can't go any further.

However, Gertrude did:

I experienced for the first time in my life not being petrified by a person's anger in your office on Wednesday. I was not afraid you would smack me.

I dreamed a horrible dream last night, a mystery of hunting for a murderer and seeing people pushed off a balcony. The murderer turned out to be a woman. I could not fall back to sleep until morning. When I awoke from this dream I said, yes, I am a murderess. I tried to kill myself. But I think the two people murdered in the dream were myself as a student and myself as a dancer and I am afraid I might kill myself as an artist.

Though Gertrude and I had long before this exchange reached a point when I could be certain that she would not again try to take her life, her words in the letter were the first direct naming of herself as a killer. I think this did occur because she had been able to accept me as a person who had been hurt before I had known her and because she had also accepted my hurt over what she had done to me. Her interpretation of the dream and of her relation to her mother rang very true. If I were to compare Gertrude's torment with that of others, I would say she has suffered more than most of us and certainly more than I have. Yet, until she could find some way in which she could perceive me as like her, she could not completely accept my effort to heal and my readiness to forget her hurting me. She could neither forgive herself nor share my gratefulness that she was still alive.

I had a similar experience with Marlene. When she was five in Europe, her parents judged it best to send her away from them to be hidden by a gentile family. The Nazi terror shortly afterward engulfed their village. Marlene never saw her parents again. During treatment she gave me many opportunities to interpret her separation anxiety. She met me during the first minutes of every session as if we were strangers on a train waiting for the other to make the first move toward friendliness. It was also a rare and heartening event when she would leave my office without having tried to pick a fight or not indicating that she felt we would never see each other again. Only during the last six months of our formal meetings was she able to say good-bye when she left.

However, my interpretation and my compassion for what misery she had been subjected to did not appear to be enough to release that sobbing through which a person reveals the acceptance of the irredeemable loss of a parent. I also knew that research on orphaned children had indicated that they do not recall having cried if they were younger than nine years when a parent died.[5] Marlene did not even recall any tears of separation the last time she saw her father when he put her on a train, or her mother in a hospital bed a few hours before she died. However, I hoped that she would eventually burst into tears as an expression of her chronic suffering over their tragic death as well as over having been orphaned.

Once we both stood by a window and my eyes filled with tears when she called me a son-of-a-bitch for losing my temper. I told her that I had become upset because I could not seem to get through to her that my compassion for her also arose from my own pain. My parents were alive, but I always had felt my father's remoteness, even to this day. Marlene, then, for the first time, began to sob over the death of her parents.

It has become a part of my faith that allowing the person to hurt me, recognizing his power to do so and affirming his need to see me as vulnerable in my own aches are necessary for the relief of his and my loneliness in the time we are together. The biggest price we pay when we are repeatedly injured is despair over whether we can even love another. My faith is that the hunger for reconciliation, the longing to be in a relation of affection, is the strongest urge in life. When it is obliterated, we wish to die or we live life as "hollow men." This is how I understand what a patient means when he says, "If I let someone get to know me, I'm afraid he will find nothing."

Changes in the Therapist During Therapy

During the many years I have been a therapist, I have gone
through some significant changes in the circumstances of my life. I
hope and I think these changes have represented a growth in that
kind of flexibility of character which I try to achieve with a patient.
In growing older I should have become wiser. I have been through a
long psychoanalysis, much, much longer than I now believe was
necessary or useful. I have been divorced, have remarried and again
become a father. My ideas about therapy and my relation to psychology as a profession and as a discipline have changed. Ten years
ago I would have been taken aback if someone had predicted that in
recent years I would be a teacher at Union Theological Seminary.
My attitude toward religion and Christians had been shaped by my
particular background as a first-born son of Jewish immigrants who
had themselves broken sharply with their religious parents.

During any therapeutic relationship spanning a period of one or
more years many patients have been unwitting witnesses to significant changes in my life. I have changed in this way, too. Patients
now are less the unwitting witnesses they once were. I now tell some
patients about a few of the important events when I have believed it
would help the patient acquire some basis for judging my opinions or
when I have been moved to do so on the spur of the feelings emerging in our contact. Only rarely have I felt that the patient abused my
confidence.

Natasha came to see me about seven years ago, partly on her
mother's urging, because she was deeply involved with a man of a
different faith. A quite attractive person, she also agreed that she
needed help for a very troublesome habit of pulling out clumps of
hair. Through the two years of our meetings she ended the affair
and fell in love with a divorced man who didn't quite fit her mother's
ideal and who in turn had little use for her mother. The hair-pulling
had abated but was not "cured." During the past five years she and
Stanley have had two children. Natasha has consulted with me a few
times about one thing or another, and there seemed to be little doubt
that she was a "successful case," even though on occasion she again
found herself pulling on her scalp and was possessed by acute anxiety.

Shortly after I published a paper which revealed that I had changed my approach to patients, I gave her a copy of it as she was leaving after one of her occasional visits.[6] I told her I would appreciate her reaction very much since I was sure she would recognize some changes in the way I conceived of therapy. She then wrote a long letter, from which I take the following extract.

My overwhelming feeling as I read it was that I wished you had felt this way during the time of my analysis. From the very beginning I think I would have felt less disoriented—the situation would have resembled other relationships, and a give and take situation is, I think, the only basis for a real relationship. Therefore it took a tremendous amount of work to learn to accept the fact that this was to be only a—should I say "giving" or "taking"?—relationship. ("Giving" in the sense of talking, "taking" in the sense of learning.) Not only that, but, as I mentioned in your office, it would have been more honest. It's unnatural for a person to become almost a sounding board. You said you were disappointed when a patient failed to ask how your weekend had been. I always felt it was taboo to ask anything about you as a person, and yet I was always curious to know whether you were married, if you lived where your office was, if you had children. . . .

I felt fortunate in having this follow-up. It doesn't happen as often as I would like. And this instance is of special interest since Natasha did improve in a relation which had much unpleasant meaning for her. I frequently wonder whether the pace of change would not have been quicker had I been as nondogmatic in the past as I think I am now. Natasha is an example of how many patients will try to take the best from the therapist and make do with his confusing messages.

When a patient has seen me for a considerable length of time, he has undoubtedly spotted contradictions between what I said last year and what I believe at this time. I encourage the person to draw my attention to such inconsistencies. In turn I try to clarify the contradiction and also affirm that I find it helpful that he confirms the fact that I have changed.

If the patient reminds me of an interpretation or reaction of some time ago which I now realize could have hurt him more than it helped him, I acknowledge this as a gift, and as an indication that the person is feeling much freer. Frank is thirty-eight and unmarried.

He was always taking his mother's side and accusing his father of being neglectful, running around and making life unhappy for the entire family. Since Frank was well acquainted with the possible interpretation of this complex of attitudes, I did not have to say anything more than "Oedipus" to him, to emphasize the hate for the father. About eighteen months later it became clear to both of us that his defense of his mother was at certain times justified, and the fact that he could express it openly to his parents was a new feature of his relations to them. In being open about it, he also revealed tender feelings toward his mother which had been suppressed along with all his negative reactions.

What do we choose to underline when a patient reveals an ambivalent relationship? Do we accent the aggression or the nascent affection? Since we all are confirmed by what another says about us, my response as a therapist can lead the patient to a belief in his meanness or to a faith in his affection. In Frank's case, the change in my emphasis had something to do with the various experiences we had had together. But not entirely. During the years we had been meeting I had re-evaluated my own psychoanalysis, largely because I had been living in a loving marriage.

I was discussing with Juliette my feeling that some of the time we had spent together might have been made necessary by my obtuseness and my overinvolvement with her when she was feeling especially troubled. She said, "At one time I think I might have gotten mad at you to hear you say that, but now I'm not. I think it makes me feel good to know that I got where I am now with some leeway and not just by the skin of my teeth." And Marlene, during the last week of our formal sessions, just before she left to get married, thanked me and forgave me when she said, as our review of the years together blurred the distinction between her difficulties and my responses to them, "I envy your patients, the new ones, now that you have changed." All patients need to feel an increasing competence in giving me the same understanding they expect from me. When they feel it, they can stop coming.[7]

Despair, Suicide and Death

Voluntarily coming for help means that the patient still believes that something matters and someone could care what he feels. When this hope goes, the wish to die can bring the person to try to kill himself. Though suicide can be interpreted as the vengeful murder of oneself rather than a hated enemy, or cheating the fate of succumbing to an unwilled death, I think that he who takes his life has given up all hope of the possibility of affection. There are exceptions, of course, as when the person kills himself under the extreme duress of torture, or when the pain of a fatal disease becomes insufferable. In the therapeutic relationship, I hear suicidal thoughts as the cries for help before the final spasm of despair takes over.[8]

I have observed this despair only in one other kind of patient. Josephine, a woman in her middle fifties, was unhappily married for thirty years to a man she could not leave and could not love. Her husband also could do neither, although his solution was to work harder and occasionally have a secret liaison which sooner or later would leak out. Josephine was learning to manage her life better when she developed an incurable cancer. Knowing she would soon die changed her severely depressed outlook into the despair that goes beyond even the desire to kill oneself.

She had always had doubts about the usefulness of our endeavor. Would it make any difference? But these were readily referrable to the deep discouragement which besets any person trying to alter the conditions of chronic suffering. The feeling about the uselessness of any struggle against the exigencies of life or against life's very condition has been, of course, made into philosophies as old as stoicism and as new as some forms of existentialism. Enduring the absurd is not an uncommon feeling. Josephine became swamped with the thought that the terminal cancer was proof of the uselessness of any struggle. "The best you can do for me," she told me, "is to help me die." This request was the one break in the monochrome of bleak and listless despair. If I could help her die in a different way than she ever thought possible, I could continue the spirit which guided our relationship before she had learned of her fatal illness.

I have not had much contact with patients who are fated to die because of an incurable disease. Psychotherapy with such people concerns itself very often with the personal and social attitudes toward death of both patient and therapist.[9] With the dying, the doctor cannot avoid these themes, which are quite readily and successfully reduced to other variables in many accounts of psychotherapy. Feelings about death can be allayed, at least temporarily, by

being ascribed to repressed anxiety about separation or to unresolved hostility. As the one irreversible fact, they are nevertheless
often given less weight in the balance of suffering than are childhood
complexes.

Through the years, I think I have come to lose any dread of dying
I have had. However, the happier I have become in my family life,
the sadder have become thoughts of my eventual death. I think this
happens with patients. An increase in their potentiality for happiness
brings with it an intensification of the suffering and pain evoked by
the shortness of life. As long as the person feels bleak about his
prospects he treats passing time as if he lived in eternity. Only when
he feels freer does he become repelled by his procrastination and
senses with more direct anguish the limit of life. The nearness of
death brings us into the most complex of involvements with our
close ones since our fantasy impels us to imagine their lives without
our presence. I cannot imagine anyone dying alone in his mind. The
dread that this could occur is very often present in patients, although
it is rarely expressed in such words. In addition to all the forces in
the social and personal history of the patient, thinking about death is
dreadful because it brings us close to the ultimate doubt and terror:
"Will I die alone?"

Isolated physical death obviously can occur, but a death outside a
relationship, no, unless long before bodily death the person's senses
have been so numbed that he is out of his mind. If he is not visibly
so, he is an automaton who keeps his anguish completely within the
prison of his rooms, or he is an inarticulate infant. When existential-
ists speak of the person dying alone, I think they confound the dread
of dying with the process of dying. They even may be administering
a form of therapy, through the attempt to persuade us that anxiety
about death is inevitable since we must feel alone when we die. If so,
I think it is a palliative and a placebo.

I know that thoughts about the brevity of life often affect my
responses to the patient's suffering. I wish to be patient with him, but
I do lapse into an irritated plea that his suffering, as meaningful as it
may be, is relatively ameliorable when compared to the loss and
waste of irretrievable time. I can become a therapeutic zealot when I
cry out to him that he get to the matter of expressing himself. It is
my belief that such exhortations also reflect my own railing against

the grief of dying. This recognition enables me to become patient again. Perhaps, however, when I am older and frailer, dying will not be anticipated with as much grief as in the past. When I was younger, I did not feel passing time with as much sorrow as I occasionally do today. This is another reason why I challenge any kind of therapeutic system which assumes that the inner workings of the mind are to be taken apart and put back together in some fashion.

We change through time, yet I have found myself talking with a patient as if the insight we have achieved together will be the way things are forever. I try to say, instead, "Here is an opening, and if it is enlarged, its contours will undoubtedly change the longer the view passing time gives you. If we accomplish anything, it is the readiness to re-evaluate our memories through the rest of time." I have changed many estimates of the events of my life. What I had believed significant became a bore, and what I now believe to have been a real turning point was in the past hardly noted or considered to be a piece of bad luck.

It is some of this that I try to share with patients who are despairing. "Look what you might miss if you die before your time. If you do kill yourself, I shall suffer, but how are you going to know?" On occasion, a patient hears this with surprise. It is as if for the first time he has thought, "If I die, I will not even be able to think again of these black moments as black or perhaps as a piece of exaggerated claim on your concern." But always I hope that the despairing person can hear me say, "Your life matters and your death will end the possibility that I can say this to you another time."

There is much in life which supports the stoical line by Boris Pasternak, "To live life to the end is not a childish task." There is much in what the patient and I say to each other which helps us to live our years with courage. The revelations of our persons to each other, before we die, gives us that strength.

6

JOY, CELEBRATION

AND PLAYFULNESS

The most humorless group of books I have read are those on psychotherapy. The only time I have laughed is when I have read a report on the growth of a child whose author relaxed enough to let the child speak directly to us. The literature on play therapy gives many justifications for using play with children: it is their particular language, in play the child projects his fantasies as adults do in their daydreams and night dreams, etc., etc. Rarely does the author say, "Playing with children is fun for me, and I am told they like it too."

Another exception which proves the rule of sobriety is the occasional study on the psychology of jokes and humor. But even then the author's illustrations, which may be funny enough, are often deadened by the commentary. I am afraid that what I have written so far and what is to follow is itself an example of what I am now criticizing. This section on joy will be considerably shorter than my essay on suffering. Of course, my colleagues and I have a handy excuse. The people who visit us are hurt, and by now everyone knows that it is sadistic to laugh at a person who falls down a flight of stairs. So I had better not laugh with a patient because I might be exhibiting the smugness in my nature that his misfortune is none of my own. My smile could be the indulgence of a superior, unreachable, enigmatic ghost, like the Cheshire cat. It could also be my participation in the pleasure of the patient's growth. But from the reports on cases in the professional and popular literature the therapist never appears to take the chance of being misunderstood. The patient has little reason any longer to expect that the therapist will remain silent or at most grunt "Uh-huh." But he has reason enough to become uneasy when his therapist chuckles, tells jokes or in other ways lets it be known that he is enjoying himself. Celebration is implicitly disallowed by the texts on psychotherapy, though the sin is one of omission, similar to the omissions that used to be made by the textbooks in psychiatry before Freud began to write them with "dirty stories" included.

Of course, the texts mislead us on this point as well as on others. Therapy is always more than what the person inadvertently demanded that it be. So there is fun in many offices after all. And luckily for all of us, patients, actual and potential, make fun of the stiffness in our public relations posture. I encourage the sharing of jokes on headshrinkers.

People are so conditioned that they often apologize to me before telling a story or sharing some good news. The person who has reached this point is nevertheless better, far better, than the patient who never shares good tidings. We have our explanations for this, of course. Masochism is among the most troublesome characterological traits to treat. We offer a cure by fighting fire with fire and must always take the patient seriously. Patients often have the idea that they are only to account for their suffering, symptoms and sorrow. Generally, I learn in a "by the way" fashion that something pleasant has entered their lives. After all, the patient has come because he is in trouble, and the sharing of pleasure evokes illicit imagery. I have never met a patient who did not need my direct encouragement to show his brighter talents. We are there to help him develop his frustration tolerance, his intelligence and his awareness of interaction among people with different social roles, but rarely do we concentrate on his sense of humor. I have never met a suffering patient who could tell me his parents enjoyed his dancing. So I say, we must learn to permit ourselves to laugh together.

There is a quality in real joy which is relatively absent in the understanding of pain. It is the same quality that separates play and work or that distinguishes between work we love and work which is a chore or which separates the game played for the fun of it from the one played to win. Laughter and joy relieve tragedy so that it doesn't become insufferably tedious, as comedy unflecked by fate becomes trivial and silly. I think I can put up with a lot of a person's anguish. One way to convince him of my free-flowing, inexhaustible compassion is to be able to share my pleasure and playfulness and to let him make me laugh. Can I enter the game without my set of rules? If I can relax enough to forget about mine or where we are going, he may even say something to relieve our gloom. Of course, I want him to give me pleasure, too, because if he can, he will experience his power for loving. That is, after all, our main purpose in being there.

For some reason, however, I remember far fewer of the many things patients and I have said which turned the neurotic gesture into delightful nuttiness. Occasionally I can recall a joke at parties or to use in a lecture. Like the one a minister once brought in about the lady who, arriving at the intake desk in heaven, was greeted with great warmth. She had led an exemplary life, and a note had been attached to her file indicating that she was to be immediately granted any wish. She modestly said this was more than she had dreamed about, but could she see Mary and ask her only one question? Most assuredly, yes, but not God? Not Moses? Not Jesus? No, only Mary. By the time she came into Mary's presence the gossip had reached Mary's ear. With all the sweetness and tenderness expected of the archetypal mother, she asked the woman what it was she wished to know. "Only one question to settle an argument with my neighbor: Did you really want a boy?"

Jokes full of meaningful references to sex roles, authority figures and genetic fate can edify our unconscious conflicts. The best, though, are the ones that are brought up on the spot and which do not bear retelling well, partly because they emerge with the attitude. "I got a million of them." When the patient and I each believe in the other's unlimited possibilities for laughter through joy and tears, we need not keep track of our funny stories. However, there are a few that come to mind as illustrations of what I mean when I say to the patient, after laughing together, "You are getting on."

Once I was explaining to a woman my attitude about her lying on the couch. I emphasized my position that, although it can be helpful, I did not make a ritual of it, and that if standing on her head helped her reveal herself, that would be all right with me. She quickly excused my "innocent" slip by generalizing, "I always thought all therapists were peeping Toms."

Jim, a seminarian of twenty-four, and I were speculating about why he had left engineering and entered theological training. A number of memories came to mind, including Sunday school experiences. Since he had been recently describing his father as a man ready to play basketball, but hardly ever there when he wanted to talk with him, I asked him about his father. "Oh, of course, when we were all around the table, things were so quiet I might as well have been in church." After we laughed Jim insisted that he was right and Tillich wrong about the nature of God. "Ground of Being? My God needs a nose, mouth and most of all a tongue."

Larry tucked his legs underneath his easy chair. When I tried to imitate him, I realized how physically pliable he must be. He caught my teasing way of drawing his attention to his effeminate and unquestionably self-effacing posture. He thrust both feet forward, slouched in his chair and asked if this was the correct way to be a man. Next time I saw him, he began the session: "You know, Bernie, when I went home on the subway and looked down the aisle, I thought everyone must be in psychotherapy."

Paul O'Brian (I mention his last name because it helps make our humorous moment a little more intelligible) apparently took my ribbing about his being a stiff to heart. In the middle of a session he fell silent and then, rallying his courage, said he had a joke for me. "Do you know about the little kid who was asked by his teacher to make up a sentence with the word 'judicious'? The kid thought and blurted out, 'My mom makes matzah balls and all the Jew-dishes.'" "Ach, bad," I said. "I don't find that funny, probably because I am myself an even worse punster." Paul chuckled and began to talk of his weekly visits to the Ninety-second Street YM and YWHA. "The other night I topped off my weekly yoga lesson at the YMHA with a trip to Second Avenue. I had some blintzes and sour cream." For some reason, this struck me as funny. "Tomorrow," he continued, "I give a lecture at my church. I'm on the circuit, and I'll tell them about blintzes and sour cream, after yoga, which is better than yogurt. It's Lent, you know."

Paul and I had come quite a way, including the fact that I had been also seeing his wife. For years he felt inadequate in his career, which he didn't even believe he had chosen. Only a month before, he had been quite paralyzed at the prospect of delivering a lecture at a convention. I had concentrated my fire on his fear of success, bred into him by his masters' voices. He had arrived after one of his speeches and, with the dryness to which his sobriety was well adjusted, he said, "The speech went well, only the mimeograph apparatus. . . ." He didn't utter a word during the next few minutes as I heaped on him my righteous indignation for his inability to celebrate. Now he was repaying me with a Lenten service delivered in a Jewish dish while communing with the gods of another faith. The saying that the good doctor is one who keeps the patient amused until he gets better should also be applied to the patient who can just as well comfort his dour caretaker.

The jokes we exchange are only steps along the way to that view of life symbolized in the theater by the twin masks of tragedy and comedy. When my youngest daughter Nadia was born, Clara, then four, drew two faces: "A Sad Face" and "A Happy Face." A patient recently lived through an incident which greatly surprised him and which I said was as profound in its simplicity as it was dramatic for him.

Albert, in his late twenties, was married, but shortly preceding the wedding his homosexual longings could not be contained. Through the years of his life with Mary, he engaged in many an adulterous relation with men.

As he and I struggled with his wish to get out of his homosexual involvements and as he was mastering his conflict, he decided to divorce his wife. However, some time after the divorce he slipped. I said that I was tired of broken agreements. Either he discontinue any sexual involvement or we break off. He decided to go on within these terms, perhaps because he understood that I don't make it a rule to change a homosexual orientation unless requested to do so by the patient. Since Albert found his acquaintance a fairly interesting person, I encouraged him to try to develop a friendship.

A few weeks later Albert described what had happened the previous Sunday. Don had come over for a cup of coffee and after some talk had propositioned him. Albert suddenly found himself laughing. "I was not hysterical, but I didn't stop until Don looked at me in a frightened way as if I might hit him. When I stopped laughing, he, as suddenly as I'd begun to laugh, began to sob." I saw this occurrence as a kind of purification of the two sides of the ambiguous relation we all take to our suffering. Albert had come a long way to be able to relieve through laughter the irony of his position in life as a man of two sexual dispositions. And I surmised that Don, who had been talking with Albert about seeking help, could, in the face of comedy, express clearly and immediately his sadness.

There are numerous occasions when a patient is thinking much better than he usually does and I have become so anesthetized by his dullness that I miss learning something new about him. However, I try to stay alert and try to make the hour go by quickly in our immersion in surprising conversation. Whether I laugh or whether the matter is comical, I can celebrate with the patient when he reveals his strength.

Mandy is two years younger than her brother Alfred, who is now twenty-seven. When she first came to see me, she was a tortured girl of twenty-three, and I mean girl. She was rather plump. For reasons not relevant to my immediate point, she had had to leave college. For a long time she thought of Alfred as the fortunate one. He was closer to her parents, especially her father, with whom he now worked. Mandy twisted herself into knots both to defy her father and to win his love. However, as she found her freedom and returned to school, against her father's wishes, she began to recall Alfred in a different way. "Since I was about seven or eight, I remember Alfred going to ask my father for something and telling him how much he loved him. My father would be brutal and deny this was so. So I was forewarned through Alfred's hurt. Do you know of any research on the greater need of older children to be dependent on their parents?"

I cited some studies and some of the controversies, including comments that older children could have a more difficult time of it. "I am an oldest son of an oldest son myself. But what intrigues me about your comment is something I had never thought of in quite that way. The younger child, if the age difference is not too great, has the same advantage as a therapist. He is a participant, but he also is an observer and, as you said, forewarned is forearmed. Of course, this need not always be the case. Yet for you this recall of the memory of compassion through which you could recognize the advantages of looking at a relationship squarely is very good. And for me it also gives another cast to the problems of siblings."[1]

The patient and I need the affirmation of each other's encouragement to be at our best as well as to reveal our worst. So I celebrate with him his best thinking as I criticize his tearing himself to shreds. I shuddered with a friend of mine who recalled an episode from his analysis. "Once, after about four years on the couch, I asked Dr. Shimorov why she didn't praise me for my good points as well as analyze my coldness, hostility, anxiety and all that. She answered that the positives would take care of themselves and that we were there to take care of the negatives." My friend, a psychologist who was well versed in the literature on reward and punishment as incentives to learn and who has also taught child development, agreed with me when I chastised him. "You should have quit right then and there, or at least asked her where she got her conscience." I hope my patients have the courage to close the door in my face if I ever imply that joy in their achievement is not called for.

There are many occasions for a party in the office. Patients graduate from school, meet new friends, stand up to a feared parent, become engaged, have birthdays and surprise us with original observations we haven't heard before. The best gift a patient gives to me is his freer imagination and his courage to look others in the face. When he can do this, we will know he does not need to come any more. It is best when the last official session is a time of singing. I am saddened when the patient stops coming and we cannot laugh, but even then his right to say no to me, a right which for all patients has been hemmed in by his childhood relations and too often reinforced by educational authorities, and a right which I try to nurture, is itself a cause for a hurrah.

Sometimes I become perversely and persistently playful. "Let's play a game. It's a new approach to therapy based on communication theory, linguistics and the analysis of all kinds of interpersonal transactions. So we can do it on the highest and most up-to-date authority. Erich Berne recently wrote a book, a pretty funny one too, called *Games People Play*, but let us not be misled as to the seriousness of our intention to help you get out of your rut." Having assured the patient that this is the latest fashion and approved for its safety though not for its efficacy, he may even be amused at the cleverness we can display in the analysis of the rules by which we check and double-check each other.

"Stephen Potter assures us that lifemanship is a game in which one is always up and the other is always one down.[2] The one down tries to get one up by playing a ploy which will get the one up one down. One good ploy to get the other down is to go down further and then jump up before he knows it and cry, 'See what you have done to me!' Jews have called this particular ploy the Schlemiel. And just to encourage you to continue with me, I remind you that the Zen masters have practiced this art for centuries, so our game partakes of the wisdom of the sages."

If he is bright enough, I can refer him to a book on computers which are wired according to certain rules. We can then figure out how he has been programmed and how I am the new data which he is processing according to the programs wired into him by some other operators. If he is even more knowledgeable, he'll catch on that this language has some semblance to other systems describing mental operation. The current slogan of the coexistence segment of the party is "rules of the game." It is, these liberals insist, a better slogan than the one that for years had been pushed by the Sullivanian revisionists: "parataxic distortions." And this one had in turn been offered as an alternative to the banner slogan of the orthodox faithful: "ego defenses."

To survive the ins and outs of party politics, we must keep up with the times, be flexible, speak about gamesmanship rather than offer incantations about motives and the psychodynamics of systems. I try to be a slippery fellow and adopt any language that is in favor with the particular voter. Except, perhaps, body language when I don't feel like holding hands or when it becomes uncleanly erotic and gets in the way. So it can be Freudian, Jungian or, better yet, our own language developed as we proceed in our conversation. That's what it is all about after all is said. We have been conversing with each other toward friendliness. That's what Dr. Schofield tells us is the nature of psychotherapy when he labels his book *Psychotherapy: The Purchase of Friendship*. I like to remind the patient that I can be thought of as a verbalizing prostitute, a whore who sells his soul. That is more virtuous than being a gigolo.

Friendship has one rule which must be agreed on by both players. They make up most of the rules as they go along and discard those which lead them to play ice hockey on the grass and football when they wish to walk in the rain. "Let us play such a game," I suggest to the patient. "You tell me what is going on in you and in me, and I'll ask you how I am and tell you if you are correct. It is a game of hide and seek, of me reaching you and you getting to me. It is a game in which I have one advantage. If you lose, I think I'll lose too, but you lose more than I do because by definition, and by your predisposition and mine, I am the dealer and 'dealer's choice,' you know. But then again, if you win, I'll win too, but you will win more than I do because you are betting more than I am. I am betting a little of my professional reputation and a little time, and you are betting your years and a 'little' money.

"But what if we can make up a rule which is as inflexible as we can make it? We decide that we both start from scratch. No inequities and no differences except those that come about as we play together. I immediately tell you about any advantages in my position, and you tell me of any weaknesses in my moves which you spot before I do. You don't think such a game is possible between us? I am the doctor and you are the patient? That's an easy move to counter. My move is: no wonder you are the patient! You fall out of the game I want to play: Mutuality. You insist on having it your way, to be the patient. All right, I can play that way if you insist until I trick you into playing it my way. When you get tired of playing inequality, you'll play another game which doesn't cost as much. Or I can say, 'When you get tired of moving like a schlemiel, when you get tired of pretending your position is weaker than mine, you will get out of this office. You may even leave before that if you decide I am crazier than you are. Like the grandma brought by her family to the psychiatrist for no reason of her own, who opened an eye after the doctor had hypnotized her, saw her most beloved son standing over her couch and asked, "Has the Nut already gone away?"

"I have some more to say. Since hypnosis didn't work well enough, let me try to persuade you why I think the best game any two persons can play is the game of Mutuality and Equality. And the best way any person can play this game is to make sure he picks someone who is different enough to make a difference and fair enough not to humiliate him. You see, I am an idealist after all, and I have faith that two persons, big and small, smart and not so clever, man and woman, rich and not rich, can meet, even if for a short time, and look each other in the eyes and gain an advantage which Abraham Maslow calls 'Synergy' and 'The Peak Experience.' Some call it the norm of love and social justice. Whatever we call it, that's what I believe we do when we play the game of psychotherapy at this time in history. We are manifesting that longing, that call to brotherhood, which has moved men to rebellion against oppressors. You and I can only play this game imperfectly because we are imperfect and because we are conditioned to a game of competition and to a rule that my gain is your loss. The dice are loaded, the cards are stacked, the house has rigged the odds against our winning. That's what makes our effort such a funny one."

7

EQUALITY BETWEEN PATIENT

AND THERAPIST

In the last decade or so, it has become commonplace to refer to therapists as value makers. The therapist has become much less an objective and neutral technician and much more a person who represents to the patient a pattern of values more or less integrated with his behavior and the community. I will cite two authorities who have helped us realize that the therapeutic relation is always expressing values, beliefs, feelings and attitudes which achieve objectivity only because they are shared and agreed to by therapist and patient. Thomas Szasz, in speaking of "the myth of mental illness," has made the sharpest critique of the notion that problems of living significantly parallel the medical concept of disease of the body. He wrote:

Psychiatrists are not concerned with mental illnesses and their treatments. In actual practice they deal with personal, social and ethical problems of living. . . .
As to psychotherapy, it should be systematized as a theory of human relationships, involving special social arrangements and fostering certain values and types of learning.[1]

And Dr. Jules Masserman, commenting on the typical distinctions psychotherapists make among such terms as "advice," "guidance," "suggestion," "interpretation," and so forth, an issue which I will discuss in a later chapter, cut through the pretense of detachment:

Actually, all of us, whatever detachment we pretend to assume or with whatever subcult we wish to identify, are duly trained, commissioned, and empowered by our society to implement, albeit with some latitude, its current concepts and procedures. Ergo, our "guidance" is oriented by our own experiences with the cultural road map and our interpretations, however tactful and periphrastic, have the same implicit deterrent, reorientative, and "persuasive" power as those of other teachers and ministers who, with us, constitute the velvet glove over the strong hand of the police and judiciary. As intelligent citizens, we can try to effect gradual improvements in the social order, but if, as psychiatrists, we depart radically from the local mores (morality), either in what we do or "advise," we, too, would be impeached.[2]

I cannot be neutral. What do I affirm? I accent five values in all relations: (1) freedom of action and imagination; (2) personal responsibility for one's contribution to any relation; (3) change as a concrete, ever-present actuality rather than a potentiality; (4) respect for and encouragement of diversity; and (5), which includes and implies the others: equality between persons. What I mean by these statements should be much clearer by the end of this chapter, but I would expect that, even as these values are headlined, most people would not question the first four statements as properly applying to therapy and that most would take issue with the value of equality between patient and therapist. Therefore, it is on this value that I will center my comments. I will describe the others—freedom, responsibility, diversity and change—largely in terms of my definition of equality, and will offer an elaboration of its usefulness as an interpretation of much of what makes for healing. And as is always the case, we labor to define what the great poets compress into a few lines. Euripides had Jocasta say to her son, Eteocles:

Nature gave men the law of equal rights,
And the less, ever marshalled foe against
The greater, ushers in the dawn of hate.[3]

And in our decade Erik Erikson, often inspiring and quotable, wrote:

The polarity Big-Small is the first in the inventory of existential oppositions such as Male and Female, Ruler and Ruled, Owner and Owned, Light Skin and Dark, over all of which emancipatory struggles are now raging both politically and psychologically. The aim of these struggles is the recognition of the divided function of partners who are equal not because they are essentially alike, but because in their very difference they are both essential to a common function.[4]

I am making a point in using the word "equality" and not "mutuality" or "complementarity." These latter terms suggest the act of sharing in an interdependent relation which, though an important feature of equality, is not synonymous with what I mean. I use this word because it denotes the formulae: the therapist's power equals the patient's power, or the therapist's stake in the immediate relationship between himself and the patient is as great as the patient's stake, or in the immediate relation the patient's good is the therapist's good.

These formulae, like all articles of faith, are considered to be true. But the norm of equality is not only an ideal. The significant interactions between the patient and myself can best be interpreted in terms of our having equal power. When I comprehend the patient's distress as arising from his feeling humiliated, his disturbance is reduced or it is released in a direct expression of feelings. Yet when I discuss the concept of our essential equality directly with the patient, I find its rationale more difficult to make meaningful to him than any other concept. I occasionally begin to doubt my wits or my five or six senses and think I must be a fanatical and blind believer in an ideal which, as attractive as it may be in principle, is never realized in practice. However, my repeated experience in all my relations—with my wife, children, friends and the world at large, as well as with patients—provides me with concrete evidence that the value of equality is not only a faith but a reasonable interpretation of the evidence of our relations.

The patient hears much about equality. Whether he has faith in it or not, I act and talk with him as if it were real. I acknowledge that my faith and fervor are reminiscent of an attitude which has fanatically excluded the reasoning of others. In science nothing is true until it is put to the test, and I am suggesting that believing makes it true. However, I think the practice of equality and the recognition of those inequities which inevitably arise do circumscribe the risks of doing harm when one appears to be a true believer. And I remind the patient that it is he who is the ultimate judge of the usefulness of our behavior. "You cannot avoid evaluating whether I am listening to you. When you leave the office, temporarily or for good, obviously it is what you make of what we said together that matters most. And the larger the investment, the more power you have."

THE LIBERATION OF CHILDHOOD

It was said that a little child will lead the way. Our unmuted reveries tell us the wisdom of the Biblical prophecy. Fragmented, joy-filled or icy and unrelieved even by hurtful violence, a memory reveals the little child in us stealthily stalking and taking us by surprise, standing beside us or beckoning us to turn at the corner. In the whole man his many selves are always equal in affectionate criticism, celebration and quiet contemplation. A sick man's selves constantly overwhelm each other until the fragments are indistinguishable. We need not try to be children again; we always are.

The twentieth century is the century of the equality of women, of nations and of races. It is the century when the rights of man have been incorporated into international convenants. And it is the century of the rights of infants and children.[5] Our formative years have taken their place within man's pantheon to creativity. Modern psychology has told us this practical ideal: dissolve the notion of parenthood as dominion over children and the parent will be rewarded by the creative life of the child. The evidence of research and clinical experience adds up to the maxim: "Parents, trust your relation to your child, respect him and he will respect you, deal with him fairly and he will be fair to you, love him and he will love you." A child can regulate his diet to make nutritional sense, a child is eager to learn, a child will become ethical and well mannered and well behaved not when he is told to do so but because he identifies with the ethical behavior of his parents.

Will this not spoil him? This word has lost its original meaning. Don't adults like to have a give and take with each other, and don't we also need to feel we are someone's precious person? Every child can become a demanding, oppressive adult, but such people have not had what psychologists tell us they need. To be spoiled means to be indulged with gifts which bribe the child to keep his peace alone and not be engaged with others in the noise of growing up. You can force a child into a mold, but he'll take his revenge on someone, perhaps on you, probably on his colleagues and certainly on those with whom he lives in intimacy.

If the parent is concerned about who pays for it, he will not dominate his child, because he will be immediately fed back the results of any input into a child we could reasonably call "getting his way." Let us say I insist that my daughter pick up the dish she has thrown to the floor. She refuses and I deprive her of the bedtime story. In the middle of the night she awakens us with the news that she has wet her bed. Who won and who lost? Illustrations can be piled on examples, as they do in the therapist's office. Every hour there is a tale told by a patient of a Pyrrhic victory. The parent assumed that his superior knowledge, experience and responsibility required his child to accommodate to grown-up influence. This assumed that the adult's power to discipline his child was greater than the child's power to retaliate by becoming sick, mad, delinquent or indifferent. All the qualities of interpersonal relations studied by psychologists have been boiled down to two dimensions in the crucible of the statistical technique of factor analysis: ascendance-submission and warmth-hostility.[6] Time and again it is shown the person who lives his relations more fully than others is more likely to have been a child who grew up where parents liked him and where parents did not dominate or submit to his willfulness.

The real child before us, if we do not force ourselves or him, is a companion, and gives us as much as we give to him. No bargain need be struck, no contract to have a friend in the infant we hold or put to bed. Duty has its hours in the nursery as elsewhere, but if the parent and child are lucky, they are telling each other stories most of the time. Allowed to take us where he goes, the child goes where we wanted him to be without our knowing it.

I heard a child of two say to his quarreling parents, "Getting noisy here," and I saw him leave after they laughed together. I heard a child of three whose mother had just admonished her with "Don't be so cranky" reply, "Don't be sad, you were crying in the morning." A child treated as an equal will say to his father, "Do you like yourself?" when his father says to him, "I like you."

Once a minister wrote to me after we had discussed the idea of equality: "Regarding equality as a fact: my three-year-old son, when I stop him from doing what he wants, screams 'Goddamit.' How he knows that that is the last thing I want him to scream is beyond me." I thanked him for the vivid example and speculated that in our deepest experience of our faith we are also blasphemous.

A child was unfairly punished by her father because he was extremely upset over a very important relationship. A short few minutes after the father took out his anger on his two-and-a-half-year-old daughter, he broke into sobs. The following day he apologized to the little girl for his unreasonableness. She said simply, "But Daddy cried." Gratitude need not be taught because it cannot. By the time we are three- or four-year-olds we are quite capable of telling others how lucky we are to have so much. That is, if we have been given the priceless gift of respect for our persons, which means a respect for the power in our being alive. The secret is as obvious as the treasure of pure air; like begets like. If mutuality and equality with our children and our childhood selves restore to us our faith and affection, then why not with our patients?

The therapist in the office serves the patient to a good measure as the defense attorney of the child within him. If it is a parent who is being counseled, it is his child who is being defended; his child and the child he was who had been hurt and sometimes crushed to a point where the optimism and enormous energy and potential for change and growth which are the child have been almost lost from memory. If it is a child being helped, it is through his hearing the therapist assuring him, "We shall overcome."

The parent, reaching across the chasm of decades separating him from his child, tries to break out of those explanations which appeared to his generation sufficient to make his suffering and joy meaningful. In trying to put behind him his own philosophy, suitable for his age and time, and trying to capture the world view revealed by his own child, he must experience himself as on an equal footing with his offspring. If I do not impose my system on my daughter but try to follow her way, my consciousness cracks as her growing pains ache. It is revelation through time and growth and change, which can reduce the fraudulence and deception of believing that when we help the child, friend or patient to take a step we are showing him the right way and providing him with the correct meaning.

EQUALITY IN THE THERAPEUTIC RELATION

Before the therapist is a patient of his own age; the opportunity and challenge lie in the recognition of their equality in confronting problems and asking the questions each asks in his other relations; the irony lies in the attitude of the doctor, that he can leave his life stage at home while the patient cannot. Before the therapist sits a youngster grappling with his career or his choice of mate. The opportunity for the therapist lies in remembering the struggle which beset him or, if the choices were clearly and happily made, the recollected humility of being a lucky person. In either case the therapist is called to be compassionate more than knowledgeable, wise more than informed and hopeful more than assured. The irony is in the doctor's assuming that age gives him the right to know better.

And when the patient is an older man, a man who, in speaking his mind, as he is asked to do, hovers over the fact of death in this life, how is the doctor to answer him? It is in the meeting of the healthy and the dying person that being and existence become starkly stripped to the essentials of what each one makes of each moment in time. No longer does the doctor have any special knowledge or even wisdom, unless he believes in or is called upon to provide a palliative, a sedative, or lies about the true condition.

I suppose my I.Q. is as high as or higher than the majority of the patients who seek me out. I am sure that the number of my years of formal education, certified by academic degrees, is greater than that of 90 percent of the people who call me for an appointment. I am taller, heavier, older and economically better off than most of them. Take any trait that can be quantitatively measured with reasonable accuracy, and I will come out ahead more often than not. Even on the vague but vital criterion, happiness and contentment with my fate, I am probably more content with my lot than most of my patients.

What has become more impressive to me than all this is the ways in which the patient endows me with significance and the negative and positive ways he asserts this power. I used to call his negative power, "resistance," but I don't any longer because I resist him as much as he does me. If I am to reach him, he must also feel I have been affected by him. If he is to change in our relation, I must change too. If I am to teach him something about his mind, he will teach me something about mine. I think that the dedicated interest I show in his thoughts is more important than the particular comments I make about his mind, but I also know that his interest in what I think is as important as my concern for him. If he agrees to what I say and my reasons for saying it, it is because I have allies on my side. Unseen are all those who have ever shown him affectionate respect. They speak again through my tongue. If he objects to something I say, I may react defensively and accuse him of resisting the emergence of some painful Freudian, Jungian, Adlerian or whatever complex. Or when I get down from my high horse, I will state that we misunderstood each other.

Can the patient and doctor achieve equality? Is the prescription by Maxwell Jones of a therapeutic community as a set of relations transcending social roles an unrealizable ideal and thus antitherapeutic? Is it possible for aides, psychiatrists, nurses, patients, psychologists, parents, wives, citizens and social workers to meet in their humanness so that their individual possibilities and talents enrich the language of mutuality rather than assert their place in the pecking order?[7]

If the doctor reveals his own limitations, does he not lose his healing power? In 1936 Carl Jung wrote:

But since all life is to be found only in individual form, and I myself can assert of another individuality only what I find in my own, I am in constant danger either of doing violence to the other person or of succumbing to his influence. If I wish to treat another individual psychologically at all, I must for better or worse give up all pretentions to superior knowledge, all authority and desire to influence. I must perforce adopt a dialectual procedure consisting in a comparison of our mutual findings. But this becomes possible only if I give the other person a chance to play his hand to the full, unhampered by my assumptions. In this way his system is geared to mine and acts upon it; my reaction is the only thing with which I, as an individual, can legitimately confront my patient.

About the same time he also commented: "I do not know which is the more difficult; to accumulate a wide knowledge or to renounce one's professional authority and anonymity."[8]

Paul Tournier wrote of the doctor and the patient:

We have both of us left convention behind, we are really encountering each other. This is what Dr. Dubois of Berne, one of the pioneers of modern psychotherapy, meant when he said as far back as 1905: "Hold out your hand then to the poor sick man. Do not be afraid of frankly admitting to him your weakness, your inborn shortcomings. Bring yourself close to him."[9]

HIERARCHY AND RESISTANCE

The very way the doctor-patient relationship is defined contributes to the patient's so-called resistance to therapy. One person comes to the other for help. Immediately the two are involved in a superior-subordinate contact, as defined by the doctor who is the expert and the patient who has learned his lesson well from all those who have taught him where to go when he is in trouble. The patient who states on the telephone, when making arrangements for the first interview, "I want to know whether you think I need treatment," is clearly acknowledging the doctor's social role as diagnostician. He may be trying to avoid the responsibility of doing something he already has decided must be done. However, this kind of request of the therapist is consistent with the professional role of a person who sells his services.

When we accent our superior skill and knowledge as the basic reason which brings the patient to us and which will make the difference, we generate resistance. When we accept the relation between the helper and the applicant as a superior-inferior one, we convert the fact that there is always some experience of humiliation in such a situation into a norm as to what the relation should be. A person resents being dependent and being reminded he is so.

In the office of the private practitioner, the patient presumably balances the exchange with his therapist by paying a fee. In Chapter XIII I will discuss the meanings the fee may have in ameliorating or intensifying the hierarchical relation. Here I only assert that the payment of a fee, though it may help temporarily in some instances, cannot settle the account through any period in which the patient and doctor become more than superficially acquainted. The payment of the fee often becomes itself the arena of resentment over the need for psychological assistance. Is it possible to equate money with persons and not irritate the patient or the doctor? The problematical aspects inherent in the suggestion that the payment of a fee also helps overcome the sense of humiliation is brought into focus when we consider the actual or potential client who can't afford the fee asked by private practitioners.

A positive step the person placed in an inferior status may take is illustrated by a personal reminiscence by Lord Clarendon, who is, as I write, Chief of the British Mission to the UN, and was formerly Governor of Cypress, Tanganyika and Nigeria. In a speech I once heard him make he said something like the following: "The small nations have a number of things in common and one is that they have an accurate evaluation of the big nations. They have to have to survive and grow. As an officer, I was always more accurate in evaluating my superiors than my subordinates." When I listen to the patient before me and encourage him to criticize me, not for the purpose of learning something about his transferences but because I know he has been sizing me up and I can learn from him, he will give me something valuable. He will generally repay my gratitude to him for helping me with a burst of trust and further revelation.

Joan was irritated with me. After having made some progress she told me she was annoyed. "I guess this is what happens to me all the time. Last week I wrote to you that I can't tell you yet how glad I am you're you, and now I'm mad."

"But, Joan, before we jump on this train, what is it that got you sore? It may be your ambivalence, but it may be I did get you mad."

"Last week when I was talking about Bob and the way I proposed to him, you had to make the point about the rights of women. My father was always speaking about women's rights, as I told you a few weeks ago, and here you went off like he did."

"O.K., so maybe you see me like your father, but I think my little speech also was aggravating because it was something you knew, it was talking down to you. I can sound like you don't know your ABC's. I have this tendency to overdo my values and sermonize. My only regret is that you didn't call me on the spot."

Joan continued about how she had for a long time assumed she knew her sister's feelings and condition better than Ann did. She would always get irritated with Ann for her hysterics until one day she telephoned her mother and unexpectedly found Ann at home.

Ann sounded depressed, but her whine annoyed Jane. "I did everything I could to check my balling her out. Before I burst out she
asked me, 'Joan, do you love me?' The question turned me around
and inside out. Ann was feeling miserable. She had tried to slash her
wrists. I was lucky I shut up. We have had many talks since, and I
have found out how my envy of her relation to my parents made no
sense."

Joan and I were talking about the common fate of all those who
are hurt and rejected. She knew quite a bit about falling in and out
of love and her ambivalence toward her father. But when I did not
let the matter rest on some abstraction, but focused on what she and
I were doing to each other, she could speak of the equality of suffering between her sister and herself. The only moral I drew for her at
the end of the session was my faith that our identification with all
those who suffer is an aspect of loving between two persons. Yet I
think that this value, to become meaningful, must be affirmed in a
concrete exchange between the patient and me in which the patient
gives me something in kind.

Personal Responsibility and Equality

Within the field of psychotherapy, even though there is considerable disagreement as to how it should occur, experts agree that the
therapist helps mobilize the patient's sense of his autonomy and
responsibility. This value is a keystone of the democratic system.
The leader is always supposed to be responsive and responsible to
the voice of the people. In the widest sense, the predominating conception of man is that he is a creature uniquely endowed by nature
or by God with the capacity for a conscience.

If I am to contribute to the patient's increased sense that his
passions will not drown him in a cascade of tears, or draw him into a
volcanic eruption or shatter him in a gale of laughter, as a therapist I
must share with him the responsibility of what occurs in the time we
are together. I am as responsible for what occurs between us as he
is. If he does not respond, then it is my stimulus which may be
mistimed. If he wishes to die, then my faith in living life to the end
may not have been adequately heard.

My training and the weight of the literature I read push me to think that the patient is sick and is therefore likely to make a sick demand of me. Whatever effort I make to help is the best I can do, and it is his avoidance of his responsibility which is the basic trouble. If the patient doesn't respond well, the fault may also lie in other directions. After all, the study of emotional dysfunction is a relatively new one, and there is so much yet to be discovered about this patient's particular illness. Or my inexperience with this type of case could be the cause of failure. But, in the concrete instance, the center of gravity is the patient's recalcitrance. He is more at fault than the doctor since it is his resistance, his infantilism, and his refusal to take responsibility for his condition. Therapy, I used to think, was successful more or less or a failure more than less. Now I try to get out of the structures forced on the patient and myself by the very words we have been taught to use when speaking of our relation: "patient," "doctor," "success," "failure," "psychotherapy," etc. I try to think: "We are here together to do something together to make our relationship grow—he and I, he as well as I—and if it doesn't work, I have failed as well as he."

Clinicians recognize that the very act of voluntarily seeking help is the most important step toward the growth of personal responsibility and freedom. The patient says, in effect, "I want a different experience." When I, the expert-doctor-therapist, immediately concern myself with the causes of his difficulties, I force him into the position of a case, an example of a class of individuals. We begin to investigate the general rules determining his behavior. However, if I try to hear the novel and the unique, i.e., what I haven't heard before, the patient and I can become aware of our equality. We are both seeking something different and new. We are both challenging each other's imagination and intelligence. Rather than question the patient only about his lives in suffering, I want to hear of his lives in creativity. The patient has withdrawn from others in fright or in anger or in response to any number of feelings which he has learned to mistrust. Why ask him only about this and not ask him about the times he has been open with others, with an enemy as well as a friend? However, even more to the point, why not always be alert to the new emergent between us, whether it be a new hair-do, a firmer step, a heartier handshake or a clear protest against my getting in his way?

The customary opening question, after some social preliminaries, is something like "Well, tell me about your troubles," or "What brings you to seek help?" What if, instead, I affirmed and asked, "Hopefully you will be able to look me straight in the eyes and discern if I am reasonably lively and relatively unhampered by symptoms. So why not tell me about your strengths, your open voices, about the time you defended your integrity rather than curled up and cried or got a headache or all those signs of fear we call symptoms?" The patient might show me a "thing or two." I read novels and philosophies to regain my hold on the meaningfulness of life in the face of its frustrating limits and its circumscription by death. Why not get this lift from the patient, who has undoubtedly been through his form of hell before coming to see me and whose roads through his inferno, though certainly not so eloquent as Dante's, can nevertheless lead me to some measure of wondrous awe over the human spirit?

The following passage in Hammerskjöld's *Markings* expresses the idea I have been reaching for in an utterly simple way:

> Humility is just as much the opposite of self-abasement as it is of self-exaltation. To be humble is *not to make comparisons*. Secure in its reality, the self is neither better nor worse, bigger nor smaller, than anything else in the universe. It is—is nothing, yet at the same time one with everything. It is in the sense that humility is absolute self-efface-ment.[10]

When life is stripped of pretense as far as the conditions demand, both persons can stand in humility. The dross of measurement has burned off.

THE PATIENT'S SUSPICION OF TECHNIQUE

I think one of my assets in my involvement with patients is a directness and immediacy of manner and response. Many people have told me that they like my spontaneous actions, just as others have criticized me for them. I agree that I rarely can be accused of using psychological jargon in speaking with them. I like to surprise myself and others. It thus comes as a shock to some patients when they become aware that a particular piece of my behavior has been calculated to bring about a certain effect. The patient may accuse me of double talk since I have de-emphasized knowledge of procedures, and yet there I was consciously employing a technique.

I think all patients notice my style, though most do so covertly. They expect a professional to meet them with whatever paraphernalia is appropriate to his trade. That's what they are essentially inquiring about when they ask me, "What school do you belong to?" But occasionally a particular patient will directly complain to me about my maneuver and call me to task for contradicting my value of spontaneous behavior stripped of mannered ways as befitting the role of therapist. Usually the complaint arises when my manipulation has distressed them, but patients have also taken note when the consequence of my technique has been pleasant.

In addition to an effort to understand why the patient had brought to my attention my technique at that particular time, I also discuss the issue on its own merits. My "defense" runs something like the following dialogue:

B. What's wrong with using a technique? Don't you make plans to get something you want or increase the pleasure in your work?

X. Of course, you don't have to tell me about artists and scientists in the laboratory. But you seemed to me insincere, you didn't mean what you were doing. It got a rise out of me because you tell me of my artifices and yet you can use yours. That's double talk.

B. You do have a point there—my mixed messages. But first, do you object that it worked or that you didn't like the result?

X. If I liked the result I probably wouldn't object so much, but why did you manipulate me to get at my complex?

B. Is your question "why" a complaint or an inquiry? If it is mainly a question, I think we're getting at the gist of your irritation.

X. My "why" was mainly a complaint.

B. But aren't you and I and all of us playing a game? Can't we examine our relation also in terms of its style? Your way of moving is habitual, your language has a grammar which gives us clues as to your intentions. Now, just because I have thought about the rules of my behavior more than you have, is that perhaps a reason why you complain?

X. It could be. You are suggesting that I envy your range and flexibility of maneuver, and that I resent your advantage over me in being more aware of what you're doing.

B. Yes, I think that is a factor. Once you're in this field, and once you engage in the task of increasing consciousness, you never—well, almost never—let go without having some sense of where you're headed. This feeling of self-consciousness at times becomes burdensome to me and to others. My friend complains that I psychoanalyze too much, and I complain that I can't stop seeing the complexities of the issues. As one patient told me the other day, "Oh, for the lovely time before I came to see you, when I could make a judgment and not give a hoot."

X. O.K., so I object because you play the game better than I, or I object because I have to accept the responsibility of my actions through becoming increasingly aware of the impact I made. That's called, you tell me, getting control. But I am also supposed to learn to let go.

B. Practice makes perfect.

X. But I'm still not satisfied with your explanations. There is still something about your doing it to me which isn't out in the open.

B. I'm glad you pursue it. In fact, your raising the issue in the first place is the sign that you are overcoming what I think is the basic problem between us which leads to your feeling manipulated. That you confront me with what I'm doing is fine. But notice, you hesitate to pursue the matter one step further. You don't ask me, really ask me, why I did what I did. Not a "why" in the sense of your needs, but the "why" in the sense of where I learned it. You object because I have the permission to penetrate your rules to discover the meanings of them and why you play parchesi when the game is chess. Usually we find out that parcheesi is the game your father liked, while chess is the game your intelligent wife is forcing on you.

X. You're preaching your doctrine of equality.

B. Exactly. But not only because I want to help you "feel good and respected." Sometimes I could sound like July Fourth. But here I'm quite serious. If you allowed yourself to try to pin me down, and I did what I ask you to do, namely, consider your confrontation, I could become aware of the repetitiousness in my style which is inappropriate to the issue between us. It would then come out that my so-called cold technique, my method which you feel as impersonal and manipulative, is actually something I do because it has some deep meaning to me. I may be following the book, or a teacher of mine, or a way my mother showed me. I think every therapist who has practiced while he is in therapy himself will tell you how he apes his analyst. It took me some time to get mine out of the office, and I'm not blaming her for my bringing her in. Occasionally I still catch myself doing something to a person which she did to me. Then I realize I was less aware than I had presumed. When you continue to object and feel I've put something over on you, it's because you don't feel you have the right to know in what relations I have learned the game, while I have the right to break into your privacy. And it's the right to inquire which I extol as a virtue. Many times, even most of the time, you will not pick up your option because the limited time we have for discussion leads you to say, in effect, "For the sake of getting on, I'll give him the benefit of the doubt."

The patient usually appears satisfied with my rhetoric. But he may still fear that he is being brainwashed and that he will not be allowed to look behind the scene and discover what the mystique is all about. We can enjoy the excitement of a contest as long as we can ask our opponent in the game to expose his sleeves so that we can see for ourselves whether he has hidden some cards which belong to another deck.

Social Class and Equality

Class differences, even in our society dedicated to the elimination of poverty and injustice, are marked by a high incidence of almost every form of disorganization among the lower socioeconomic groups. It thus hardly seems to make sense for me to argue that in the therapy situation there is an essential equality between the middle-class therapist and the lower-class patient. But consideration of the class variable brings to our attention something that is largely overlooked in the relation between patient and doctor of the same class that is of fundamental importance to the outcome of the therapeutic enterprise.

Long before middle-class persons became patients and doctors, they had a long training in common ways of thinking about the causes and amelioration of pain. For example, middle-class doctors and patients essentially agree that it is wise to think and plan ahead and that it is wise to be aware of oneself. Psychotherapeutic methods and theories, largely developed by middle-class doctors in their work with middle-class patients, are based on the idea of reasonable and, if need be, protracted discussion before any action is taken. Foresight rather than hindsight is the motto. What a critic of the middle class would call inhibition and conformity, the middle class person considers to be the virtue of prudence and circumspection.

Cultural differences have been credited with making the professional lives of middle-class doctors more difficult when they engage themselves with lower-class patients. The usual theories and techniques do not work. And since the therapists who continue to work with lower-class patients wish to be successful, they are forced to abandon their conventional modes of thinking. This may have a liberalizing effect. Dr. John Spiegel found it necessary to modify the principle of nonreciprocity in talking with Irish-American, lower-class patients.

We answer personal questions about ourselves and do not hesitate to reveal our own value attitudes upon a variety of issues. Although our *therapeutic standards* [my italics] have made us somewhat uneasy about such conduct, we have gradually become more comfortable with it. Especially has it become easier as we have come to understand how the Irish-American patient perceives non-reciprocity. Failure to answer a question, directing it back to the patient, or interpreting it are perceived as evasive maneuvers.[11]

In attempting to change the troubled poor, the expert also changes. Those who do not give up by saying that lower-class persons are on the whole too sick to benefit from standard procedures meet the challenge by becoming revisionists of theory and inventors of new approaches. The development of family counseling, group work, home visits, conferences-in-the-street, settlement house projects and the entire gamut of approaches which have come under the rubric of Community Psychiatry stem almost solely from confrontation with lower-class patients. In turn, these approaches have affected the practice with middle-class patients, though I think far too slowly.

To rephrase my definition of equality: the power of a person or a group is equivalent to the power required to move them. This principle is directly adapted from Newton's Law that every action has an equal and opposite reaction. Those therapists who try to meet and help people in different cultural frameworks must expend an unusual amount of energy together and by themselves to feel useful and successful. Failures can be readily rationalized as due to the unreachability and incurable sickness of the patient. But this is only another way of saying that the therapist doesn't wish to invest the energy and time to keep knocking at the door.

I think I'm making a quite obvious point. The investment of power or energy in forms which vary from the large government grants, through intensive and concentrated courses in training personnel, to in-service seminars and conferences to exchange ideas and get new ones is, I think, evidence for my argument. And for this investment "to pay off," the experts who meet other cultural groups must first develop a deep respect for the great power of these groups. I do think it would be most important that I convey to the lower-class person, in whatever ways it makes sense to him, that our enterprise is a joint one requiring the full cooperation of both of us, and not only his. I am there to learn *at least* as much from him as he is from me.

I should be there to learn of the so-called communication networks which every group develops to survive and to resist the incursion of dangerous forces. I should learn their language. My success as a student must depend on the openness of my teachers, the people to whom I reach out and say I want to be with and of use to. I think that without my attempt to have the community of disadvantaged show me the way I would fail.

By now the principle is widely accepted that prejudices of all kinds are reduced or eliminated when equal-status, face-to-face relations are established.[12] And again, the correlation of this principle with the basic findings of the group dynamics movement, the experience with self-help programs and so on comes to mind. It is this repeated discovery, that the community therapist does not bring cold solutions to the situation and that he is not there to manipulate, which releases in the people the power previously expended in destructive forms. Delinquency, psychoses, drug addiction and the entire range of social diseases are signs of hatred and rebellion against the forces which have kept them in repression. And it is the increasing awareness by the economically better situated groups that the ghetto is a highly costly condition to themselves as well as to the ghetto dwellers that also becomes a key motive in inducing the recognized leaders of a community to join forces with the disadvantaged. We are our brothers' keepers, in this sense, and they have kept us too.

My direct experience as a therapist, I repeat, is for me the most persuasive evidence that a healing effort will fail if the power of the patient is not recognized as equal to my own. As difficult as it may be to demonstrate this, with middle-class patients who come voluntarily it is easy in comparison to the strangers on the far side of the city, whom I must seek out to help. These displaced persons have been beset by decades of suspicion and hopelessness. If I come not looking down my nose but straight into their eyes, the aversion may change to confrontation and cooperation.

8

SELF-KNOWLEDGE OR

REVELATION OF SELVES?

The Socratic dictum "Know thyself" is followed as a self-evident principle by most therapists of the West. As teachers of any subject matter are expected to impart sound knowledge, the therapist is generally expected to teach his patient how to relate to others through increasing his knowledge of the strategies he uses in conducting himself and through showing him the motives which impel him to distort reality. Psychotherapists are by definition experts in human relations. We are engineers of the heart, operating through techniques of the mind and erecting our bridges on the foundations provided by all the behavioral sciences. Much of our time with patients and colleagues is taken up in discussions which emphasize this view, and I am no exception. But I have become uncertain whether this makes for change.

In what ways does the therapist gain his knowledge? I do not know of any research on the hypothesis that the single most potent influence on the style with which the therapist practices is his own analyst during formal training. I believe it is far ahead of the other sources of knowledge, and that a survey of therapists would show that the second ranking influence would be the student's supervisors with whom he discussed his cases. By the very nature of the supervisory process this means the student also discusses his own difficulties. Formal courses and the voluntary reading of texts and periodicals presenting formal statements of therapies and the latest research reports would be lowest on the list, even following the vivid and occasionally tragic encounters with particular patients. In sum, therapeutic skills are mainly learned in intensive relationships with particular people as the "physician heals himself." Common experience leads us to the conclusion that we learn best when we climb into the pit and look up rather than survey the depths from the safety of a closed fence.

Personal therapy for the doctor, the so-called training analysis, too often, however, becomes a discipleship. Instead of leading us to be humble with the knowledge of how difficult it is to cut through our dispositions to see as we have been taught to see, we become adherents to the school of our therapist. This allegiance is strengthened by the usual circumstance that we limit our exposure to only a small number of analysts and supervisors who fit our bill. Therapists do appear to take a very long time extending their perspectives beyond the reference group in which their professional membership was certified. In 1954 Werner Wolff found that 70 percent of Freudian, Jungian and Adlerian analysts believed their form of therapy best even though there was no systematic evidence for this claim.[1] I would guess that today, more than a decade later, the results of a repeated study would be about the same.

The norm of equality between doctor and patient helps reduce the omnipotence of the therapist's knowledge and ideas. It helps convey to the patient a commonplace in scientific progress: it is always an outcome of an "innocent" question seriously considered. How the therapist meets the patient's doubts about the efficacy of the relationship reveals much about the therapist. Too often, the therapist considers the patient is resisting the therapist's process when doubts in all their variations are expressed. The first hypothesis, if not conviction, is that some painful material is being held back from consciousness and that the patient converts his lack of candor into a spate of criticism.

The patient's criticism is most easily discussed when it is direct, but that is when the person has become much less the patient. My sensitivity and my vulnerability are revealed when the attacks are indirect, as through increase of symptoms, the portrayal of authority in dreams, the way I am greeted in the waiting room or left at the door and so on. Of course, indirect and evasive attacks are the sorts of character difficulties for which the patient needs help. But what do I teach the person if I deem these means of dealing with the therapeutic relationship primarily a resistance to therapy? Do not I then imply to the person that he must learn to conform and to accept something which in its very nature is ambiguous and unclear? If I immediately think of it as resistance and do not convey to him his absolute right to question and disbelieve, do I not interfere with the growth of healthy skepticism and the development of his own unique ways of thinking?

The patient must be helped to be critical of me and of the relationship, because his being in therapy is in a significant measure an abdication of his freedom. Patients have become accustomed to say, "I must learn to trust you." And when I hear this, I respond, sometimes a little bluntly: "I am not asking you to trust me if you mean by trust a dedication to therapy and to my knowledge. I only ask for consideration of what I say, as you ask me to consider what you say and not automatically to believe or reject your constructions of your experiences." The concept of trust is too heavily laden with the necessity of accepting a relationship in which we are relatively helpless. Between equals there is the deep tolerance of disagreement and the conviction that the relationship might end.

I think, too, that requesting trust and interpreting doubts about the efficacy of therapy as resistance is most damaging to the patient because it plays into an assumption of innocence, namely, that suffering can be eliminated. It also reinforces another idea peculiar to the age of science. Knowledge about the way things work has given us immense control over objects. In human affairs, the fact that we appear to know more does not necessarily lead to mastery as it does with objects. Indeed, it may lead to a great deal of hesitation which appears to others, of different beliefs, as paralysis. Therefore, when I express my wish to be successful with the patient by proffering to him a choice interpretation based on the reasonable study of people like him, I may be increasing his expectation that the outcome of therapy is the obliteration, now and forevermore, of anguish and sorrow. The more distraught the person, the more he cherishes the hope of a permanent cure, and patients are supported in this "Before the Fall" fantasy not only by our optimistic-positivistic culture but by the very way we respond to their suffering. Knowledge of self, we imply, will set everything right.

No two exponents of psychotherapeutic orientation stand at more opposite poles on the question of the superiority of the therapist's knowledge than do Freud and Carl Rogers. It is useful to juxtapose a quotation from each to illustrate the divergence between psycho-analytic and client-centered therapy. In 1898 Freud wrote:

Having accurately diagnosed a case of neurasthenic neuroses under observation, and correctly classified its symptoms, one may proceed to transpose into aetiology the symptomatological knowledge so gained and may fearlessly require the patient's confirmation of one's surmises. Denial at the beginning should not mislead the physician; every resist-ance is finally overcome by firmly insisting on what has been inferred, and by emphasizing the unshakable nature of one's convictions.[2]

In 1951 Rogers wrote:

This formulation would state that it is the counselor's function to assume, insofar as he is able, the internal frame of reference of the client, to perceive the world as the client sees it, to perceive the client himself as he is seen by himself, to lay aside all perceptions from the external frame of reference while doing so, and to communicate some-thing of this empathic understanding to the client.[3]

It may seem unfair to juxtapose two statements separated by fifty years. Though the dogmatic position taken by Freud in this quota-tion was modified by himself and his followers, the heavy emphasis on accurate diagnosis based on as complete knowledge of the patient as can be obtained is still the prevailing theme today. Carl Rogers has virtually stood alone in his consistent criticism of diagnosis, prognosis, analysis of resistance and like methods.

Whatever one may question about the Rogerian orientation, such as the assumptions that any person can actually be nonjudgmental,[4] or that any therapist can keep his knowledge from influencing his responses, Rogers and his students have repeatedly affirmed that equality between client and counselor is the normative relation and that the goal of therapy is self-revelation. The client-centered coun-selor is supposed to have an attitude of unconditional positive regard toward the person before him, and try to implement this by empathi-cally identifying himself with the person's revelations. The consist-ency with which the counselor maintains the client's internal frame of reference determines how deeply the client will reveal himself. It is the baring of one's heart and soul to another who loves him and demonstrates his readiness to be with him in his suffering which Rogers defines as healing. Rogers considers the differences between intellectual insight and emotional knowing, between thought and feeling or between actions and experiencing as irrelevant to the counselor's efforts to be in a healing relationship.

Though I have been at one time a Rogerian—in fact, my first official study of counseling occurred in a class with Carl Rogers in the winter months of 1941-42—it is apparent that I am far from nondirective. However, through these most recent years I have come to agree with Rogers' emphasis on self-revelation rather than the imparting of knowledge as the primary contribution the therapist makes to therapy. When I change my emphasis of "Know thyself" to "Reveal yourselves," I believe the distance between the patient and myself is reduced, especially if I also practice what I preach much of the time. It helps, too, when I reveal my selves and speak them spontaneously.

In psychotherapy the past is an emergent in the relation to the therapist and assumes a meaning in the process of being told different from what it had before. It is revealed in a new way to the patient through the therapist's activity and one's agreement or disagreement with the therapist's reactions. In revelation we thus experience not just the discovery of something suppressed but something new that was not there before. It is information reorganized by the context in which the two beings—in becoming—meet.

If the therapist assumes a superior attitude and the patient endows him with superior power, the self concept emerging through the revelations will be of a different order from what it would be if the two met in mutuality and equality.

Psychoanalytic concepts and interpretations of the origins of guilt and guilt feelings extended our perspective on the ubiquitous and pervasive sense of sin and evil. Psychoanalysis helped us become freer thinkers, because it was based on democratic values and the possibility of extending experience through the elimination of hypocrisy. However, in an effort to eliminate the confessor-priest quality from the therapeutic relation and thus separate scientific therapy from priestly healing, psychoanalysts may have reduced the power of their ministrations. We confess when burdened by a sense of being sinful, and we confess to he who may be able to forgive us. Our confessor answers us as an equal or as a superior.

When we meet a person with our own revelations that our hands, too, are dirty, guilt gives way to regret. When I am revealing my selves to another and he his to me, the sense of change, growth and passing time possesses me as much as our immediate exchange. As we experience change, we experience loss and the inevitable and irreducible deprivation that is our lot as we move toward death. We stand in mutual recognition of the fact of existence: when we are most alive, we are most experiencing our limited life. We go on because we are changing.

In my accent on self-revelation, I try to use whatever knowledge I have, or, much better put, whatever opinion I maintain, as a provocation to further revelation. "Knowledge of oneself," I say to the patient, "is an aspect of experiencing which must change through time. Self-knowledge gained with one person will change when we open our frailties and strengths to another's attention. There is always the opportunity for revision through a present challenge, unforeseen and unpredictable, that is, if we affirm the value of self-disclosure and learn to do so. My faith and my goal as a healer are in the releasing communion in which one person is ready to be with another when a revelation of joy or suffering occurs."

Whitehead said: "Expression is the one fundamental sacrament. It is the outward and visible sign of an inward and spiritual grace."[5]

9

HOW THE THERAPIST'S SYSTEM

CORNERS THE PATIENT

Psychotherapy as a talking cure enables the patient and the therapist to discover the contradictions in the patient's life. They explore the double messages he has received from his parents which have made it difficult for him to behave with relative equanimity and dignity in the face of the essential ambiguities of existence. Dr. Gregory Bateson and his colleagues have described this in a theory of schizophrenia as the double bind.[1] The parent who instructs his child, "Don't do what I say, only what I do," is presenting the child with an insoluble dilemma. Inconsistency in parents from one time to another is difficult for a child to comprehend but nonetheless can be understood. However, those messages which say to the child that in effect he is damned if he does and damned if he doesn't are the most distressing. What is a child to do when a father tells him not to back off from a fight except if he is at fault? What is a child to do if she tries to obey a mother who tells her to get a well-paying job and at the same time urges her to do what she most wants to do.

In my efforts to clarify these mixed messages which have left the person in such a confused state, I can neglect to assess the double bind into which I place him. Sometimes a patient does evoke and encourage my self-criticism, and I realize that I have been tying him up. When I have understood my contribution to his block or his resistance, I could readily ascribe this to the mistakes any person makes in trying to help, i.e., it is an error which is par for our course. However, what I can't quite excuse myself for has been neglect on my part to inform the patient directly that what I offer as help can actually contribute to his disturbance. Though my comments are intended to precipitate the complexes which presumably he has been keeping from our attention, the therapeutic situation is itself full of ironies. And since it is my responsibility to help him become aware of the double bind in which he has been caught and in which he often places others, I am required to bring mine into the open before he brings them to my attention. I'd like to review a number of these double binds.[2]

THE BENEFICENCE OF THE THERAPIST

The first way we corner patients is with the notion that we are, by virtue of our training and the awareness of our blind spots, impartial and objective toward all people. A good therapist is supposed to approach the patient with particular traits and not others and to reveal his judiciousness, acceptance, interest, understanding, sagacity and discernment in a fully disciplined manner. We say to the patient that he can take a risk with us to get over his fright. We may quote a cliché such as "Nothing risked is nothing gained." "But what do you risk?" the patient could ask. If he could speak back to us in the words Dr. Shoben used to compare the clinician's attitude toward his patient with that of the audience viewing a tragic play, he probably would never need to see us again.

The psychotherapist, like the audience at a play, enters the special world of his patient under conditions of safety. . . . The fixing of appointments by clock and calendar rather than by personal need and desire; the relative anonymity of the therapist, who rarely talks about himself; the limitations of contacts to the practitioner's office, and the emphasis on the therapist's discriminating between his emotions and judgments and those of the patient and on his attending to the latter without distortion from the former—all these factors underscore the effort of the clinician to attain something very similar to the calm, god's-eye view of the audience at a tragedy.[3]

Dr. Shoben only appears to be loading the case since no one has claimed that the ideal therapist should be Jovian. But we have claimed that the best therapists are those who possess the qualities included in the following conclusion reached by Hans Strupp, who has been more active than anyone I know in carrying through systematic research on the qualities in the therapist which contribute to his effectiveness.

There appear to be distinct qualitative differences, consonant with skills in empathizing with and responding to patient communications, between the protocols of highly experienced and inexperienced therapists. These differences are not easily specified objectively, but sophisticated judges have no difficulty in assigning a protocol to the appropriate group. Differentiating characteristics appear to be: a certain respectful warmth, incisiveness in phrasing a comment, responsiveness to the patient's feelings rather than manifest content of his verbalizations, a quality of humaneness, ability to adapt the patient frame of reference without "taking sides," etc.[4]

No one dedicated to the cause of love and the triumph of hopefulness will deny the solidity of these virtues. The paradox for the therapist, and most markedly for the patient, is in the way these virtues are to be made manifest. Almost by definition, the patient is a person whose parents have been found wanting in these virtues. Therapists should be different and are undoubtedly kinder, more understanding and listen better to the person than have his parents or those with whom he is at present living. I know I can be for a period of time because among other reasons I remind myself that the patient and I will separate after a brief period of time.

How does the patient discern these ideal qualities and differentiate them from good manners? How can the patient be sure that the therapist means what he says and feels what he does? The doctor has been trained to be warm, but is he so or is he exercising a technique? What patient hasn't turned on his therapist and covertly if not overtly accused him of being a machine and going by the book? A therapist tells his patient to let go of his feelings, all of them, spontaneously, but as a therapist, to be effective in his work, he must always be understanding, calm, measured in his words, and in a way which other therapists would judge to be so. No wonder the analogy between audience and clinician occurs to Dr. Shoben, though he neglects one significant fact that makes quite a difference: the audience pays the price of admission.

If we believe what we read in the cases published for professionals or laymen, practicing these virtues is as easy as sitting quietly enraptured at a play. Rarely does one read of an account where a therapist became furious or complained intensely to the patient that he had been hurt or told the patient that a certain piece of behavior was at the least uncalled for if not downright unacceptable. We are supposed never to become exasperated—never. Now most therapists will privately admit that they occasionally do, but in public the description offered by Dr. Strupp will be accepted without any demurrer.

Well, I am no longer abashed at losing my temper. If I try to help the patient realize that anger is an experience which occurs and, though explainable, needs no justification, then I am entitled to the expression of this feeling as well. Afterward, if I realize that I have been unfair, there is time for contrition and discussion. However, if I respect the patient, why should I not let go without the fear that he will fall to pieces? For many patients anger has become synonymous with rejection. It need not be. The definition of rejection which makes most sense to me is: indifference to the other person, which involves an absence of honesty and effort to clarify one's own position.

The patient must wonder what is going on that makes it possible for the therapist to be so calmly judicious with him when he supposes that at least on some occasions the doctor becomes angry or hurts people he claims he loves. He may ask himself, "Is it because I am paying him to be kind?" The fee, if the therapist hides his full response from the patient, can become a payment akin to the one made by the customer at a carnival who gets rid of his aggression by hurling balls at the head of a hired goof. If we encourage honesty in the patient and do not behave this way ourselves, then our message is a double bind. "Become sensitive to the feelings of others, but do not worry about mine! You can be sure I will not get angry, though I may tell you when I feel good. My affection for you, which you can assume I have or I wouldn't be seeing you, includes my criticism of your behavior in different relations. But never should I speak in anger because it will show my unresolved countertransferences."

If I ask the patient to take a risk with others by being sensitive and even hypersensitive to another, then why shouldn't I risk the same with him? I believe that my readiness to take such a chance with my own imperfections is as important a contribution to our relation as are my other qualities of understanding, tolerance, reasonableness and so on. In my attempt to be judicious, can I not be passionate?

PATIENT, TAKE RESPONSIBILITY!

Perhaps the most sacred of instructions to all patients is: "Take responsibility." The Rogerian approach, for example, strikes this bell almost in every moment of the session. The client's attempt to get the counselor to commit himself should be answered with "And what do you feel?" or, better, "You wish to know how I am feeling." The nondirective counselor is not supposed to admit openly his feelings to the client.. He defends his being by reflections of the client's feelings. He asserts that it is his unconditional acceptance of the client which makes the difference, but he never lets on what it is in the client which calls for total acceptance.

The psychoanalytic systems appear to be more flexible and variable on this issue, but when it comes to a test between the patient's opinions and the analyst's, the weight of responsibility usually ends up heavily on the patient's end of the seesaw, even though he remains up in the air.

In a psychoanalytic type of relation the patient is helped to reveal his unconscious affects and ideas through free association. The analyst's interpretations are presented to release the blocks in the patient's associations. The deeper meanings of his symptoms and complaints will become evident, it is stated, when what has been repressed returns. The analysand is thus implicitly forgiven his aberrant relations because they are caused by forces beyond the reach of his ego or self. Thus it follows that he cannot really be held directly responsible for his disturbances with others. Yet, when he acts in a way which the analyst evaluates as defensive, the patient is told he is resisting. But how can he help that if his resistance is generated by unconscious processes? Perhaps the analyst must learn to speak directly to his unconscious. Or perhaps he could make plain to the patient the criteria he uses for judging when the patient's aberration was not of his making and when he is deemed to be able to will it otherwise.

The patient knows from the beginning that he is being put into a diagnostic category which also carries with it a prognostic rating. The prospective patient who asks, "Do I need special help and if so, what kind?" is only requesting information he has the right to expect from a doctor who traditionally diagnoses and prescribes. Most therapists do think in these terms, and their acumen, fortified by years of training and experience in special testing procedures, gets to work immediately. They are inwardly asking: "Is this person neurotic, borderline or psychotic? What kind of neurosis? Is expressive or supportive therapy indicated?" And so on.

From the beginning we lift up the patient's head and say, "Stand on your own feet," and then we tell him, "We know what makes you tick and what you need for your particular illness." If I tell the patient he needs help, then it follows that I should know when he doesn't need a therapist any more. Diagnosis leads to prognosis. My opinion that a patient should or should not go on can be useful, but it also contradicts my message that the person should become freer, accept his feelings and be responsible for them.

Lana, an unmarried graduate student in social science, came immediately to the question on the telephone. "I want to consult with you to decide whether I need help and if so whether I need psychoanalysis." It is possible that Lana already had decided that she needed special help, but was leaving the question open so that she could size me up before she acknowledged her decision to me. This inference can be made about every patient since they are not directly encouraged by us to "diagnose the therapist." It is thus safer to speak of the question of need than of "Do I want and need you?"

In Lana's case this possibility became a probability after we talked for a half-hour. She frequently played it safe with men. In a later session she confessed that during the first interview she had even lied to me. However, when we met I answered her wish to have me recommend a course of action with the acknowledgment of her right to expect such a procedure and then continued, "You and I can agree or disagree about the need or wish for a therapeutic relationship. But when you come down to it, the decision you are faced with is whether you want to spend your money and take your time to come to see me because it seems worth while or whether you would like to do this in another way."

My immediate attention was given to the paradox in which every patient and I are implicated. By coming to an expert in mental health, whether he is in a clinic, a hospital or private practice, the patient has made the most important diagnosis. When he begins considering psychotherapy, he is in effect saying, "The approaches to a fuller life which I have tried have failed and those I haven't tried are either unavailable to me or I'm afraid to try them or I'm pretty sure they will not work." From the very beginning I emphasize the fact that every human being is a psychologist whose years of experience equal the number he has spent in thinking about his relations. Coming to see me means that he is considering arranging a kind of case conference where we are both colleagues, he the expert in his experience and I with some experience of my own.[5]

All patients are soon told that they must take the initiative for the hour by bringing in problems and commencing the interaction. Never mind the doctor's specially heavy step as he comes to fetch you in the waiting room. You are to take responsibility for your hour. The therapist, no matter what may be on his mind regarding the patient or someone else, is taught to wait for the patient to begin, to open the hour and tell his doctor what is on his mind, while the therapist is supposed to be warmly, attentively responsive but always following the patient's lead.

But what if some bright, philosophically minded patient turns to his therapist and talks back? "I thought you are supposed to have a deeper and broader grasp of issues than I. Does it really mean that I have taken the initiative by coming and opening my mouth first? You've been around for some time. Long before I even thought about being a patient you proclaimed your availability to the public. By some twist of our paths, years later I emerged from the crowd and our consultations began. Who took the initiative and who is responsible when the fate which brought us together included the responsible actions of family, friends, teachers and colleagues, as well as our own?"

ADVICE AND INTERPRETATION

The difference between advice to do something and an interpretation of one's thoughts seems plain and obvious. I'm about to show, hopefully, that the presumed differences are largely spurious and are based on artificial distinctions about the nature of human action.

Only the unsophisticated patient who comes for a quick remedy does not understand our professional posture that direct guidance is bad because it will make him dependent, or cater to his infantile longings to be taken care of. Many patients will soon recognize whether their therapy is real analysis, according to the relative ratio of advice given to interpretation of the unconscious. A patient would say to me, "I want to ask for your advice, but I know you're not supposed to tell me what to do because it will make me more dependent." "That's right," I used to say, "think before you speak and act—outside the office, of course, not here." And when a patient got smart and retorted, "I know better what I think after I act or speak," I would label him an impulsive, acting-out type. It is common knowledge that therapies featured by advice and support have a considerably lower status than insight therapies like psychoanalysis or even nondirective counseling. It is much less often mentioned that this has a lot to do with socioeconomic variables than the efficacy of the kind of therapy.

Why should an intervention into the person's expressions, in the form of an interpretation, be any less directive or humiliating than a suggestion as to how to proceed outside the office? After all, the therapist is sought out because the patient has some faith in his power, and as a doctor he usually does many things to enhance his power, including setting the requirement that whatever he says should be very seriously considered.

The ambiguity involved in the distinction between direct guidance on the one hand and interpretation or reflection of feelings on the other can be underlined in the following illustration. An interpretation is made and the patient returns for the following session declaring he had acted on the insight given to him by the therapist. How is this release of action to be evaluated? Did the patient slavishly hear the therapist's interpretation as a call to do something because the patient is an obedient, acting-out type who jumps to conclusions? How much thought should the patient have given to the interpretation before acting? Who is to judge what kind of action is appropriate to an interpretation and what kind of action is precipitous?

Carl Rogers was correct when he argued that an interpretation is essentially directive and judgmental. This was, I think, the significant reason why he first called his approach nondirective. However, the dilemma remained. The so-called nondirective counselor also had to select from the client's welter of ideas and had to make the selection on the basis of values·and feelings of which he was both aware and unaware. Rogers failed to realize that any person we endow with power to make a difference to ourselves becomes willy-nilly a directive person.

Another illustration. The patient is judged to need some practical counsel. He is a highly dependent type who flounders about in his work and marriage. When he asks what he should do in a concrete situation, the therapist makes a suggestion. This passive-dependent and weak patient returns. The crisis still exists. The patient has not followed the advice. His need for help apparently has turned into a resistance. Is the advice faulty or insufficient? Or does the patient need an interpretation of his ambivalent attitude toward the doctor and other authority figures? In a few moments supportive therapy has become expressive-interpretative therapy dealing with deep transference material. I could go on with other examples which show that a therapist is essentially satisfied when an interpretation given to a patient with a so-called weak ego results in a reorientation of the person's attitudes or when a particular suggestion to an analysand with a strong ego was converted into what the doctor judges very appropriate behavior. All these illustrations emphasize that the evaluation of whether a particular person or a method is more or less coercive would depend on the social system in which the practice appears and the coerciveness of the therapist himself.

Coerciveness is an inner attitude of superiority, which, like any attitude, is manifested in a variety of ways. I am coercive when I think I know something, withhold my opinion and go about furtively setting up the situation so that the person "discovers it for himself." Am I coercive if I am told by the person that he has something on his mind but refuses to tell me, and I then insist that I need to know? I am if I reject him for not telling me and do not grant him the right to say no to me. But I don't think I am coercive when I confess that his secrecy makes it very difficult for me to listen to him without feeling he is leading me a merry chase.

If we are candid, then, we are less concerned about the particular form of the stimulus which prompts further exploration and deeper experiencing. An open mind is concerned with the values manifest in the variety of ways different people disclose themselves. An open-minded person presents his own thoughts as clearly as he can, defines how strongly he is convinced of his position and conveys his readiness to change his mind. If we don't emphasize that it is the clarity of our thoughts and the exposure of our assumptions which are the heart of the matter, we confuse the patient. We distract his attention from our own muddledness by drawing his slavish respect to the high and low of interpretation and guidance.

There is much in our own systems which is as confusing to the patient as it would be to nonpatients, the so-called normals. Anyone in his reasonably right mind who has tried to discuss the concepts and assumptions of any theory of personality with a proponent of the theory soon gets a sense of what a patient may be up against. Take the concept of an autonomous self or ego, about which I will have more to say in a later chapter on the self. Alan Watts has done much to bring our attention to the concepts of Zen Buddhism and their significance for Western psychotherapy. The major tenet of Zen is that the belief in an autonomous ego is an illusion. He argues with cogency that all therapeutics, if they are effective, serve to demolish the dichotomy between self and others, between subject and object and between ego as active or passive. The therapists do this through a kind of double-bind judo administered to the patient. Referring to the therapist's response to the patient's demand to be freer and more spontaneous, Alan Watts wrote:

To this end he knowingly or unknowingly engages the patient in a double bind. It is therapeutic because the therapist does not really want to dominate the patient for his own ends [hopefully, I add] and because it is going to be directed in such a way as to reveal its own contradiction. In short, the patient becomes involved in a relationship which he can not define or control however hard he may try.

And a little later:

In short, the therapist is directing the patient to try to control the relationship, but making it appear that he is not being directive at all and that everything is happening on the patient's own initative.

The outcome for the patient is:

He does not learn to be "himself" as if that were something one can do; he learns rather that there is nothing he can do not to be himself. But this is just another way of saying that he has ceased to identify himself with his ego, with the image of himself which society has forced upon himself.[6]

The patient's very wish to disengage himself from the image forced on him, through a deliberate act that he learns, is itself as paradoxical as "kissing one's own lips." This is successful therapy. But what if the therapist takes his system so seriously that he does not acknowledge that he, too, is caught in a system? He can and does double-bind the patient for years in the name of discovering the fundamental real self.

10

THE DEFACEMENT OF PERSONS:

TRANSFERENCES AND FIGURES

No one can speak with his positive voices of experience and not be against something. So far in this book, I have been critical of all systems of therapy. In this chapter I will concentrate my "rebellious" attack on the Freudian denomination. I "pick on" this school for a number of reasons, including the fact that it is a popular sport to take a crack at the biggest and most influential fellow. Dr. Roy Grinker, a leader in the education of psychiatrists and psychotherapists, writes: "American psychotherapy has imitated and closely approached the psychoanalytic model with only a few exceptions. . . . The basic core of our pedagogical process in psychiatric training is the psycho-dynamics of Freudian psychoanalysis."[1]

I also "pick on" this system because I have been a missionary of the Freudian school. I have practiced as a Freudian and have been analyzed by a Freudian whose own analyst was one of the six to whom Freud gave special finger rings as a symbol of their mutual, secret and exclusive devotion. If my howl sounds mongrelized, I still can whimper about my pedigree and my right to yelp because I have gotten the words almost from the horse's mouth.[2]

Looking back I realize more and more how much I have been always restless with systems, and yet despite this how much I pushed aside many criticisms I read and heard of the Freudian system because of my absorption in it. And by that I mean my personal analysis, which took me almost as many years to get out of as to be taken by it. Today I think that whatever I gained through my own patienthood was achieved in a quite inefficient way, though it did teach me the lesson not to follow a methodology. I am as convinced of this as I am sure that my own analyst believes even more now than eight years ago what she pronounced in my last session: my cure was incomplete and analysis was interrupted. It is possible that she might call my present views on therapy a sign of unresolved transference. This concept of transference, which is at the very core of any psychoanalytically influenced therapy, has been used as an explanation of different ways of thinking. It is this concept with which I will be largely concerned in this chapter.

I am, of course, joining a long line of very reputable psychotherapists in criticizing the standard operating procedure of psychoanalysis. Karen Horney, Harry Stack Sullivan and Erich Fromm are best known in America for their cogent analysis of the orthodox group. Though I also differ with these giants, their work contains many of the points I will be making, or belaboring. Carl Rogers, unlike most revisionists, began outside the establishment. His nondirective or client-centered approach tried to place the person who came for help in the center of the relation rather than such abstract categories as neuroses, resistance and transference. His system has been recently thought of as a forerunner of the variants now labeled existential therapeutics. The latest sign of the reformation of American psychotherapy has been the organization of the American Association of Humanistic Psychology under the leadership of such people as Abraham Maslow and Charlotte Buhler. This group represents itself as the Third Force, in contrast to Psychoanalysis and Behaviorism as the other two forces which almost from the beginning have dominated American psychology and psychotherapy.

TRANSFERENCE AS AN EXPLANATION OF SUFFERING

The most reliable data used in treatment by the analytically oriented therapist are not the patient's memories but the patient's behavior with him, which presumably repeats his childhood experiences with his parents. Usually an interpretation of this "transference attitude" is resisted. The mobilization of resistance then serves the analyst as an indicator that he has hit pay dirt, i.e., has touched some buried unconscious conflict. In the analytic relationship the patient's neurosis reveals itself in a transference neurosis, which is then directly amenable to the intervention of the analyst. When a "pure" type of psychoanalysis is conducted, the analyst is supposed to be influencing the patient only through the interpretation of the transference neurosis and the underlying unconscious conflicts generating its manifestation toward the neutral doctor.

The basic assumption underlying the therapeutic usefulness of transference-resistance interpretations is that an understanding of the regularities and lawfulness of behavior brings about change. The therapeutic relationship becomes a kind of laboratory in which the analyst searches for the most general explanation of the diversity of phenomena appearing in the office and appearing in the patient's daily life as he selectively remembers them. In this laboratory the analyst is geared or programmed by his training and experience to observe three related but still different levels of regularities.

1. The deepest level is that of the universal complexes or phases of psychic development which all humans in all cultures presumably must go through. This level includes the fate of the so-called instincts. The Oedipal complex is the classic example in the Freudian system of a universal complex. The archetype of the female, the anima, and the male, the animus, is an example of a universal complex which would be attended to by a Jungian analyst.

2. The second level of psychic organization includes the cultural mores which have shaped the individual's orientation to authority, children, the weak, men, women and so on. The neo-Freudian theories of Horney, Fromm and Sullivan would tend to focus on social influences on psychological malfunctioning.

3. The third level includes the particular patterning of experiences the child learned in his own family.

The analyst gets the hang of the patient's ramblings and incoherent noise. He then thinks he is able to predict the person's actions because he has found the modes in which the patient is consistent and the reasons for apparent inconsistencies. In other words, the person is cased and there are no surprises. The analyst is in this sense not doing anything different from what the ordinary person does who thinks about his friends. But just as the common person's categories for placing people (occupation, religion, income, birthplace, accent, race, age) can become rigid and dogmatic, the analyst's uncommon categories can also lead to uniformity and conformity.

It is obvious that no one can suspend completely some ordering of his observations of another person into a set of categories, i.e., an order imposed from without. Language and its grammar are themselves an ordering reality. In any relation there are structures and regularities. Most of the time we hardly notice some of them, while others rise sharply to our attention, especially when we feel uncomfortable. The balm I am pleading for lies in the reminder that it is the common experience of all of us that abstract categories of behavior offered as explanations do not serve to free the person from his anxieties in meeting people unless they are offered in a personal way. The "objectification" of a relationship must include the recognition that our own judgments are relative and are open to criticism and continuous evaluation. When a relationship becomes nonsurprising, i.e., predictable, it has lost interest for us. And it has become so not only because we may have been perspicacious but because our partner has submitted himself to routinization.

Of course, any expert in human relations will insist that his concepts which order behavior into a system yielding "nonsurprise" are superior to the ideas of the common man, even the well-educated one. The analyst believes he differs from the common person in his accent on unconscious processes. And though analytically oriented therapists differ among themselves in the relative emphasis each gives to the three aspects of unconscious process listed above, they maintain that the common person hardly thinks of these matters at all. With this claim I would agree. Dynamic psychology has brought a different perspective into our ways of thinking about loving and hating, especially in its emphasis on the development and growth of persons.

However, let us consider the patient and why he comes for treatment. Before the person has become a patient he has been trying to break out of the stupefying and demoralizing experience of going around in circles. Usually after an extended period of frustrating attempts to grow, events provoke him to turn to a professional therapist to make a difference. If he chooses to settle down with me for regular visits, he has made a judgment that I do make a difference, and will continue to do so.

Now if I emphasize the regularities in his behavior and attitudes, he may learn something about his past involvements. However, I believe he will learn and change only if the new qualities in his attempts to find a measure of reasonable liveliness are also heard. I am affirming that what has gone wrong is that in his other relations the patient's creative sparks have been doused by the categorical enclosures imposed by others.

I know that if I look for the common features in any batch of data brought to me by a patient, I will find them. I certainly can give him some other rules by which to play the game of life. And my rules are different enough from his to prove diverting for a while. When he tells me, "I've never thought of that before," I don't flatter myself about my wisdom in finding a truth. Rather, I hear his recognition of a different and new handle with which to pick up the hot potatoes. I'm afraid that when we look for regularities we overlook the uncommon qualities and the differences which every person must also always present as long as he lives. He comes to see me to make a difference, and if I do not listen to the differentiations he has made and is constantly making, of me as well as others, I will indoctrinate him into yet another system which may flatten out the courage we always need to meet the unknown and unpredictable future. This is what Erikson "grudgingly admits":

And we were dismayed when we saw our purpose of enlightenment perverted into a widespread fatalism, according to which man is nothing but a multiplication of his parents' faults and an accumulation of his own earlier selves. We must grudgingly admit that even as we were trying to devise, with scientific determinism, a therapy for the few, we were led to promote an ethical disease among the many.[3]

And I think that this is what Thelma also was telling me. She visibly cringed whenever we discussed her father. During one session, after receiving a reply to a letter she had written to him, she re-experienced the anxiety that had possessed her ever since she could remember. That she also admired, even adored, him was plain, but his constant effort to instruct her in a bombastic and superior tone put her off. She remembered how much she wanted to say something to him. "I would say to myself, 'I'll count to three and I'll speak,' but I never got past two."

Thelma's gift of concreteness and immediacy in a relation made it very easy for me to discern important parallels between the way she remembered her father and the way she behaved with me. After some reflection on the facts that she would often remain silent for a number of minutes, that she seemed at moments frightened of me, that I was also her teacher and, of course, that I was a man, I suggested a typical transference interpretation. Thelma rejected the idea on the spot. The next day I received a letter in which she explained why she disliked the connection I made between her father and myself.

Let's not create problems that don't exist. "A relentless teacher." Yes, he is. But I don't believe that I am fearful of you because you are that, too. I don't think I am fearful of you period. Oh, in some degree I suppose I am. There are times when I feel myself—what's the word I want?—feel myself shrinking when I know you are about to ask me a question or suggest an interpretation. But I really don't think that it is enough of a problem to be considered a problem. I mean, you don't for one minute think that I could talk to you the way that I do if I was really afraid of you. Your "teaching" is something that disturbs you far more than it does me. Really, in that sense you don't resemble my father at all. I always felt he wanted to destroy me. I certainly don't feel that's true of you. In fact I feel just the opposite, but just the opposite. It's important to me that you understand that.

I wrote and thanked her for the differentiation. My own disposition to abstract relationships and to emphasize the worst or least common denominator was sensed by Thelma as complicating matters. It was the difference that mattered.

TRANSFERENCE AND THE LAW OF EFFECT

There is another assumption implicit in the use of the concept of transference as an explanation of suffering. Not only is it assumed that the discovery of consistencies and regularities of behavior will bring about a change. The analyst also assumes that the patient will learn best when his mistakes are emphasized, i.e., when the patient is punished by being made aware of his distortions of reality. In experimental psychology this notion of learning has been subsumed under the classical Law of Effect.

This law explained that the kind of connection that occurred between a stimulus and a response depended on whether the response was a punishing or rewarding one. In the analytic situation the punishing aspect of the analyst's interpretation of a transference distortion is heightened by the implication that it is the patient's fault because he must take responsibility for his personal actions. The analyst often says to his patient that he is not casting stones at him. However, when the patient is confronted with an interpretation which implicitly or explicitly says, "It is your characteristic modes of relating which give trouble to others and to yourself," the patient is being jolted rather than rewarded, and besides the blow to the person's self-esteem, let us not forget what a double bind it is to insist the person take responsibility for his unconscious. The patient, having come to set a different course, is supposed to learn how to be different by being told how he is doing the same old things over and over. Described this way, therapy is seen to be based on the same belief which I think most people have: "Show the sinner his waywardness, and in his suffering he will confess and be saved."

Though the patient's unconscious patterns of relationships revealed in the transference should include positive as well as negative qualities, the tendency is to accent the negative features. The patient's sickness must be exposed, and the best way to expose his illness is to bring about a regression in which his nefarious childish ways will erupt. The patient is ill because he avoids conscious suffering and does this through those mechanisms of defense most characteristic of him. If he is an obsessional person, he most likely will repress feelings and intellectualize. If he, or rather she, is an hysteric, she will repress ideas and act out her feelings. Either way the patient is doing and experiencing in the wrong way. He is not thinking well enough and not feeling deeply enough. The confusion is also compounded by the therapist's personal and often arbitrary definition of how thinking is to be distinguished from feeling. I shall pick up this point a little later.

This notion that people learn best through punishment rather than reward has been demonstrated to be largely mistaken through a variety of researches with different kinds of animals besides human beings.[4] Yet this is not the worst aspect of the punishing attitude taken by the analyst toward the patient. The greatest irony lies in the fact that the best candidate for analysis is usually described as an intelligent individual, with a good capacity for developing relationships and a strong ego. And yet he is the very one who is not trusted to use his high intelligence and draw his own conclusions about his quirks, since this is regarded as a form of intellectualization. Rather, the ideal analysand is encouraged by the impersonal demeanor of the analyst to revert to infantile behavior and exhibit his worst selves, to become dependent, angry, demanding, etc. This regression is justified as the one in which the person's true and deepest selves emerge. The irony is that the most complex intellectual theory of human behavior became the most anti-intellectual therapy, that is, it denigrated the analysand's intellectual powers to the level of a defense. For example, it became customary to counsel an analysand not to read too much psychological literature while in treatment. If the person happened to be a psychologist and was very much involved in his field, this counsel was a handicap.

The pessimistic and demonic view of human nature implicit in this conception of therapy has been amply criticized by many who, though recognizing the manifold ways in which the devil manifests himself in men, did not conclude that the inner and deepest truth is that we all have the souls of unredeemed sinners.[5] The cultural and social forces affecting our views of human nature have been exposed repeatedly through historical studies. No one can become neutral toward human nature, including, and perhaps especially, the analyzed analyst. The more the assumptions, beliefs and values suffused through all psychoanalysis were exposed, the more Freud and his followers became great storytellers and philosophers.[6] And from my point of view, therapy is just about that, the telling and sharing of stories, of experiences, of persons facing and not defacing each other. How much comfort it would have been to Freud's patients if he had been as candid with them as he was with Oskar Pfister, the Swiss minister who became a missionary for Freud's ideas among clergymen: "I cannot face with comfort the idea of life without work; work and the free play of the imagination are for me the same thing, I take no pleasure in anything else. . . . In the words of King Macbeth, let us die in harness."[7]

TRANSFERENCE AS A DEFENSE FOR THE ANALYST

The concept of transference also has another function besides serving as a tool for the elucidation of the structures in the patient's character. The analyst defends himself against the patient's intense feelings toward him by becoming a symbol. If he is loved or hated with any intensity beyond some normally expected expression of liking or annoyance over some untoward event, the therapist understands that it is not himself who is the culprit. The patient is re-enacting a fantasy. Thomas Szasz, from whose paper on transference I borrowed the heading of this section, convincingly showed how interpretations of transference can be used defensively by the analyst. He wrote: "It introduced into medicine and psychology the notion of the therapist as symbol: this renders the therapist as a person essentially invulnerable."

The concept of transference was very useful at that time in Vienna, when the entire notion of intense sexual feelings directed toward the physician during the talking cure would have been considered obscene had these feelings been believed by the physician to be realistic. Dr. Szasz wrote: "It suggests that, in psychoanalysis, what stands between obscenity and science is the concept of transference."[8]

I can illustrate this a dozen times over, as can any therapist. Here is one example.

Joan, a long-legged and rather attractive brunet of twenty-six, was unmarried. Her dresses often revealed her shape to good advantage, and she often crossed her legs in a way which exposed her slip and even her garters. At times, in case I missed the point, she fingered her skirt near her thigh. Following the analytic system, I brought to her attention her behavior, stressed its sexually provocative aspects and tried to relate this action to the events in her life. This wasn't too difficult to do since she brought forth much material about her frustrating involvements with men and her inciting them and then pushing them away. At the age of thirteen her father once found her talking to a brother as she stood in the bathroom dressed in her underwear. An unusually cold and indifferent person, who hardly talked with her, he this time became furious and accused her of being a whore. "No wonder she repeated this behavior with me," I thought. "I am a father figure from whom she wants love in any form."

Joan readily accepted transference interpretations of her relation to me as a symbol of her father and brother. Yet, if anything, the skirt rode up even higher on her thigh. Finally, I said directly to her, "Joan, I am distracted by your legs. They arouse erotic thoughts in me and I can't listen well." She immediately countered with a series of fantasies of sexual relations with other men. "What about me?" I asked, excusing my apparent vanity. She fell silent. I forced the issue, and she began to speak haltingly about my lack of interest in her, or when I showed interest, it was on matters she considered irrelevant or silly. Her silence was also interrupted by a reference to her father and a particular memory, but I cut her short with "I know that often enough I've pushed you off by referring your feelings to me as a problem with your father and brother." She burst out in a laugh, "And was I relieved when you did!" We both participated in an ironic situation which, when recognized, was quickly released by knowing laughter.

Another example also shows how patients hand me a transference interpretation in order to avoid the immediacy of our own relation. Andrea had warned me not to give her advice. She would listen carefully to interpretations, but any suggestion I made about a current dilemma was repulsed because "It will make me more dependent on you. I'll feel closer to you, like with my parents. . . . When I was ten, they were having trouble with my younger brother and I became a counselor to my mother." I turned her back to our relation and again discussed my ideas as to why advice need not be any more interfering and binding than an interpretation. "In fact, Andrea, your rejection of advice is a bind on me, because I'd like to give it if I have an idea and think it can help." After a few moments, she timidly spoke of the arousal of erotic interest in me.

In earlier sessions she had revealed that she was always afraid of becoming "a nymphomaniac" when she felt close to and dependent on men. Of course, she was most virtuous, but her memories of her brother attempting intercourse and of being molested by an older boy were for her strong evidence of a wickedness in her character. Again, a transference reaction could be discerned and interpreted. Instead, I asked if she thought I recognized her sensual interest in me only because she confessed it. "If I observe fire in your eyes, there must be some delight in mine." She responded with relief and with the pleasure any woman can have in being experienced as an attractive person by a man whom she admires. Andrea also could know in this way that she could not seduce me by thoughts and without our mutual willingness to go to bed.

I am not supposed to respond to the patient at his level of discourse; instead, I am supposed to analyze his productions. But is this concept necessary? Must I interpret the patient's responses to me in order to protect myself against charges of obscenity and vileness of temper? A code of ethics is by itself not enough. The patient's basic reliance must be on my character, which will come through for better or for worse, and on his own right to keep a watchful eye on me. It is not correct to pose the alternative as one between reacting to the person on his own terms and analyzing his productions. I am at the same time a symbol and a real person. He may endow me with traits I don't think I possess, and then I am a symbol for him. I may provoke his behavior by qualities I think I do have, and then he is realistic. However, what is the truth in a particular instance is something he and I must mutually try to discern rather than either of us arbitrarily imposing our own version on the other.

Transference as a Device for Controlling the Patient

Dr. Szasz made another point in his paper which is crucial to my presentation. He connected the concept of transference to the mind-body problem encountered by every physician in the diagnosis and treatment of bodily illness. In his first book, *Pain and Pleasure*, Dr. Szasz dealt with the question: When is pain real, and when is it mental?[9] He answered this critical question in this way. When the doctor can find a somatic cause for the patient's complaints, that is, a diagnosis based on available knowledge, he will agree with the patient that his pain is real. When the patient and the doctor have a conflicting opinion about the sources of the patient's pain, and this conflict cannot be settled by the available methods of examination, the doctor will be inclined to the judgment that the pain is in the patient's mind. The physician arbitrarily concludes that the complaints are unrealistic. If the physician is psychologically oriented, he will decide that the pain is caused by unconscious mental attitudes for which he has no responsibility. If he isn't inclined toward the psychosomatic hypothesis, he may dismiss the patient as a malingerer and a crank or even admit to ignorance.

If we take this medical model of the doctor-patient relationship and transpose it into the psychotherapeutic setting, which is exactly what Freud did, the doctor is again the judge as to the difference between "real" and "unconscious" suffering.[10] In the analytic situation any complaint which the doctor believes is inappropriate to the situation as defined by him is then judged to be caused by unconscious complexes. The doctor, of course, hasn't contributed to this reaction except in the sense that he is there as the agent for the manifestation of these complexes in the form of transference attitudes. The doctor may be at the bottom of the well, but he claims he has been placed there. The best criterion the doctor uses to assess the presence of a transference reaction is the patient's resistance to the expression of whatever it is the patient is *supposed* to be expressing. In classical analysis the patient resists when he breaks the basic rule of free association: to report whatever enters his mind.

Transference, we have since learned, is a two-way street, and the doctor's side is conventionally given the name of countertransference. He is supposed to be aware of it, to analyze it and, if necessary, to discuss it with a colleague, a supervisor or his own analyst. But not with the patient. The analyst, in effect, says to the patient, "I will observe, reflect on and interpret the contradictions in your history, your memories and your dreams. I will indicate how your feelings toward me are distortions produced by your neurotic development." Yet, within the therapeutic situation, the doctor rarely engages with the patient in a critique of the relation itself. "Learn from the mistakes I point out to you, but I can't acknowledge that I may learn from those you point out to me. Your criticisms are too full of shale for me to discern the true oil." Inside the office it is the patient who is sick and the doctor the clear-sighted one. Though countertransference feelings are expected, otherwise the doctor could be accused of being cold and indifferent to his task, it is the analyst's position which is relatively sound. As Menninger put it:

The analyst is a relatively fixed point. By reasons of training, dedication, interest, experience, tradition, and other factors, he has great authority. The patient on the other hand, has great potential freedom of motion, but *relatively little power* [my italics]. The only thing the patient can be authoritative about is the way he feels, and he is not always very sure about this.[11]

Menninger's statement reveals the essential superiority with which the analyst approaches the patient. I draw attention to the phrase, "relatively little power," since my interpretation of the patient's great though negative power differs from Menninger's view.

Not everything is transference, of course. If the analysis is not progressing, and the patient becomes angry, he may have a right to complain. However, it is the doctor who is authoritative and who will have the final word within the confines of an office into which no one looks. Dr. Szasz raised the ethical question created by the privacy of the therapeutic situation: "No one, psychoanalysts included, has as yet discovered a method to make people behave with integrity when no one is watching."[12]

The cultural definition of the doctor's role, giving him the authority formerly reserved for the priest, together with the patient's great need for compassion for his suffering, both conspire to give the doctor the benefit of every doubt. If the patient complained to friends or relatives about his doctor, few would be sympathetic since going to a therapist is by conventional definition a sign that something is quite wrong with the person. Psychotherapists also have directly reinforced the stereotyped notion that patients are not to be believed by repeatedly telling the public how much people resist facing their problems. "We are attacked, attacked, attacked," is the refrain only rarely uttered publicly in such strident terms. But in the office and in scholarly papers erudite terminology is used to convert criticism of the analyst, who may be unfair, into an irrational and unconscious aggression.

Dr. Szasz rendered a proper indictment, but I don't think he went far enough. Any approach to a patient is potentially wicked which places the person in an inferior position and constantly emphasizes his weakness and relative lack of power. This will itself encourage the person to maintain his "negative will," as Otto Rank called it and which Freud called resistance. And when this is reinforced by the notion that the person's resistance rises out of the depths of the unconscious, which by definition is beyond the person's control and only decipherable by the analyst, the relation will become wicked if not tragic.

Transference and Faith Cures

It is inevitable that terms used by social and psychological scientists must differ in meaning according to the person using the term and according to changing times. Transference was not only a word referring to the patient's inappropriate attitudes expressed toward the doctor—as judged, we should remind ourselves, by the doctor—but it also had the meaning of a capacity for relationship and even of faith. Analysts do speak of transference cures when they refer to a rapid abatement of complaints. The patient has a "flight into health" when symptoms disappear without real understanding of the origins of his difficulties. Obviously, from the point of view of the rational therapist, such faith cures are superficial at best, and at worst an avoidance which will lead later to an even worse disturbance.

Of greater moment, however, is that from the early years of the psychoanalytic movement the capacity for developing transferences was considered to be a major criterion for recommending psychoanalysis for a patient. Here the term is used as a synonym for a good ego. Patients who could not attach themselves to the therapist and could not stand the frustration of relating to a person playing a role, such as those diagnosed as schizophrenic, were to be given other kinds of therapy. The diagnosis determined whether therapy was supportive or expressive. In supportive therapy the doctor was not to conceal his real interest in or affection for the patient and was cautioned not to analyze the patient's attachment. He was not a "symbol" but a "real" person, and through his reality he would bring about a cure. On the other hand the classical analytic situation was the paradigm of expressive therapy. The analyst was to remain as neutral and impassive as possible so as not to dilute the transferring onto him of attitudes belonging to other significant people and thus make it possible for the analysis of the transference neuroses. Lewis Wolberg, in his long handbook on the techniques of psychotherapy, introduced a discussion of transference with the following comment:

Before taking up this process, it is necessary to emphasize that in supportive therapy, and in directive forms of reeducative therapy, it is usually unwise to delve into the nature of the relationship with the therapist. Such a move tends to challenge the foundations of faith on which success in treatment may depend. Indeed, one often strives to perpetuate in the patient the illusion of the therapist's protective powers, no effort being made to peer into the irrational sources of the patient's dependency need.[13]

In other words, analysis of transference, initially associated with Freud's psychoanalytic system, gradually became linked in practice with all so-called depth therapy. Any system which deplored its use was considered superficial, supportive, ameliorative or re-educative and based on magical faith. Psychoanalysis became the prestigious form of therapy, and any other type was for weaker, sicker and by extension inferior persons. There were some exceptions to this notion, the most widely known being John Rosen's direct analysis with schizophrenics in which he approached them with a no-holds-barred, intensive confrontation and interpretation of their deranged thoughts and behavior.

As I will discuss in detail in the last chapters, there are no studies which can prove that one therapy results in a deeper change than another since it is impossible to make such a comparison. The word "depth" eludes definition and varies in meaning from person to person. Is symptomatic relief of mental distress always a superficial change analogous to taking an aspirin? Karl Menninger and his associates in *The Vital Balance* tell of the radical changes that occurred in long hospitalized and neglected psychotics, who were well on in their years, when an unrelieved dreary routine was suddenly altered by an experimental and massive dose of old-fashioned care and affection. This was supportive therapy with a vengeance, and some of the hopeless cases were able to resume responsible living in the community.

Does the exhortative and mutual uplifting approach of Alcoholics Anonymous, which makes it possible for many of their members to retain jobs, support families and stay out of other trouble, affect a less significant change than the long psychoanalysis of a gifted individual? Obviously, many nonrational values determine presumably objective judgments. My argument, that in any form of therapy the doctor's values and needs affect the relationship as much as his theoretical and empirical knowledge, would lead to the inference that the differentiation between supportive and expressive therapy could be based on such factors as the social and occupational status of the person, his financial resources, the time the therapist wishes to devote to him because of a research project and so on. The socio-economic aspects of diagnosis and treatment have already been amply documented by a number of studies, of which Redlich and Hollingshead's is perhaps the best known.[14]

TRANSFERENCE AND THE NEUTRAL PASSIVITY OF THE ANALYST

Psychoanalysts have justified their effacement of their real selves as an essential requirement for the emergence of the deepest layers of the patient's personality. The primitive forces in the id, it was maintained, would arise in the analytic relation through the transference of the unconscious onto the analyst, on the condition that the analyst would remain impassive and neutral. The ritual of the couch, Freud confessed, was introduced because he could not face patients eight to ten hours a day. But it soon became the platform behind which the analyst hid. Out of sight he could easily refrain from personal comments and advice and refuse to answer the patient's inquiries. Modifications of these techniques did occur. The couch might be abandoned, the analyst might wish the patient a good weekend, but the basic attitude was maintained: do not reveal your true self. In short, neutrality and impersonality would contribute to the patient's experience of isolation and hasten a regression resulting in an eruption of his oral, anal and phallic fantasies.

The concept of motivation used to justify this procedure is that of the so-called pleasure principle. The human animal is at the core seeking direct gratification of his needs. According to this principle only the environment interferes with an immediate discharge of tension arising from the tissues. So, if the analyst stays out of the patient's way as he removes the patient's defenses, the libidinous and hostile beast within will come out.

It took many years before the analyst's neutrality and interpretations deprived the patient's defenses of reinforcement enough to soften them and allow the impulses clear expression, as judged, of course, by the analyst. Yet it was also possible that the inactivity of the analyst might prolong the time before the patient's strongest feelings would emerge. And now, after many years of research, an outstanding student of psychoanalytic theory broadly hints that this situation has been the result of the impassivity of the analyst. It looks as if isolating a patient on the couch reduces his passions rather than arouses them. Dr. Robert Holt does not discuss psychoanalytic therapy per se in his review of the laboratory studies on isolation. In these experiments the subject is cut off from familiar environmental stimulation. He lies on a couch in a soundproof room, his eyes are covered. Dr. Holt draws the following implication of the results of these studies for psychoanalytic theory:

As I read them, the facts lend themselves to the following conceptualization: the cognitive processes of a subject in an isolation experiment undergo relatively little take-over by drives because the deprivation of external input directly interferes with the usual drive processes themselves. Quite the opposite of being given free rein, the drives seem to act for the most part as if they have been impoverished. I realize that this is a radical conception to psychoanalysts, but I believe that it is in good accordance with many facts, and points to a need for a fundamental reconsideration of the psychoanalytic theory of motivation.[15]

Of course, the laboratory situation in which the subject is isolated is not strictly comparable to the analyst's office, where he sits out of sight of the patient. We can suspect that some if not many analysts will object to the extrapolation of the results Dr. Holt was reviewing to the results the analyst is attempting to achieve with the analysand. The patient can move freely, he can keep his eyes open, he does hear noises, the analyst does speak to him from time to time. However, analytic therapy, to repeat, has been following a theory of motivation which has been found deficient, and it is hardly possible any longer to maintain that personal distance from a patient will breed a familiarity with his true nature.

When I read Dr. Holt's paper, I had an image of hundreds of patients, including myself, who through years of lying on the couch were caught between the requirement to free-associate in order to become aware of the beast in their unconscious and the fact that an impoverished human environment interfered with the direct expression of their affects and impulses. I shuddered a little but became more tranquil when I thought of how progress is often a breaking out of the ironies propounded by systems. I was only one of many who had been caught in the mixed messages of an approach which interfered with the very goal it was trying to accomplish.

I close this section with David's dream. It is presented, of course, as an illustration and not as proof. When he had this dream, David was a twenty-six-year-old man about to complete his studies for the ministry. A few months after leaving therapy he was married to a woman whom he had courted, on and off, for almost as long as he was in treatment. He and I had a first round which lasted about six months. He then left for another city, where he entered analysis with a Dr. Herid. After about one and a half years he returned to New York to complete his studies and we resumed our dialogue. I should add that David possessed all the qualifications required of candidates judged to be suitable for psychoanalysis.

On his return David pointedly told me that in his relation with Dr. Herid he learned how it felt to meet a silent analyst, in contrast to my "noisy" style. But besides his criticism of my ways, he also reported the comment of a friend who was also seeing Dr. H. "He's got laryngitis today, but I guess that doesn't make much difference." About four months after he resumed with me, he had the following dream, which I asked him to write down.

I was sitting on a chair which was balanced on a 4′ x 4′ timber running horizontally from front to back. Both the timber and the chair seemed to be resting securely, although the rear end of the timber appeared to be suspended in mid-air. The timber was situated halfway down what I recall to have been an excavation ditch; the front end of the timber was secured in the earth ahead of me. The ditch was a large ditch so that I had no feeling of being cramped in, but I was very aware of being partially underground.

Directly ahead of me and somewhere above me, sitting on a chair resting on the earth at the point where the timber stuck into the ground, was Dr. Herid. There was no verbal exchange between us; in fact, I was not aware of a "relating" as such.

The only activity going on was being undertaken by Dr. Herid. He had a very long-handled hoe and was busy scraping a combination of mud and feces off of the timber directly under my chair. I was looking down, over my left shoulder, concentrating on what he was doing. The only feeling I recall at the time was the feeling that what he was doing was important and that I wanted to sit there and concentrate on his scraping so that he could clear away all of the mud-feces.

Then the dream-content shifted. Dr. Herid became Dr. Steinzor. The ditch became something of a basement room or furnace room, but still with earthen walls and some piles of dirt on the sides. The timber was gone. Dr. Steinzor and I were sitting on chairs which were resting on the earthen floor. The chairs were close together, and we were at eye level with one another. Both of us were heavily engaged in a conversation and leaning forward slightly in our respective chairs. There was the feeling that both of us were expending a great deal of energy in an attempt to communicate.

When I heard this dream, I confessed to David my full, even smug, satisfaction. "You could be considered to be indoctrinated by my ministrations and trying to buy me with flattery. But I still maintain that you are like most of us. The more passive our friend, the less responsibility we take for our relation. And one possible solution is to do what you did in the dream, concentrate on what the other man is about and try to force him to do all the dirty work."

In 1937 Freud reminded us of the original spirit of psychoanalysis: "Finally, one must not forget that the relationship between analyst and patient is based on a love of truth, that is, on the acknowledgement of reality, and that it precludes any kind of sham or deception."[16]

Yet in the search for truth and knowledge the analyst literally masked himself by sitting behind the couch, while armed with a conceptual system unmatched for complexity and virtuosity before or since by any other ethic of personality development, with the possible exception of Carl Jung's. With the degree and prestige of the doctor and the excitement over a new method to relieve suffering, the analyst could use his judgments of what was transference and what resistance to defend himself against the patient's versions of truth. Erikson, who was most sympathetic to the psychoanalytic tradition, struck directly at the ambiguity of a healing relationship which, on the one hand, stood for truth and honesty and for the uniqueness of the whole person and, on the other hand, insisted that the analyst had more virtue than the patient:

As we grow beyond our early childhood, more and more classes of men become the "father" of our newly-acquired insights and techniques: grandfathers, uncles, neighbors, and fatherly teachers. If we call such fathers "father surrogates," we empty an important function of its true significance in an effort to understand its potential perversion; this may lead us, as therapists, to cut off our own noses in order to present impersonal enough faces for our patients' father-transferences.[17]

ABSTRACTIONS OR CONCRETENESS IN RELATIONS: STRUCTURAL CONCEPTS OR PROCESSES

So where does all this critical analysis of the defense mechanisms, transference-resistance, leave the patient and me? Whether he has read much psychology or not, the patient manifests a definitely strong loading of abstractions and generalizations regarding his life. His explanations regarding his behavior often do not agree with mine, but he does give his version of the reasons why A, B and C and even Q and Z belong together. As for my side, I have been trained in scientific theory and thus seek general explanations. I am an intellectual type of person, at least in the sense of having a faith in the discovery of laws. Am I going to appear before the patient and say to him, "I have nothing to say to you about possible connections because this will distort our relation"? What do I say to a patient when I think I see a possible connection among a variety of events, including his behavior with me? I present my view as an opinion, which is a pointer and no more than that. And if it doesn't move the patient to a new revelation, I tell him that my inference didn't serve its purpose of stimulating him. It may have been poorly worded or poorly timed, which amounts to the same thing as irrelevant. I emphasize that he is not resisting.

I think it does make some difference when we redefine transference in terms of "laws of learning." The patient usually can grasp more concretely the idea of a habit as an explanation for a response to others and can much more readily understand resistance as a feeling of rebellion against a sense of humiliation than he can understand some hypothesized switchings in his thought processes. I think it makes better sense to talk to each other in terms of exaggerated reactions and an adequate sense of proportion which may need to be accounted for by both people.

Here are a few illustrations of the way I speak with a person about the more than a dozen mechanisms of defense defined by psychoanalytic theories of the mind.

Perhaps the most commonly known and discussed defense is projection. I speak of it to a patient in the following way: "You say I feel something which I don't feel. Maybe I am denying something and I can turn my attention to my thoughts if you wish that. But if you prefer, let us assume for the time being that the feeling you ascribe to me is completely justified in some relationship, that you are confusing that relationship with ours and that all we need to do is discover in which relationship you were fully in your right mind in feeling persecuted."

I define rationalization as follows: "You are presenting a reason for your behavior with which I do not agree. It is not crucial that you agree with me. Just try another explanation than the one you gave. Go try someone else's explanation, against your grain. Through the very act of trying you will change. If it is for the better, then my explanation becomes right. If it is for the worse, you can always go back to yours or, even better, try still another."

I define intellectualization as a form of expression which I find boring because I cannot tell whether the person is interested in what he is telling me or is also bored. If he can show me what is so fascinating about discussing the recent ideas of Tillich or of Elliot or of any other expert on the issue at hand rather than his own encounter with a colleague or his wife or his mother, then I probably will no longer experience his presentation as dry and devoid of affect. The extent to which my own values, hobbies and fascinations enter into my judgments regarding intellectualization is extraordinary and is most easily recognized when I remember how passionately I have debated theoretical ideas and how many of us invest as much as one-third of our lives in experiments and keeping up with the literature. That is why I am loath to tell a person he is thinking rather than feeling.

I define an hysterical defense as a communication in which my own "logical and reasonable" needs to speak clearly and to understand another's language are being thwarted. For example, I say something to a young woman and she begins to cry. I suppose she may be telling me that I have offended her. I think tears in women have a number of meanings, one of which is: "You bully, look how you hurt me." Women are the weaker sex and are permitted to cry when feeling hurt while men, as little boys, have been told it is shameful. So when there is a sign which I call hysterical, I am in effect saying that the patient is unfairly using the language she has learned instead of the one I think she should use. Usually, after a variety of encounters on these matters, the patient learns my language because we get on better that way, and because in coming to see me she has implied that her language has not gotten her anywhere in her struggle for self-respect and for equality.

I speak with a person who doesn't make sense to me in terms of misunderstandings about "truth" rather than of displacements, transference and so on. Modern linguists differentiate types of signs, distinguish between signs and language symbols and identify the different rules used in various languages. If we followed this mode, we would also find it unnecessary to dichotomize a person's expression into thinking versus feeling. It would then no longer be required that I postulate some repressed idea (for the hysteric) or some repressed feeling (for the obsessional), but rather to consider that in a particular communication network the person has learned to speak through certain types of signs. When he did so, friction was reduced because a consensus as to meanings was achieved between himself and someone who mattered to him. When a therapist tells a patient, "Your thought lacks feeling," or when he remarks, "The intensity of your feeling is inappropriate to your thought," he is really expressing a difference in the value given to a particular idea. When it becomes clear to the patient that the therapist disagrees with her signs and that he wants her to speak a language he can understand because he feels it is the right language, then the patient, if she is bright, will learn to speak the new language in tones of moderation.

There are levels of complexity in different types of language. Scientific language varies in clarity and levels of complexity depending on the phenomena being described or explained. Artistic and poetic communications, which are usually considered to be the language of feelings, also vary in levels of complexity and clarity. Seen this way, the elimination of confused communication, as I have been repeatedly stressing, depends on an increasing consensus between two people as to the signs and symbols best used to convey to each other the meaning of experience. If I nod, am I thinking or feeling? If I grunt with pleasure, is this a feeling or a thought? I don't think it is possible for a human to feel without thinking. When I hear something unclearly communicated, I may ask, "What are you feeling?" or I may ask, "What are you thinking?" It amounts to the same question. When agreement is experienced, there is usually a release of energy and an assertion of freedom. When the new language is different enough from the old language so that the person senses the kind of pleasure one has in living another way of life, the therapeutic endeavor becomes successful.

I believe that what really makes a difference is the apparently mystical but nonetheless very concrete experience of a confrontation in the immediate relation out of which the patient and I, in surprise and excitement, realize that we have never been here before. Not that the rest of our talk is sounds and alarums signifying nothing. It is preliminary negotiation and education in speaking each other's language. We are disarming each other of conventions in which we are cloaked willy-nilly, and disclosing ourselves person to person. When I speak to a colleague of mine about our work, he and I make most sense to each other when we tell each other stories about our patients. That's what essentially goes on in the professional journals: stories in the form of case reports, hopefully not spoiled by too many program notes.

I think what happens when the patient and I experience each other's values and presence is that he goes away and draws his own conclusions. When the therapeutic relation becomes differentiated from others, the patient begins to differentiate his important relations and in so doing may see the general assumptions which had forced him to be the same old way no matter with whom he was speaking. If it is necessary—and I stress the *if* rather than the necessity—his own mind and his own need to make an aesthetic system will provide enough explanations to keep him busy and warm. One of the few positive conclusions I took from my own analysis was: Well, everything is possible, so since it can become a witch's brew or a birthday party, I'll take my pick as to whichever pleases me at the time.

That is one principle with which I meet a patient: Let's differentiate ourselves from others and the integration will take care of itself. When we differentiate the relation, we acknowledge its reality; my theory emphasizes the reality of concrete relations rather than self or man, or father, or child. These are categories, which are, like words, only symbols and pointers and only a part of reality. In the following chapter on dreams I will illustrate through night stories patients and I have exchanged how I think we can differentiate relationships in a analytic fashion which is based on the faith and experience that true living is meeting, as Buber would say.

Buber, in his great work, *I-Thou*, first published in 1923, characterized two possibilities of relations in his opening words.

To man the world is two-fold, in accordance with his two-fold atti-
tude.
The attitude of man is two-fold in accordance with the two-fold nature
of the primary words which he speaks.
The primary words are not isolated words, but combined words. . . .
The primary word I-Thou can only be spoken with the whole being.
The primary word I-It can never be spoken with the whole being.[18]

Our truest beings are lived in the present, while our relation to
objects is always in the past and dead.
The I of the I-Thou is always in equality with the Thou, while the
I always precedes the It.
Ultimately, for Buber, the I-Thou is the I in relation to the eternal
Thou, but this fullness of relation to one's God is often apprehenda-
ble in concrete, mutual, intense dialogue with another. The I-It relation is the relation of the I to objects and their usefulness to the I. It
is a relation to parts of the Thou which thus become objects. In its
ultimate form, the I-It relation is a monologue with a fragmented
part of the I, devoid of relation to other selves, and leading to
suicide or madness.

I I

ON DREAMS

From Joseph to Freud, king and commoner have granted the interpreter of dreams great power. The dream man may be shunned for a time if the meanings he gives to our dreams are alien to the community, but if his imagination does not quail he will be revered sooner than later.

Throughout history it has been believed that the unravelling of dreams would give a man the wisdom unavailable to him in any other way. Whether dreams were interpreted as oracular revelations, creative acts, reflections of the devil, reveries satisfying our frustrated waking ambitions or any of the other ways they have been interpreted, all who concerned themselves with dreams assumed that understanding them would give us a reach into the depths of our souls unavailable through any other means. Freud called the dream "the royal road to the unconscious." And though the Freudian unconscious was more of a hell than a heaven, a Divine Comedy without a Paradise, untold blessings were held in store for the traveler who took the dream road to his innermost soul.

In calling the dream "the royal road," Freud was not different from any other of the great wizards of antiquity. But when he did so, the analysis of dreams became the *sine qua non* of depth therapy. It was his book on dreams through which he gained the attention of those of the intelligentsia who were searching for the keys to the soul. Freud's masterwork began to guide us in the learning of a new language, that of dream images. But even today we have still a way to go before we become as familiar with the picture language of our night thinking as we are of the words of our waking thoughts.

Even a brief summary of the qualities of dreams helps us understand why they call for special interpretation. In dreams we shatter normal and common sense, we defy the rules, logical and illogical, which we have been painfully taught. In dreams we are most willful and most helpless. We experience in them heroic glory and every devastation but our own death. What we think is least important during the day becomes the kernel of great drama. Our own five senses are transcended beyond the imaginations of any but those we too often call deluded. It thus is not so strange that the great leap forward Freud made in bridging nineteenth- and twentieth-century psychotherapy was made on the basis of *The Interpretation of Dreams*.

Today every educated patient in offices on Park Avenue, in community clinics or in mental hospitals knows something about the value most psychotherapists give to dreams. The typical patient often apologizes to the therapist, "I forgot my dreams," "I didn't dream last night." Nowadays therapists can agree that the patient has forgotten, but he cannot agree that he hasn't dreamed. Hamlet must be corrected when he says, "To sleep, perchance to dream." To sleep means for certain to dream.

What Are the Relevant Facts About Dreams?

In recent years we have discovered immense and startling new knowledge about sleep and especially about dreams. Until Nathaniel Kleitman and E. Aserinsky connected electrical leads from the eyelids of sleeping subjects to recording pens, the significance of the dream in the total mental economy of people could only be speculated about.[1] Only in the last decade have some solid answers developed about the importance of our dreams in everyday life. None of the various theories and observations on people had been able to provide any solid answers to such questions as "Is dreaming a sign of personal disorganization?" or "Is the often reported disclaimer, 'I never dream,' a true report?"

Since Kleitman and Aserinsky published their original work on dreams, many others have also demonstrated that everybody dreams every night.[2] The average adult has from four to six periods of dreaming in a night, totaling about 20 percent of the typical eight hours of sleep per night. The number of minutes taken in dreaming increases from the first dreams, which occupy about ten minutes, to the fifth period, which may last as much as a half-hour. The interval between dreams is usually and regularly about ninety minutes. When a person is asked to act out one of his dreams, he takes as long to do so as the time in which he did the dreaming. (Of course, the actual verbal report of a dream takes much less time than the period of dreaming.) Dreams do not occur in a flash. Researchers know this because rapid eye movements (Rems) usually signal the start of a dream and a typical rapid brain wave of low amplitude always accompanies it.

Another, and perhaps the most pertinent, fact about dreaming has direct implications for the therapist's response to the patient's dreaming or his nonrecall of his dreams. Dreaming occurs at a stage of sleep which appears to be characteristic of mammals. This type of sleep is apparently as distinct, physiologically, from other stages of sleep as it is from wakefulness. For instance, a dream may be affected by an external stimulus, but only if this stimulus is applied during the so-called D-state of sleep.[3] The percent of time spent in this type of sleep is highest in infancy and lowest in old age. This proportion of dreaming sleep is very important to preserve. When it is curtailed, the person will become restless and make up for it at another time. Thus we cannot yet conclude that it is dreaming that is necessary. It may be more appropriate to infer that it was the type of sleep rather than the dreams which subjects must make up for when their dream-sleep is interfered with. No therapist is warranted to say to a patient that his not remembering his dreams is a sign of disequilibrium. After all, if dreams are just a kind of background, incidental noise in our sleep, why bother to attend to them? Studies have been undertaken to distinguish between recallers of dreams and nonrecallers. Though some differences have been found, they do not suggest so far that the nonrecaller is a more disturbed person than the individual alerted to his dreams.

The hallucinations of the psychotic and the imaginings of the sleeper have been often compared. Vivid visual and auditory sensations swirling up from within have been induced by psychedelic drugs and by perceptual isolation, like that occurring in highly monotonous surroundings when the solitary person is, or believes himself to be, cut off from human contact. This suggests how much the person's mind must continue organizing his memories and sensations into some meaningful framework. When the usual definitions and orientations are interrupted as when we are asleep, or drugged, or cut off from others, the human organism presses on toward other ways of expression. If this formulation makes sense, it helps us understand why the interpreter of dreams has such a hold on our imagination. He steps in when others have left us.

It seems that the dream we tend to remember most is the last one we had before waking, and this tends to be more vivid and bizarre. No one has claimed that the remembered dream is randomly selected, but clinicians have usually not considered other factors determining the recollection of a dream besides emotional drives. There is no clear evidence whether the series of dreams we have in any one night are usually linked by a common theme or whether they represent a five-ring circus with no meaningful connection among them. However, there is some association between what Freud called the day residues, that is, those experiences during wakefulness of which we may have been aware dimly or even not at all, and the content of our dreams. Laboratory research work on subliminal perception has demonstrated how unseen stimuli are distorted, elaborated and transformed in our dreams. Some dreams appear to pick up broken-off events of the day which we pushed aside to get on with our business.

About the content of dreams, the data are in dispute since assumptions about the human condition play a larger role in their interpretation. The best study on a nonpatient population is Calvin Hall's. Of his findings and speculations, I select a few that are most relevant to my arguments. Not only do the majority of dreams have an unpleasant tone, but the proportion of unpleasantness in dreams increases with aging. Dreams containing fear, anger and sadness occur about twice as often as those containing joy and happiness. Rarely do dreams concern themselves with widely publicized events. Rarely does the dreamer involve himself with prominent people or those he meets on TV or in the newspaper. The cast of characters most often includes the dreamer himself (nearly always) and those with whom he is emotionally involved. Before adulthood we dream of our parents, and afterward of our lovers, enemies, spouses and children. Our dreams tend to be the stories we most likely would tell only to intimates. They speak of personal and private, hearth-bound relations. If you had to bet on who was dreaming about you, it would be safest to choose the person who enters your dreams. And finally, color appears to have no connection with any other variable, though it occurs in some measure in about one-third of a random series of dreams. However, a significant minority of people never report color in their dreams.

Because most of the systematic research on dreams has been carried out in the United States, the question of the applicability of these results to other cultures does arise. It is not too likely that the findings about the need to dream or the frequency of dreaming are exclusive aspects of the American dream. It is somewhat more likely to suppose that Dr. Hall's results are culture-bound. Hopefully, comparative studies will soon appear.

In line with my discussion of the therapeutic relation as an inner sanctum, I would tend to interpret Dr. Hall's finding on the relative paucity of important public events in dreams as also a product of our culture rather than a universal characteristic. I don't believe we need conclude that the ignoring of global catastrophic events is a universal trait of men, as we might from Dr. Hall's finding that not one of his subjects dreamed of Hiroshima during the days following the dropping of the first A bomb on man. Perhaps we Americans, with our stringent avoidance of death themes, had to deny the catastrophe before it entered our dreams, or, if it did, we dreamed of the terror at those times of night which precluded easy recollection on awakening. Nuclear bomb dreams might then have been relegated to the vast majority of forgotten dreams. Avoidance of the meaning of nuclear bombs is also, we should remember, a characteristic of many Americans who think of peace marchers as radicals. The fact that among remembered dreams we rarely report public events which have a large influence on our lives is to be investigated rather than accepted as normal. Could it be that the patient who does dream of public personalities is an unusually broad-minded individual?

SOME IMPLICATIONS FOR THE THERAPIST OF DREAM RESEARCH

There are a few tentative conclusions the therapist can draw from these findings.

1. The most important one is that dreams should not be approached as pathological expressions. Since psychiatrists and clinicians made the most noise about the meaning of dreams, in intellectual circles at any rate, an association developed between dreams and psychological deficit. Though Freud maintained that dreams preserve sleep, and thus implied that dreams were biologically necessary, the educated public followed the emphasis given to dreams by clinicians and tended to equate dreams and their contents with neuroses. This traditional attitude among modern therapists has persisted despite the hard data discovered since Kleitman's first report in 1953.

If the clinician believes that remembered dreams are signs of "disturbances in personality function," the patient will tend to remember and report disturbing dreams. It hasn't been demonstrated at all that remembered dreams are more indicative of pathology than forgotten ones, though it has been demonstrated by Calvin Hall that about two-thirds of remembered dreams are the unpleasant and painful ones. It should be noted, too, that Dr. Hall's finding does challenge the common notion, supported by many clinical authorities, that we usually forget painful events. It would take a sophisticated researcher a great deal of time and effort to test the hypothesis that remembered dreams are signs of a pathological state. But it is certainly illogical to argue that a painful dream is a sign of personal disturbance. The fact that about two-thirds of our remembered dreams are painful and the obvious point that pain and disorganization are not synonymous preclude the conclusion reached by most authorities.

It is simple arithmetic which warns us that the number of remembered dreams is a small percent of the thirty-five or so dreams we have in a week. Are the remembered dreams, even if they could all be reported to the analyst, more or less pathological than our unremembered ones? To be consistent with the notion of repression as a sign of disorganization, the clinician should tell the person that his remembering a dream is a sign of increasing integrity. Systematic research may yet give us some clues as to whether remembered dreams are more or less like clinically noteworthy symptoms, but until then therapists must be circumspect in their judgment about the dreams patients remember.

2. The fact that any one dream is only one of about thirty-five weekly dreams requires the interpreter to beware of bias in drawing any conclusion about it. A number of factors determine which dream the patient brings to his therapist. Among these would be the qualities of the relationship between patient and therapist. Even in classical analysis when the patient comes five times a week the number of remembered dreams must always be small and the number reported even smaller. What is told to the doctor is, then, a summary of a selection from a set of dreams most of which have been forgotten for reasons no one yet knows. If the therapist has a psychoanalytic orientation, he should not only tell the patient who denies that he dreams, "You are repressing," but also tell the patient who does report his dreams, "The important ones may be just those you have forgotten, I mean repressed." The forgotten or nonreported dream may be the significant one.

Occasionally a patient will say, like Andrea did, "Oh, I forgot to tell you a dream I had about six weeks ago. I was at my wedding, dancing and singing. A large group of friends were there, and I was very happy. It wasn't clear to me who my husband was." Andrea told me this dream after she met and fell in love with Charles, whom she eventually married. Between the night she had this dream and the week in which she and Charles found each other, Andrea was more disturbed than usual. I was in fact wondering at that time what was going on in her which made her present herself as "worse" than she had been. The forgotten dream was like a prophecy, but she found it necessary to forget it, or perhaps to withhold it from our attention. Why she did so is not immediately relevant, though I imagine one could come up with a number of useful speculations. The chances are good, however, that had she told me of her dream at the time she had it, our relationship would have been considerably clearer and I for one would have been spared much. But again, that could be the point of her forgetting to tell me.

3. The need to dream suggests that there may also be a need to tell one's dreams, at least for those people who have a fairly devel-

oped need to share their personal thoughts. This is true for patients who come voluntarily. It may be that healing lies in the sharing of the dream with another person, especially the person one dreams of, rather than in its interpretation. In my view the encouragement to reveal oneself through all means, including dreams, is the healing force, rather than the insights derived from dream analysis. Insight, so to speak, follows rather than precedes change. Insight is hindsight.

4. The fact that the patient is in the office suggests that most if not all of what he says is tinged, lightly if not heavily, with peculiarities. Are his dreams also? Yes; if we want to see pathology in them, we will. All the known facts about dreams have not yet revealed how to interpret the content of any particular dream. This still remains the responsibility of the patient-doctor pair and is affected by the idiosyncrasies of each. Whether the dreams of the average outpatient are wilder than those of the nonpatient remains to be discovered through research. Those of severely disturbed and hospitalized patients do appear to be different in quality from nonhospitalized people, but so does much of their behavior and thinking reveal the emptiness of human relations reflected in their dreams. But even in the case of a psychotic his telling of the dream could be seen as a restitutive effort rather than as a focusing on the content as a sign of his emptiness. It is the interpreter who still is responsible for accenting the problem-stating or the problem-solving features of our dreams.

The Attitudes with Which I Listen to the Patient's Dreams

I lay no claim to originality in the way I interpret dreams, only a re-emphasis and reorganization of the ideas of others. The dreams I will report in the next chapter to illustrate my "theory" probably will be differently interpreted by the reader. This should be so because it is in the nature of dreams, as it is in the nature of all stories, for the listener to conjure up his own meanings.

An interpretation is always a hypothesis and cannot be objectively proved true, as I have affirmed at a number of points in this volume. Interpretations that are "true" are those which appear to the therapeutic pair to be true, i.e., have consensual validity. One would tend to think that those interpretations which the patient accepts as true make more of a difference than those he does not accept, but I am hardly sure of this. Often enough it is the spurned idea which precedes the person's originality. When there is a wish to talk together cooperatively, the truth or falsity of any particular point is irrelevant.

An interpretation of a dream may appear to be validated by other sources besides the patient and myself. This occurs because he and I share values developed in situations in which we both have participated such as socioeconomic groups, educational programs and religious associations. I emphasize the commonality of intellectual or cognitive values in the discussion on dreams because relative to other contents discussed in therapy these common values we share tend to be ignored. The interpretation of a dream would appear to be more influenced by the therapist's categories of thought than those of the patient's because the dream is relatively peculiar and confused to the patient and the psychotherapist has often assumed the interpretation of a dream as his special province.

An humble doubt regarding the real truth is called for by the very nature of all human relations, whether they are experienced in dreams, in conversation or in the usually unrecognized communion of gestures. The interpreter of dreams is required to tell us his values, the frame of reference in which he tends to place the communicated dream. To repeat one fact as evidence: no one knows how it happens that of all the dreams the person has a particular one is remembered, which of all remembered dreams is reported and even whether the analysis of dreams is necessary for therapy to effect a deep and radical change in the person's life.

Carl Rogers does not ask for the client's dreams, and his clients rarely speak about them. Psychoanalytically oriented therapists do not require all their patients to talk about their dreams. For one thing, experience has shown that a person can chatter through telling his dreams as he can chatter in any other way. The practice of asking the patient to keep a pad and pencil on his night table isn't much in fashion today. Many patients have caught on anyway and the instruction would be superfluous. For another reason, therapists discourage some patients from talking about dreams because the patient has been judged to be a psychotic or a "borderline" case whose hold on reality is very weak. Presumably it then follows that a discussion of "crazy" night thoughts might further blur the already marred distinction between the pictures in one's mind and "those out there." Here again is another illustration of the two unproved and unprovable assumptions that dreams more than any other of our thoughts reflect our potentiality for disorganization and reveal the depths of our nature which day thoughts and behavior cannot reveal.

As I commented in my opening paragraphs, the idea that in the deciphering of the dream man penetrates his most obscure secrets has persisted from antiquity. The fact that it is a primitive thought doesn't necessarily make it irrational, but the very perspectives on man formulated by psychoanalytic theory, of the Freudian, Jungian or Frommian brand, as well as the recent facts about the physiological function of dreaming, do suggest that "the dream as the touchstone" is a magical thought. As it is imbalanced to ignore our night thoughts, it seems to me quite exaggerated to give our dreams greater significance than the meanings of our hours in sunlight. From one point of view, my argument is simple and obvious. Is man's degradation or glory or insecurity or creativity more truly represented after we shut our eyes than when we are moving about? A discussion of a dream gives us another opening to the creativity and imagination lying fallow in all too many of us. This is a large contribution of the psychoanalytic tradition which provided a necessary corrective to the relative neglect of talk about dreams by Western philosophers. But even as interpreters of dreams and great humanists, the leaders of psychoanalysis were possessed by the magic of nighttime, "the royal road to the unconscious."

I think of dreaming as an activity in which we continue our daytime activities. I do not think the meanings we give to dreams need be any deeper or truer than those meanings we discern in fairy tales, historical records, space travel and so forth. The dream takes form in poetic symbols which are often very surprising to the dreamer, but that is because we modern dreamers have not listened enough to the music of the spheres and because we leave fables and stories to kindergarten teachers. The dream is itself a symbol, as well as composed of symbols, and, like any other aspect of our life, can be shared with ourselves and others. It is a symbol of the process of imagination, which is new largely because there has been a false division between poetry and science.

My emphasis on continuities rather than discontinuities is based to some degree on the fact that the experts on dream interpretation always have, and probably always will, vary in the schemes they use for unraveling a dream. I can be accused of playing it safe, but a prudent eclecticism makes sense to me on other grounds as well. Freud spoke of dreams as wish fulfillments, and he included nightmares and other dreams of dread in his theory. Jung, accepting this as true for some dreams, also insisted that dreams could reflect plans for the future. Dreams were not only regressive but prospective. Fromm in turn agreed with both but pointed to the problem-solving qualities of some dreams. One or another authority lent his prestige and his sagacity to the language of dreams by stressing their reflections of sexual urges or aggressive drives or as adaptive coping with the variety of stimuli impinging on every person.

The dreamer could be, on any particular night, a frustrated lover, a terrified hater, a thoughtful artist or an expansive thinker wrestling with the conundrums of his daytime professional pursuits. Make an inventory of all the kinds of italics given in particular interpretative frameworks and you have a list of all the possible ways of deriving the meanings of our existence stressed by different philosophers, which they derived from an inspection not of dreams but of mankind's directly recorded daytime productions. Freud used dreams to reveal the meaning of neuroses and other characteristic conditions of men, but he also used waking creations to throw light on dreams. This is, of course, a commonly accepted principle in modern dream interpretation. One cannot understand a particular dream without understanding the whole dreamer.

The recent evidence that dreaming may be as necessary for preserving our minds as are all the nutriments necessary for preserving our bodies also supports, I think, the emphasis on the continuities between waking and sleeping reveries. If dreaming is necessary to preserve sleep, then from a psychological point of view it follows, I think, that dreams need not be considered any less or any greater distortion of reality. Dreams, as "crazy" as they sound on reporting, seem only more "crazy" than our wakeful thoughts because we are unfamiliar with their language and because we have been conditioned by modern instructors in dreams to think they are more difficult to decipher. If we would put aside our awe of dreams, as a person entering an art gallery should set aside his awe, but not his wonder, appreciation would follow with a little effort. As I must read a new poet over and over again in order to appreciate him, or if I am interested in oceanography, I must work at its vocabulary, so I must also work humbly at learning the new dream language of every person. A nightmare of the wildest and most terrifying sort is hardly more terrifying than, let us say, the columns of a sensation-seeking newspaper, or what happened at Hiroshima, or our own daydreamed fantasies, occasionally brought to the fore at moments of respite. Yes, we can and do dream morbidly during the day, and we often, I hold, dream creatively, lovingly and joyfully at night.

At this point I wish to state a central theme of my attitudes toward healing, because in the discussion of dreams it is even more important to make this attitude evident to the patient than in any other topics which arise between us.

Healing occurs in a relation which helps us believe there is still promise even when we feel at our worst and which helps us become attuned to the voices of skepticism when we tend toward euphoria. Whenever a patient presents me with a thought, dreamed or caught in a moment of respite during the day, I may or may not speak about it with him. If I do, do I accentuate the positive without eliminating the negative or do I accent the negative and imply to the patient that at bottom his soul is blacker than he imagines? Erich Fromm appears to be making this point: ". . . we are not only less reasonable and less decent in our dreams but . . . we are also more intelligent, wiser, and capable of better judgment when we are asleep than when we are awake."[4]

We therapists take on a great deal of responsibility when we make a choice in which we express a crucial, perhaps unprovable assumption that the patient is more disturbed than nonpatients. My bias, as I have affirmed, is to the contrary. Patients, I believe, reflect the acute sensibilities often avoided by most men who lead lives of quiet or noisy desperation. The act of coming for help is still, unfortunately, an act of deviance. It is still too often taken as a recognition by the person and others that he is not normal and is ill. The therapist helps the patient accept this deviance as also an indication of refined sensitivity to the hypocrisies of our times.[5] He helps the patient to realize that his talking critically and angrily about his parents is evidence of his caring for them. He and the patient learn together the timeless longing for harmonious and creative meetings. If this is what is accented—taught, if you will—the patient will get out of the inner sanctum more quickly and act more socially responsible than otherwise. The majority of patients need more help in recognizing their ethical yearnings than they do in analyzing their displacements, condensations and all the defense mechanisms about which they are quite often aware. "You are better and stronger than you think you are, rather than worse," is what I wish to convey to the patient as I help him experience how he hurts himself as well as when he hurts others.

When it comes to interpreting dreams, the therapist needs to be more humble than ever, for all the reasons I have been giving. Fromm made an interesting point when he wrote:

Dreams give us a clue to the qualities of hidden desires and fears but not to their quantities; they permit of qualitative but not of quantitative analysis. In order to determine the quantity of a trend discerned qualitatively in a dream, other aspects must be taken into account; repetition of this or similar themes in other dreams, associations of the dreamer, his behavior in real life, or whatever else—like resistance to the analyst of such a trend—may help to get a better view of the intensity of desires and fears.[6]

This could be as well applied to any other thought production in the therapeutic relationship. It is particularly important to apply it to dream thoughts since they are shrouded and decorated and poetically phrased in a language which is learned by both the dreamer and the analyst relatively late in life. And always I must remind ourselves that any single dream is only one vision of the myriads of visions and only one enlargement of the hidden thoughts of the patient. The dream he recounts may just as well be a transient one, a trivial preoccupation rather than an experience cast up repeatedly on the shores of memory. I hope every patient who brings me a dream for interpretation hears me say to him:

"You want my reactions to your dream. If I give them, we join in the assumption that the dream must have a particular meaning. Despite tradition, any dream and all dreams may be as decipherable as the meaning of life itself. Move the kaleidoscope a fraction, recall and tell the dream again and the pattern may change. I do try to decipher some of my dreams, but often I conclude with the thought that dreams are always pointing to potentialities and possibilities which can never be fixed.

"But if we want to try to analyze your dream, and thus make it our story, I ask you to keep in mind that what I say is what I think at this time. I know I am selecting something and ignoring more than I select, as you have done in reporting this dream. Your language is to be respected, as you are in your realized feelings, in your hopes and as yet unrealized potentials.

"Furthermore, your remembered dream may be an expression of a complex which doesn't frighten you so much and so you can speak about it at night. The dream may be telling of a barrier overcome as well as being a warning of what lies ahead, or a statement of your present frustration and condition. I think it can be all these at the same time, and you and I, out of our intuitions, choose one or another perspective from which to analyze it."

An Approach to Three Classes of Dream Figures

There are three dimensions of a dream which I try to distinguish with the patient: the real humans or things he knows personally (the proper nouns), the persons or animals or objects he doesn't know directly (the common nouns), and the fantastic, unearthly, as yet unnamed images.

1. *The Proper Nouns:* Since I consider suffering beyond that embodied in simple existence to be an outcome of a sense of isolation, of anxiety in contact with another person, of a feeling that no one hears or cares and an unsureness about the clarity of one's own feelings, I first select the elements in a dream which have to do with the real people in it. I ask the person to tell us whether his feelings and thoughts about the person he recognizes in the dream are similar to or different from what he senses in his waking relationships. Does the dream tell us of feelings which were important to the person but which were given less significance in the waking contact because other needs and pressures dominated the situation? Perhaps the person is dreaming about the other individual because he wants to review the relation or complete the picture and integrate all his possible feelings into the light of day. "My assumption," I say, "is that you are occupied at night because you were not as fully clear

about the relationship and attentive to it during the day. You are saying to your friend or enemy, 'I take notice of my experience of you.'"

2. *The Common Nouns:* Then I ask the person to turn to unknown figures, animate or inanimate, and to try to understand what they may symbolize. Here I affirm that his associations and interpretations are as good as mine and that mine are as worthy as his. Yes, the dream may disguise some truth, but the deciphering of the displacements and condensations is a mutual task. Walter Bonime's continuous emphasis on the cooperative action of patient and doctor in the decoding of dream symbols is, I hold, the most valuable aspect of his book, of which I have been critical.

3. *The Unnamed:* The third class of dream figures and their meanings includes all the elements which are at the time shrouded in an unrelieved haze. They may never be understood, as much of life will never be comprehended. If the patient or I have some special aesthetic inclination to wring the dream dry, then we might pursue particular fragments and bring to bear every possible association. However, I am inclined to be a cream skimmer, to get the available nutritives easily so that the patient, fortified with the sense that he does have a perspective, can then more actively participate with others outside of the office.

12

DREAMS TOLD AND UNTOLD

IN THE OFFICE

I have argued that some screening process determines which dreams are remembered and also which dreams the patient presents to the therapist. It follows that the illustrations I will give are not random.

Since the patient's dreams are not excretions of a disease but communications affected by his present interactions as well as trodden dispositions from the storehouse of past experience, so are those dreams about which I am writing. Most of them are from patients I have tried to help, a few are from the publications of others and some I have dreamed. Some examples are only fragments of longer dreams, selected because they best illustrate my point of view. Some are given because for some reason I remember them well or have, in the midst of a session, decided to jot them down or, on taking leave with the person, asked him to write them up. I can be certain, of course, that my coverage is not thorough, but I do think I have touched on most of the important issues. And I hope it is seen in the ways the patient and I discuss dreams that I do not follow any special technique. For example, I don't see what special virtue there is in the "common and unquestionably important procedure for the therapist first to hear a dream and then to direct the patient to associate."[1] Let there be a free flow of dialogue rather than ritualization of technique.

DREAMS ABOUT THE THERAPIST

The patient's dream tempts therapists who are sensitive to the significance of the therapeutic relation to use it as the means for understanding the "deeper" levels of the transactions between them. The therapist often assumes that any unexpressed attitude toward him which possesses the patient will eventually appear in a dream. He is then especially ready to translate dream symbols elaborated by the patient's associations into categories describing the patient's feelings toward him. I have done this also, and patients have accepted or differed from or been indifferent to my interpretations in which I have taken any figure and said that was me.

I do not doubt that some of our reinterpretations do help the patient become more direct about all his feelings, that is, more genuine in all his relationships. But I also do not doubt that our readiness to see ourselves in the disguises of the dreams also increases the patient's strong inclination to overvalue the help we can give him. In doing so he becomes more rebelliously passive in his relationship to us as well as to others. Rather than incur this I discuss the patient's feelings toward me as expressed in a dream only when I appear as myself. I presume I am represented in some dreams through other figures, but if he must disguise his feelings, then the chances are as great that the figure I think is me may be somebody else.

Dreams, as I have experienced their telling, can be used by any patient to avoid talking directly about something important to him, as they can be used to get to some perspective. However, when the patient says to me, "I dreamed you were . . ." then it is I who avoid the recognition of myself if I imply that someone else lies behind the figure of me. First, we must discover the sense we have of the reality of our relationship; then we can proceed to differentiate it from others.

When I appear as myself in a dream, I am very much inclined to believe the patient is telling us something true about me. Since he certainly selects some features for articulation and may consign others to an unbroken silence, the selected traits he ascribes to me in his dream are often exaggerated. However, any quality he gives to me I accept as relatively true for us in our relationship and thus as an aspect of myself. And rarely does the patient tell me something about myself which I do not recognize as valid in some way.

Joanne, in her mid-twenties, has been trying some new ways to break out of an alternating cycle of short-lived involvements with men followed by long periods of loneliness. The boy friend of the moment is usually quite as unkind to her as she is insensitive to him, and this appears to confirm her dread that she and a man will never be able genuinely to wish each other well. One attempt she has made to find other relations to engage her interest in her participation in a chapter of CORE. Shortly after joining in the civil rights movement, she described a long dream. In one scene she enters a political club and sees me as the leader of the group. My first comment on her dream was that putting me in this setting was quite insightful of a significant aspect of our relations and my activity in it.

"Joanne, you know of my social and political interests. You know I have encouraged you to be a good rather than bad Samaritan. I myself have dreamed and daydreamed of being a politician and lawyer who could do something about unjust laws. But even more, I think all therapists are acting on the basis of their values and are using their power for social ends. Hopefully, the politician you see me as in your dream is using his power openly and not covertly manipulating the group as professional politicians supposedly do."

One of the dreams Walter Bonime reports is that presented by a social worker, about thirty years old, who, during the second interview, held two months after the first, reported that a few weeks after the initial session the analyst appeared in a dream as a chauffeur. "You had voluntarily been coming to my house for our sessions. After one session you were chauffeuring me about the city with your car." After some discussion in which the patient "spontaneously" spoke of his feelings of dependency and the way his mother would push him to do things, Dr. Bonime comments: "At this point the interpretive hypothesis was offered to him that the dream of the analyst-chauffeur represented his demand that I take the initiative and the responsibility for his getting well." According to Dr. Bonime, the hypothesis was verified because in succeeding sessions "the tyranny of the patient in all his significant relationships—with his wife, children, supervisor, parents, and friends—began to show clearly."[2]

I think Dr. Bonime's interpretation is a feasible one and according to his account led to the productive analysis of a general trait of this patient which is often labeled passive-aggressiveness. Yet, if I were the therapist, I would have accented the patient's expression of a reality of the therapeutic relationship and spoken to him as follows: "I'm not sure whether you are openly dependent on me or see me as subservient to you at the moment. We will probably explore this theme in our relation as well as in others. But you do express a truth for us. Yes, I do come to your home, in a manner of speaking. You open your doors to the privacy of your marriage when you become a patient. You place yourself in my power, too. A chauffeur is someone who is hired, as I have been, and though he is usually considered to be of a lower status than his employer, in this dream I am chauffeuring you in my car. You have placed yourself in my power, that is, under my influence, and you express this realistic feeling by making me the driver, and the driver of my car, not yours. As long as I have my hands on the steering wheel, I might take you where I wish to go rather than where you guide me. There are thus a number of elements in our relation as doctor and patient which are quite accurately summarized in your dream. You probably have thought about them since you dream directly about us, and I want to know more of your feelings about having placed yourself in my hands."

Speaking this way to a patient helps him learn to affirm the reality of the present situation as well as go on to clarify the confusion of past with present relations. In placing the analyst in the role of chauffeur it is possible that the patient is transferring onto the analyst an attitude developed with parents and crystallized with other authoritative persons. The analytic situation, however, has real elements of driving and leading the patient, and if all goes well, he will not be taken for a ride. Perhaps Dr. Bonime's patient was inquiring how the analyst felt about the power given to him in his act of coming for help.

Joel is a second year-student of the ministry who dreamed about me the night before our second session. The first meeting was on November 21, 1963. During this first session he informed me that he had decided to come for help after considering the recommendation of a supervisor. His difficulties became apparent to him about three years ago during his last year of college shortly after his mother died. His account during the first hour underlined three themes which were to recur throughout the seven months we met. He longed for a close relationship to his father, he felt disturbed because he could not grieve over his mother's death and he wished to develop his love for Sal, with whom he recently had become engaged. We set another time on the following Tuesday before we made any final commitment about meeting regularly.

A good part of our second meeting was taken up with the exchange of feelings about the assassination of our President. Joel spoke with evident distress over his efforts to avoid expressing his sadness. He did not call Sal, he could not look at the funeral on TV, and when he was in the stacks at the library, he almost cried but something held him back. He had thought of calling his father but refrained from doing so because he did not want "to interfere in his friendship with a new girl friend." Then he told me his short dream. "I was coming to see you and you said that I did not need any help. I asked you for some other names."

He was puzzled about the dream since he had about decided that he wanted me to be his therapist. I agreed that I had become quite important for him. The fact that so soon after we met he was reporting having dreams of me indicated that. But the dream appeared to say that he felt I did not want to see him. Joel thought that the way I questioned him during the first hour implied that I was dubious about his need for help, and I affirmed his impression. "Though it was possible that behind me stands your father, since I had not actually told you I did not wish to see you, the fact is that I had wondered about the need for therapy. In thinking about our first discussion, I realized that I had jumped about quite a bit in the way I questioned you. There was something on my mind that day, I recall, which may have affected my way of talking with you. However, I also had the distinct thought from what you told me about your life that you were growing, with considerable distress of course, but you were changing more than you recognized. I think that my judgment, which I expressed to you, could have been taken by you as one of not wishing to see you. If this was the case, it may be another expression of the sensitivities you have so clearly described. The first point to reiterate is that your dream also did make good sense in our relation and indicated more than an unjust displacement of some of your feelings onto me."

Joel's dream could have also meant that he had decided to seek out someone else and didn't really want to work with me. Since there was no way of discovering the real truth, the only thing we could do was to recognize this possibility. I asked him if he wished to go ahead. He decided to make a contract.

Joel was quite a dreamer, or rather he reported many dreams, which we used fruitfully. About three weeks later, after we had been considering his difficulties in expressing angry thoughts and after he had spoken with Sal's parents about their plans to marry, Joel had the following dream:

I followed Joe Kennedy, Kennedy's father, into a hotel room. In this big room, an intense beam was focused on me and pressed me against the wall. I had to take out my keys and as I did, a lot of old pictures tumbled out, including a copy of Life magazine. Many of my relatives were all around the room. This X-ray beam inched me along the wall, and the purpose of the investigation was to find out if I was an assassin.

Who could the operator of the beam be if not I? Joel had no other possibilities in mind. He accused his father of indifference and not of active, almost persecuting surveillance. The possibility that I was behind the X-ray also was suggested by the reference to Kennedy. He followed Joe Kennedy into the room and our second meeting followed President Kennedy's death. Also, the grouping of relatives, the exposure of old photos, which could represent memories, and the copy of Life all could easily symbolize aspects of therapeutic work. I also accepted part of the responsibility of his portrait of me as the operator of the beam, if indeed it was I, since I had put considerable emphasis on the problem of his aggression. "However," I added, "since the person behind the beam remains anonymous, I will suspend for the time being any acknowledgment that I could use such a long-distance and remote way of forcing you to confess. I think I am a very direct person and would more likely rattle you to your face. Therefore, it is also possible that you are describing the remoteness you feel in your relation with your father. As long as you did not identify this operator, let us be tentative in our interpretation."

A month before we stopped formal sessions, Joel dreamed: "I call my father long distance to tell him I am sorry he cannot come for my wedding. He is very glad I say so. I look up and we are sitting across a desk and do not need a telephone." I approved also the fact that Joel had already told the dream to Sal, who had recently come to accept his sadness about the distance between himself and his father.

Laura, a young woman, is Ronald's second wife. I had been seeing them both for some time. I experienced her husband as a more cooperative person than she was. In fact, there were many times when the discussions between Laura and me suddenly changed from a brief consideration of some issue into a tense petulance on her part and an irritated silence on mine. Our work had been going slowly. However, we both managed to have the fortitude to stick it through and directly discuss our difficulties with each other. She then presented a series of dreams in which I figured prominently and in which she appeared to have revealed her contribution to our involvement and, by inference, to the very severe marital disharmony between herself and Ronald. I asked Laura to write them down after she had reported them to me since I might find them useful in a book I was planning to write.

I am out for a walk with Ronald—it seems we're window shopping or something—not always together—wandering leisurely about. I run into you a couple of times and you "role play" with me the casual meeting of acquaintances, giving me some assurance that I can manage this.

A while later I am going to meet Ronald. I stop at a door stoop, noticing that in a pile of dirt there seem to be some good fossils. I spend several minutes pawing through the dirt. Most of the specimens are broken but I find three or four that are worth keeping, and I start off again to meet with Ronald. I've been delayed by the fossil hunt so I hurry. Then I see him walking with you and a little girl (I assume is your daughter Clara). I run to catch up with the three of you. You, Bernie, notice how fast I can run, and even remark upon it to Clara. I catch up and you say something about wondering just how fast I can run. There is a place just there marked off (⅛ of a mile) (also I am confused—it seems you wonder if I can run eight miles an hour, which seems real easy to me in the dream). I say, sure, I'll let you time me. I hand you my purse and put my fossils in your hand. I take a position to start and decide not to run in my coat (I am wearing slacks and a long coat), so I hand my coat to Ronald, who is standing nearby. You give a signal and I make a very cramped start, so I stop and say, "Let's try again." At this point I wake up.

I told Laura that much of the dream spoke for itself and affirmed many of the experiences we had had together and those she had described in her relation to Ronald. Her portrait of me as challenging her to race symbolized the pressure I had put on her, which at times, in my irritation with her, had become touched with sarcasm. After all, the marked-off distance of an eighth of a mile is quite short. She was also correct in seeing me as feeling equal to her husband (we walk together), while she is treated as a little girl.

For good reason I drew our attention to the fossils, which appeared to symbolize the good and bad remnants of her childhood. ("Most of the specimens are broken but I find three or four that are worth keeping.") She remembered that on one vacation Ronald and she had looked for fossils in central Ohio. Also, they had traveled in Europe the previous summer, and it was she who first drew attention to fossils in the stone floor of a Swedish museum. This recollection she counted as among the happiest of her three-year marriage. Laura remembered that one of the few happy contacts with her father, a man who had had four daughters and no sons, involved hunting for fossils. Some of the numerous meanings of the fossils in her dream were thus elicited, and both of us agreed that it was possible she was here recognizing an aspect of the tendency to confuse Ronald with her father.

We also briefly touched on her mentioning Clara, about whom I occasionally spoke. Her wishes to be close to Ronald and me, perhaps to have a child with him or perhaps to be a little girl like Clara with the two father figures, were raised as possibilities. Other themes, such as the race and her handing her unnecessary coat to Ronald for safekeeping, were not discussed, though at that time I think they spoke of her cognizance of the way she felt therapy as an unburdening and also as a competitive encounter. Again, she was correct on both counts, whether we consider her feelings as displacements or symbolizations of the actual therapeutic relation. She and I were in a race with time, and though running eight miles an hour is an easy feat, therapy is a pressured experience no matter how much the therapist tells the patient to relax. How can Laura accomplish it when her difficulties make her life more troubled than it need be and when life is short enough? How can Laura not feel in a race with me when I not only try to help her reveal herself spontaneously and in her own time but also provoke her anxiety when I point out to her that she both runs away from her feelings and cavorts like a young child? Therapy is a digging around in the dirt not done at leisure, as has so often been implied by the doctrine of free association.

In the first part of her dream Laura also anticipates that she and Ronald might meet me outside the office. This is a distinct possibility since I occasionally visit the library of the school where Ronald teaches. She perceives me as helpful to her in dissolving the formality of our sessions in the office. In this she also anticipates the future and the possibility that we might become friends.

In the following hour Laura gave me a fossil, a trilobite she and Ronald had found before they were married. I received this interesting present, which had much value for her, with appreciation. About five months later she reported a dream which reflected a radical change in her feelings about our relation:

There is a little interlude in which we are talking about dreams, then rather suddenly you turn to me (you are standing at the window—I think I'm sitting in the chair, not sure), you say joyfully that you're having an erection. I take this as your saying to me you really like me. I come over to you and you put your arm around me. We sit down on the couch and embrace. We start to recline, but I say that I don't want to go so far as to have intercourse with you, but I am glad that we can be close. We sit up and embrace—I awoke at this point with a happy feeling about the dream.

When I awoke I immediately reflected on the sexualness of the dream with the reflection that Ronald is my husband and I want to be intimate only with him but that I was happy to have this feeling of closeness with you. I felt that the symbolism of the erection was rather strong, but it didn't really worry me. In the dream I was happy about the relationship and found it easy to make myself clear about how I felt. I also did not feel that I was putting you in a bind.

I had very little to add. I expressed my pleasure in her own sense of closeness in equality. I confessed that I never believed I could be sexually aroused as long as she played being a little girl. But now that she was able to say no to me without having to fight me, it is possible that she would become a fuller woman who could arouse in me an erotic fantasy.

Margaret, an unmarried young woman of twenty-three, and I had been through some experiences that were very trying for her, including an abortion. These events intensified the bond between us, as must occur when one sets aside one's doubts about consequences and chooses to intervene actively in the life of another.

Margaret felt that all was well because it ended well. She often enough expressed directly and in dreams her gratitude for the direct help I had given her. I was relieved about the outcome, but I reminded her that it was reasonable to expect that she would harbor resentment about her need for my help. About a year after the abortion Margaret had this dream: "You had died. I was very unhappy and I called your wife and she was the only one who would comfort me. She was the only one who could help me because you had trained her to be a therapist."

It occurred to both of us that her dreaming of my death could be a disguised expression, veiled in crocodile tears, of a murderous resentment toward me. It was also possible that the dream which brought in my wife pointed to her hate for her father, who she felt at the time had made it very difficult for her to be close to her mother. These interpretations were both possible in the light of the many present and past memories she had related. We discussed these possibilities, and then I asked what trait of mine was she alluding to through imagining me as dead? I could think of one basic fact in our relation. I was her doctor and she wished the therapeutic relation to end. Perhaps she was expressing this wish and at the same time her sadness over it.

Her recognition that I still would provide for her by training my wife to care for her was rather mixed in this dream since there are other ways of symbolizing separation. Though she had never met my wife, she knew Luciana was also a psychologist and that I had told her something about Margaret. That my wife was the only one who could comfort her suggested how much Margaret still felt like an inferior little girl who could not comfort a person who would grieve over my death. Her need to give had been as frustrated as her need to receive, which always is so with children who are kept at a distance by their parents. It was this theme which made most sense to Margaret. She represented our separation as doctor and patient in the most radical way, and this seemed to reveal for us once again how little confidence she had in becoming a giving and loving woman.

We tease each other if we are friendly and mock each other if we bear ill will. The patient may present me in a comical image or in an

unflattering pose, to which I may immediately object, but if I consider
the portrait I can almost always discern in it something true of
myself. To call the part of Margaret's dream in which I was dead
plainly a transference of murderous impulses would be pleading innocent to my contribution to the situation. I would then only be
preaching and not practicing an essential in every loving relation: to
realize your part in the situation as it unfolds.

Even though I do not appear in the following dream, it does
appear to involve the therapy relation. Max, a thirty-eight-year-old
bachelor, and I had been discussing the possibility of his not having
to see me any more. Two sessions after the one I'm about to report,
we did terminate our formal arrangement. He returned from a
Memorial Day weekend and said he had had a wonderful holiday.
That was evident from his suntanned face and his new jacket. I
wondered how he would be feeling since he had decided to take a
long weekend and this had meant cancellation of a scheduled session. Neither of us could be sure that he knew I really meant it when
I said that the decision to stop was completely his. I had also raised
the possibility of visits P.R.N. Max and I had been seeing each other
almost four years, a span of time neither of us had believed was
overly long in view of his serious disturbances and our common
orientation to psychoanalytic concepts. The "new policy," then, was
to be tested in practice, and with some trepidation Max chose a long
weekend.

Max wasn't sure where to begin and what to speak about. After
this confession, which he often made with much anxiety, like a
frightened schoolboy who hadn't done his homework, he told me
that he did not experience any regret over missing the hour. On the
contrary. He then said he had a long series of dreams and remembered only one part, which itself was vague. "I am up before a judge,
not on the charge for which I have been convicted. Then he tells me
that the Supreme Court has handed down a decision to review the
sentence of three to five years I received. I don't know what to do
about it."

He quickly made the obvious interpretation which had crossed my
mind. "The three to five years refers to my time with you, and the
review is what we are doing now." I added that the image of a
courtroom was one he was likely to choose since he had always felt

on trial. I was his fourth therapist. We had been reviewing our relationship in a mutual acknowledgment of how he had often mis-led me and how I had too often tied him up with double messages. His sharp critique of my behavior with him had helped me think through the ironies in my therapeutic efforts. I had appreciated Max's incisive critique, and his thoughts came to me as we discussed the dream.

"Max, it may be itself an injustice to you to focus only on the implications of this dream for our relations or even what it may be revealing about your past misdemeanors and crimes. I have often told you that I believe you demean yourself by focusing on narrow matters and how often you have profound thoughts about broader issues. I recall our discussion on survival in an atomic war and our talk about Kennedy's assassination, and in sharp contrast I recall my impatience with the petty details on your job which you bring in here as symptoms to be analyzed."

Max objected to the way I put my point. "You're exaggerating." I did not agree with him. "Of course, there is no way of objectively deciding who is right. We'll leave it as a difference of opinion." After this comment he added, "Oh, by the way, I've taken care of those little details regarding that project I've been assigned to do. What the fuss was about, you tell me."

"The Supreme Court," I continued, "has recently handed down some pretty important decisions. Today there was one on the NAACP and Alabama. Why not suggest that your dream is also saying something about our culture?"

"Bernie, that is possible. Those who were in jail and were re-leased, they lost a piece of their lives, too. So justice was finally done through a new interpretation of the law. What is gone is gone. In the dream I didn't feel I was fighting the judge; he was there, as was the Court, pulling things together and weighing them. It was the ad-versary I was against."

"The trouble is, Max, that here I am often the judge and the adversary. The numbers in the dream do suggest our relationship, in which it is true that you've been for almost four years for a crime you didn't commit."

"Bernie, I think every patient really knows that when you are sitting there in judgment you are in conflict yourself. You can't be both judge and partisan. You must be involved with or against, but you can't be the impartial judge."

Our session ended soon after he glanced at the clock. As we parted we shook hands in a gesture of which he had been fearful in the first years, which then had become routine but only during the last months had become an expression of a particularly good meeting.

DREAMS OF SOCIAL SIGNIFICANCE

Erich Fromm reported the dream of a man who fled Germany after Hitler's rise. The patient's antipathy to Nazism was felt, in Fromm's words, "not just in the conventional sense of an anti-Nazi 'opinion' but passionately and intelligently." This political conviction was perhaps freer from doubt than anything else he thought and felt. One can imagine his surprise and shock when one morning he remembered clearly and vividly this dream: "I sat with Hitler, and we had a pleasant and interesting conversation. I found him charming and was very proud that he listened with great attention to what I had to say."

Fromm cites this patient's dream as an example of a wish fulfillment type of dream. The patient's central problem is described by Fromm:

. . . his attitude toward authority: he exhibits an alternation of rebelliousness and submissive admiration in his daily experiences. Hitler stands for the extreme form of irrational authority, and the dream shows as clearly that, in spite of the dreamer's hate against him, the submissive side is real and stormy. The dream offers us a more adequate appreciation of the strength of submissive tendencies than the evaluation of the conscious material permits.[3]

Since Fromm knows this patient well, I am not on an equal footing in questioning his interpretation that the patient reveals in this dream his submissiveness to irrational authority. Perhaps some unreported associations made it possible to link the person's central problem of authority with the manifest dream, though the central problem of the human condition, according to many of Fromm's writings, is the one he ascribes to this patient. Of course, I agree very much with Fromm's general view. Yet I interpret this dream in a different way because the patient says that Hitler was listening to what he had to tell him and not that he was listening to Hitler. The dreamer did not say what he was telling Hitler.

Fromm cautions us not to reduce this conflict with authority in the person of Hitler, as he says Freud would, to a representation of the young man's feelings of hate and admiration for his father. This might be so, in that "the blend of rebelliousness and submissiveness came into existence and developed in the relationship to the patient's father." Yet it also is the adult patient who is rebelling and submitting. Fromm also asks us not to place in doubt the patient's sincere anti-Nazi convictions. I agree with both these requests, since reducing a strong feeling in the present to a childhood conflict reduces the patient's current experiences to shadow plays in the night. However, in his own way, according to his own convictions about the central problems of patients, Fromm may be reducing the patient to a problem rather than affirming for the patient a critical insight into broader issues than those usually considered to be legitimate for therapeutic discussion.

Clearly, since the patient never actually spoke with Hitler the dream in which he does is a wish fulfillment. What possible wish could he be fulfilling? One answer would accept the manifest dream as standing in its own terms. I would speculate that the patient wants to appeal to Hitler's better side. Despite our hatred of Hitler, we might surmise that someone could speak to him and be heard. What a fantasy of love, to imagine that if I could have spoken to Hitler, he would have listened and the world would have been spared its greatest catastrophe! Fromm's patient did not remember what he told Hitler, but could we not suppose that the patient spoke with a belief that even the devil can be reconciled with words of love? Or is this a completely grandiose, world-saving wish reflecting a presumed omnipotent fantasy of childhood? Yet the longing to reconcile with love those who are hateful and harmful is a basis of the faith of deeply religious people and of psychotherapists. Here, in this dream, Lucifer incarnate and the outcast sit down and meet in equality. The lamb leads the beast. Daniel goes into the lion's den.

My suggestion may be farfetched and grossly inapplicable to this particular patient. I hold no particular brief that it is better than

Fromm's interpretation. My point is that psychotherapists tend to neglect the transcending aspirations of men when they meet the "sick" person.

If I read the literature on dreams correctly, a subtle bias may have been affecting the interpretation of the Negro figure when he has appeared in dreams. Rather than being recognized as representing the theme of inequality and prejudice, the Negro has been seen as a symbol of primitive impulses, unrepressed, powerful sexual urges and the dark side of our unconscious. Ralph, an unusually gifted writer and teacher of about thirty-five years of age, whose knowledge of mythology and primitive religions often edifies and enthralls me, dreamed the following: "I am in my apartment and look down into Harlem the other side of 125th Street. I see a basement full of Negroes drinking and conspiring to some delinquent action."

Ralph's proclivity to transfer his own feelings into abstract forms was recognized by him long before he came for help, and we had discussed this often. In this dream he could be representing his looking over rather than directly experiencing his antisocial urges or his passionate feelings. His poetic imagination can encompass what his behavior with others usually conceals. Among other reflections on this dream, I commented, "You may be, like so many of us who are on the side of civil rights, showing here the influence of our dominant, popular cultural attitudes toward the Negro, which at best recognize him as the creator of jazz, at worst as a criminal, but at all times avoid entering into a heart-felt communion with him."

Ralph, with whom I have rarely experienced a feeling of competition, accepted my comment as interesting, and we discussed this phenomenon in the light of the various protests of Negro leaders against white liberals as well as harshly prejudiced people. A few months later he reported the following two dreams, revealing the influence my values, as well as his own, had on his reflections while asleep. They were recorded by Ralph after the session.

In the first of the dreams I find myself in a very large, empty room. The room is perhaps an empty store, facing on a busy street, resembles 125th Street in Harlem. It seems that there is a large plate-glass window, facing the street, but that the window is so grimy that one cannot see through it to the street. I am seated near the end of this long narrow room at the end farthest from the street. I am practicing the clarinet, playing music which is placed before me on a music rack. While I am playing the door opens and an enormous Negro woman, dressed elegantly, with furs around her shoulders, enters the room. She is carrying a small brass musical instrument, a *Flügelhorn*, which is tiny when compared with her mammoth size. I am cowed by her, but fascinated by the *Flügelhorn*, which I want to play. I get up, walk the length of the room, and ask the woman if I can play the *Flügelhorn*. She looks down at me coldly, says, "No, you do not play well enough," and leaves through the same door. With my feeling of disappointment and, I think, of shame as well, yet agreeing with her judgment, the dream ends.

All that I now remember from the circumstances immediately preceding the dream is that I had been invited to play for a concert in an ensemble otherwise made up of Juilliard students. I had accepted and had been given the music to practice. I had not been practicing regularly for some time, and I found the music very difficult. P.S. After the dream I practiced like hell.

During the session in which Ralph reported the dream, we noted the elegance of the Negro woman's dress and her authoritative manner manifested in a setting that was shabby and could represent his often experienced "closed-in feeling." Despite his fine sensibilities, Ralph usually met another person as if a translucent distorting screen separated the two of them. We speculated that the Negro woman might be a voice of wisdom through whom he was acknowledging the limitation of his existence: "One can't play everything." In his case the limitation had become enormously oppressive since his beloved wife had died. The Negro woman, a "Mammy" figure, could also represent courage in the face of adversity. But Ralph also portrays her negatively. The woman is ostentatiously dressed. Many of us perceive this style as vulgar, and I think this reflects a racial prejudice rather than a matter of taste.

Ralph and I thought that the second dream, which had come to him some weeks after the one just discussed, but which was reported in the same session, did reflect the use of the Negro as a figure from whom one can learn about life. I should preface the dream with the note that Ralph is an unusually sober person. I had never heard him even consider entering a bar.

In the second dream, some weeks later, I find myself in a bar in Harlem, seated at a table in a dark corner near the back of the room.

There are perhaps four or five other men at the table, but the only one that I notice is a Negro, seated across the table from me, with whom I am engaged in an enthusiastic conversation, made spirited also by a double Scotch which each of us has just consumed. I call the waiter and order two more double Scotches. Then (and this part of the dream has become unclear to me) I say that this isn't the way to get any work done. No—first my Negro friend says something like, "That's the way to go, man," and then I say, "This isn't the way to get any work done." Yet in the dream I feel a great sense of well-being and pleasure in his response to my ordering two more doubles. Then I make the remark about not getting work done, and my friend begins to tell me how drinking is the way to get work done, is how he does it, and I am listening with fascination when the dream ends.

As I was on my way to the box to mail this, something "clicked" about this dream. I did have it distorted. My Negro friend says, "That's the way to go, man" and I say, "Yes, that's how I get work done." Then he replies to me that that is not the way to get work done, that he can't work that way, and that I don't mean that I do. I lose none of my pleasure in his "That's the way to go, man." But I am listening intently to what he is saying when the dream comes to an end.

Ralph is loosening up, in his music, in his relationships and in his work. Despite the high opinion his colleagues have of him, Ralph has been dissatisfied with his achievements, as he wrote in his associations to the first dream. He has been having a great deal of trouble in completing a book for which he had already obtained a contract.

His postscript to the account of the dream, added as he was about to seal his letter, is evidence for my interpretation of the Negro as a figure in our dreams. When Ralph first wrote down his dream and as he first recounted it to me, the Negro friend is counseling him: "Abandon yourself to pleasure and you'll get your work done." Ralph first thought he disagreed, even though he was enjoying their drinking together. However, he then recalled in his postscript that the conflict between pleasure and work is not a necessity, it is a distortion of memory. His companion in the bar says that drinking and work really do not mix and then Ralph says they do. He has it both ways. The Negro is equally conscientious and free and so is Ralph. Ralph, who feels so personally oppressed, identified himself in his dream with the most oppressed figure in our communal life, except for the Indian. He and the Negro are equals, and they join together in the liberation of pleasure and its possibilities for enhancing good work.

The next two dreams were reported by Lucy, a thirty-two-year-old married social scientist, born and raised in Spain. She married an American lawyer and after some years of indecision became a naturalized citizen. Their marriage is an unusually intense one. I have chosen the first dream because it lends itself readily to a psychoanalytic interpretation which may be as "true" as those meanings Lucy and I chose to give to her dreams. The second dream, the last one Lucy described during her final session, is as fine a dream as a therapist could wish to receive at any time, but especially at the end of formal therapy. Both dreams, we agreed, clearly revealed social class variables.

The first dream, one of many Lucy reported during our therapeutic relationship, directly represents the most significant situation in which all educated women find themselves. Lucy was in the throes of deciding with Morris, her husband, whether to have another child. According to her report, her husband was uncertain about his wishes, though he assured her that he was inclined to go along with her decision.

The conflict between having a child and working full time need not reflect a regressive disturbance involving the unresolved Oedipal conflicts of a little girl. If the therapist does refer the choice of child versus career to an historical situation, the patient will be usually persuaded that her current distress is only a repetition of repressed conflicts. However, for an active, intelligent woman committed to her field and trained to make a social contribution, becoming a mother involves a necessary and sharply felt compromise if the woman does not wish to turn over the task of child-rearing to a nurse. After we discussed this dream, I asked Lucy to record it in her own words.

Simone de Beauvoir and Sartre were standing in a room, a kitchen; they had a baby, a few months old, he was somewhere in front of them, not clearly, either sitting or lying down. Then Simone and Sartre felt clearly that they did not want the baby, that he interfered with their freedom and creativity. Up to now the dream was like a still picture with no movement. In the next scene, Sartre moves over to the baby and starts feeding him, sitting at a table with food that Simone had prepared. The focus is on Sartre and the baby. Simone is in the background. And then the baby dies. But it is not that I see him dying, nor that he falls still. He just was not there any longer and Simone and Sartre felt free. This "feeling free" I experienced myself in the dream at this point; it was not expressed by S. and S.'s words or movements, but I knew they felt free and I felt free too.

Lucy later summarized our associations as follows:

I think of Simone de B. and Sartre as persons having a definite direction to their lives and identification as writers. Especially Simone de B. appears to me as having been able to follow this one purpose—to be a writer—keeping it paramount at the expense of all other possible purposes she might have realized, particularly having a family (the kitchen, her husband feeding the baby and the baby himself). This purpose, shared by Sartre (shared in the double sense of wanting to be a writer himself and wanting Simone to be a writer too), appears to me as having a very potent, almost magical, power. I see it as inspiring all their actions, thoughts and decisions, also when they are not aware of it. In the dream, as soon as they realize that they don't want the baby, they take an action which is apparently "normal" (i.e., most common: feeding a baby) and which is apparently opposite to the feeling of not wanting the baby; still their action leads to the realization of their wish.

My associations go to the recent Democratic Convention, to Johnson and H. Humphrey; they have had one direction in their lives, they have successfully followed it, they must have taken—often without thinking about it—the right decision.

It is not magic in the sense of thoughts becoming reality without action. It is a very patent attitude, in the sense of inspiring the action that leads to the main purpose, without going in other directions.

I associate the act of feeding the baby in the dream with a process of "incorporating," meaning that successful people incorporate what stands in their way, making it disappear as an obstacle, through a normal (socially approved) action. It also means that the recognition of my feelings (we don't want a baby) brings a solution of the conflict, even when the action does not seem directed to such a solution (feeding instead of getting rid of).

I did not tell Lucy that I was not convinced about her interpretation of the baby's dying. The baby could symbolize the obstacle to her career, but it also was a real person in the dream with whom a relationship existed. Getting rid of it in the way it occurred in the dream could also reflect the magical faith of young children who believe that they can do something and then undo it at will. There may have been murderous feelings reflected in the dream which Lucy had toward a younger brother whose birth, five years after hers, was greeted with the relative exaltation boys receive in Spain. Lucy's use of the baby may also have touched on a situation she directly experienced. Simone de Beauvoir, with whom she strongly identified, of course, has written vividly on the difference in treatment of boys and girls. It was on my suggestion that Lucy became acquainted with de Beauvoir's work. She had previously studied Sartre's philosophy but had only heard of de Beauvoir. Lucy was taken with the autobiography of this outstanding woman intellectual of our times. The fact that I had been the "matchmaker" probably had a bearing on Lucy's use of de Beauvoir in her dream as well as in her waking thoughts. If this is so, it was a sign of our increasing consensus in therapy, which it had been my intention to achieve in the first place.

Lucy and I had discussed discontinuing our regular sessions since there was much evidence of her wish to enter fully into her marriage with Morris. When she brought in the following dream, I exclaimed, "I can't see why you have to or need to or want to come to see me in my office." She agreed fully that my "nudge" was called for, and so our final session was arranged for then and there. She sent me a recording of the dream a week later.

I was in a classroom in high school with some of my old friends; the teacher—a woman—was giving oral exams in history. I was anxious that she would call on me as I knew only my recent history not the past lessons in the book. She calls the girl whose name is just after mine, Zapata, and then the boy whose name came a good deal before mine, beginning with L. (his appearance reminds me of a boy with the initials G.B., which are also the initials of my adolescent love). L. excuses himself since he had been absent on account of illness. At the teacher's request several boys and girls leave the room to get coffee for everybody. I give some suggestions, but the teacher reproaches, scolds me: "You think you can help me when I have been in this school for so many years and I know better than you."

Next, Morris appears as I leave the classroom without a word or any reason, just as a matter of fact as if following an impulse. Several scenes follow, when Morris and I get ready for a trip, with some misunderstanding and uncertainties. The next clear scene: Morris leads me, I with him, without effort, with the same naturalness with which I left the classroom. He leads me into the park that was behind the school. I am naked and we are going to make love. I am already lying down on the grass and Morris is about to come next to me. But some children come along and also a policeman. He did not censure us. We get up and start walking toward the school. It is all natural, effortless. I did not get dressed but I am not naked either, as if a light cloth were covering me to my knees. As we walk, I ask Morris: "Have we forgot anything?" and the policeman says, "Some day Negroes' belts will be found in the park," and we both know that he means that also Negroes will be free to let down their pants and have the pleasure of making love in this park.

Lucy and I did not interpret this dream, but when she sent it to me she added the following:

It may be interesting that I had this dream shortly before Morris and I returned from our long weekend. The dream points to the defiance of a strict and rejecting authority and then meeting a lenient authority, the policeman, through Morris' love. In it I feel a different orientation on returning to the city (the school is my job and other duties and trials). I am not anxious about the lessons I know and hopeful others will find the freedom I once lacked when I felt enslaved. The orientation is toward freedom, also for the slave.

I shall let the patient have the final words in this chapter.

13

THE FEE AND PAYING FOR "IT"

The patient and I cannot ignore the complementary questions: What am I purchasing? What am I selling? The evasion of this issue will corrupt the effort as much as the patient's deceptions, and as much as the deception the therapist practices when his personal values and social attitudes are hidden behind his theories and procedures. Obscuring the question of payments or remaining silent about them is as much a violation of the spirit of psychotherapy as is silence on sex. In fact, some patients and some therapists are as frank in discussing masturbation as they are reluctant to discuss how they make out with their income.

THE THERAPIST'S VESTED INTEREST

From a strictly economic point of view, the "industry" of psychotherapy is a fair-sized enterprise. I remember reading a *New York Times* report that about eleven thousand patients are presently in psychoanalysis, a figure which includes only those patients who are being treated by members of the American Psychoanalytical Association. At an average fee of about twenty to twenty-five dollars per session, with about three to four sessions per week over about a forty-five-week year, a conservative estimate of the annual turnover in money is thirty to fifty million dollars. I don't know of any figures giving the number of patients seeing other than "official analysts," but it is a fair guess to say that about seventy-five million dollars could be changing hands.[1]

In the literature specifically devoted to a discussion of fees and the frequency of sessions, the emphasis is placed on the meanings the payments of the fee have for the patient. There are conservatives and liberals who debate the merits and demerits of stringent regulations. But rarely does the writer more than glance at the likelihood that the economics of the psychotherapy industry tends to perpetuate the conditions of practice and the theories about cures. Can a person who makes a decent living pretend that he does not tend to protect his achieved standard? We require judges to remove themselves from hearing a case if they have been involved with the disputing parties, and lawmakers are not supposed to have a vested interest in legislation. As imperfectly as the ideal is achieved, the exposure of conflict of interest as an impediment to fair play cannot be abandoned without a return to autocratic rule. The therapeutic relationship is concerned with this issue of conflict of interest in all areas of living, and it must concern itself with the meaning the fee has for the doctor as well as the patient.

I must discuss the question of money with the patient and how my practical and emotional investment in the fee affects our struggle together. I think this must be done even when the therapeutic work is conducted in an institution where the client does not pay the therapist directly. The therapist and patient practicing in an agency, so often degradingly referred to as "low-cost clinics," are in a sense even more involved with money problems than is the therapeutic pair on Park Avenue. The patient in a clinic is there because, among other reasons, his choice of therapists has been directly affected by his low income. Agencies often have a means test: anyone above a certain income is not eligible for service because the facilities are so taxed. And the therapist? Is he there because he is learning his craft and does not yet have his time filled by private patients, or is he there because he wishes to devote his time and experience to others who cannot afford his private fees?

The patient must wonder about the therapist's motives in a society where earning capacity is one of the most significant indices of power and social status. We need also to remind ourselves that the patient and therapist in an agency are both there because the agency's existence has been made possible by voluntary contributions and by public monies. Someone is always paying for it, even though the therapist does not collect the fee from the patient. Does it then follow that a social service is a charity inducing a sense of inferiority and inadequacy or is it an accepted activity which brings into light the often invisible and reciprocal duties, responsibilties and relations between the person and his community? When a community recognizes and accepts its obligations to provide a service, such as social security, welfare payments or police protection, then those concerned are not in conflict about nonpayment or low fees. It doesn't come about easily, however. The most recent example of the emphasis on the fee as a sign of good doctor-patient relations is the conflict over Medicare. The Federal Government has issued a set of rules to guard the "traditional ties" between patient and physician. The set of rules pertains solely to the size of the fee and the terms of billing and collection.[2]

On the other hand, the specter and onus of socialized practice have been raised less often in the area of family counseling. In some communities, usually the smaller ones where private practitioners aren't available, the family agency is utilized by all social classes.[3] Perhaps in the future the right to adequate help will be completely separated from the question of economic resources. But a community where the amount of money a person has isn't the measure by which needed attention is given to him may be the kind of community in which its citizen members need less special psychotherapy. That may be utopian, but so are the central values of psychotherapy, when we measure the possibilities of their realization against the actuality of achievement.

In a lively discussion of the "tinkering trades," Erving Goffman, a sociologist, places the question of the size of the fee and professionalism in the context of tradition. He writes:

Traditionally a fee is anything other than what the service is worth. When services are performed whose worth to the client at the time is very great, the server is ideally supposed to restrict himself to a fee determined by tradition—presumably what the server needs to keep himself in decent circumstances while he devotes his life to his calling. On the other hand, when very minor services are performed, the server feels obliged to forego charging altogether or to charge a relatively large flat fee, thus preventing his time from being trifled with or his contribution (and ultimately himself) from being measured by a scale that can approach zero. When he performs major services for very poor clients, the server may feel that charging no fee is more dignified (and safer) than a reduced fee. The server thus avoids dancing to the client's tune, or even bargaining, and is able to show that he is motivated by a disinterested involvement in his work.[4]

However, can I really maintain a "disinterested involvement" without being rigid and applying a standard fee to all who seek my help? It seems to me that the fact that I earn a living by engaging myself with suffering people means I am involved in an ambiguous and potentially ironic situation. After all, a crucial social value which has made possible the emergence of psychotherapy as an institution is the pricelessness and immeasurable dignity of an individual life. The therapist and the patient must share in this belief or they would not participate in a relationship which calls for concentration, usually over a long period of time, on refined and highly subtle aspects of human interactions. Yet the fee I ask appears to be for my skill, education and service, which are an extension of my person, and thus I appear to be selling myself. And the fee the patient pays is in some measure blood money, that is, a payment to ease his guilt for taking my help and my time. Who does not believe that "You get what you pay for," and who does not often feel, "I'll make you pay for it"?

Neither the patient nor I can get away from the dilemma, occasioned by deep-seated complexes about the money value of man, the status of earning power, the fact that psychotherapy is not yet accepted as a necessity for anyone who wants it, and the close correlation between the dollar and exploitation.

THE SIZE OF FEE: A MEASURE OF MOTIVE?

It is fairly common knowledge that some therapists tell a patient that the fee he pays is an expression of his motivation for help. For example, Menninger asserts that a psychoanalysis will not proceed well unless the patient is making some financial sacrifice, that "if money is a serious problem, psychoanalysis is not the treatment of choice."[5] Obviously psychoanalysis, being the deepest and most arduous treatment, requires the greatest motivation and thus a larger sacrifice. This opinion, exemplified by Menninger, is itself worth analyzing. It is as complex an opinion as is the complex of motives which brings the person to the doctor and which hopefully unfolds in the therapeutic reaction.

One implication of this opinion is that the higher the fee the person is willing or ready to pay, the more he is motivated to get out of his devious maneuvers with others. Stated this way, the therapist's attitude on the size of fee is a distortion, to say the least, and exploitative, to say the worst. If a therapist as defendant or plaintiff in a damage suit knew that the judge conducting a hearing would be receiving a cut of the settlement, he would protest vigorously. The patient appearing before the therapist is involved in a damage suit and is paying a fee to the therapist, who cannot help but make judgments about the damages and is at the same time collecting a fee. Doesn't the patient have the right, indeed the obligation, to inquire of the therapist about his attitude toward money and how he fixes his fee?

When a patient asks, "Are we getting anywhere?" he may be attempting to divert attention from a shameful revelation. But his question is a realistic one: "Are all this time and money I am spending worth it?"

One example of my attitude about the reality of the expenditure of money is my reply to a patient who asks, "Do I need therapy?" "Do you want to spend your money in this way rather than in another?" Whatever else money may mean to the person, consciously or unconsciously, the readiness to invest a certain portion of income (and for the patients I meet, usually a high proportion) is, for those who have not inherited wealth or who are not dependent persons, evidence of reponsible work.

Real financial difficulties may also develop in the course of therapy. A patient may lose a job for reasons beyond his control, or leave a well-paying position because therapy has helped him get out of a situation throttling his deeper interests. How these issues are met varies, of course, with the person, but whatever I do, I must recognize with him that I have a vested interest in trying to clarify his financial state.

In a frank and realistic discussion on fees Frieda Fromm-Reichman wrote:

Psychiatric services—that is, the attempt to help a person overcome his emotional difficulties in living—are priceless if successful or worthless if they fail. It is through these attempts, nevertheless, that the thera-pist makes his living, so that the settlement of his fees has to be deter-mined by the market value of psychiatric services at a given time and in a given area. The degree in variation of these fees must be in proportion to the financial status of the patient and according to the number of pa-tients whom the psychiatrist has accepted at both average and reduced fees at the time.[6]

She is telling us that the fee has to do with the market value of a professional and is therefore regulated by the same economic factors that regulate the employment of any worker for a specified time. I set my fee according to the standard of living I want to maintain and the fees other professionals ask with whom I may be competing. If there is a big demand on my time because the supply of therapists is limited, my fees tend to go up; that is, I feel I can afford to ask a higher fee for the hours I wish to devote to practice. This may enable me to spend more time in research, writing, teaching or with my friends.

And when the patient is asked, "What are you paying for?" he usually answers in some variant of "Your help and your skill." This answer is expected. On the bills of most professionals there is the phrase "For Services Rendered." One distinction between the la-borer's status and the professional's is that the worker often feels he is putting in his time while the professional believes he sells his skills. Thus the payment of a fee has been rationalized as the equal-izer between patient and therapist. Though the doctor may believe he receives from the patient such "by-products" of the therapeutic relation as material for research and special satisfaction in helping a person who will help others, it is the money which the patient gives to the doctor which presumably balances the account.

The number of years I have attended to my work should have made me a better helper, and presumably my reputation and my professional credentials are among the criteria used in selecting me. That, I agree, makes it seem that the fee I ask is for my skill and experience. Yet the person's own pocketbook has already set a limit on the therapist's fee. According to my own appraisal of my skill and years of experience, I ought to ask twice the amount, but apart from any feelings about this being an unconscionable sum, I couldn't even get it. Rich people hardly ever approach me, and when they do, am I to give them better service because they pay me more for it? And if the patient were to pay me more, would he get more, or if he were to become delinquent in his payments, should I withhold my attention? There is an old tradition among physicians, supported by ethical codes and by the state, that a patient cannot be abandoned in the middle of therapy. Of course, what we do in psychotherapy is in many respects not analogous to medical treatment, but this code of physicians stresses that once the patient and the doctor are in a continuing relation, the fee should become extrinsic to their effort.

In community agencies where people often go because they cannot afford a private therapist, the prevailing idea that the therapist is selling his skills contributes to the client's notions that he is receiving less adequate help because he is paying less. This attitude could affect the outcome, of course, as could the possibility that the staff of such agencies may have less experience. The notion that low cost means low skill is in part a consequence of the idea that the therapist sells his special skill and knowledge.

There is another point of view which proclaims that the patient is purchasing not skill or services but the therapist's time. This claim is also concretely manifested in the bill the patient is given, which usually contains the date, the number of sessions and the fee due. In the past I have argued—and that is the word for it—that I do not sell my skills because I cannot measure them, but I do sell my time because it is measurable. Dr. Fromm-Reichman in the above quotation said as much when she wrote that the service is priceless if successful and worthless if it fails. Since it is impossible to measure skills or meter attitudes and it is obvious that we measure time, why not then take the position that the therapist sells his time and not his skills? Yet the answer to this might be: "It may be a convenience to think of it in this way, but when you sell something, you are giving it away, and just as it is obvious that we can measure time, it is plain that you can't give time away. You are living in time, too."

I agree with this argument that all of us are equal in living in irretrievable time. It is impossible for me to give away what I am also using. When a patient arrives late, he may excuse himself by saying, "Well, I wasted my time." The therapist who agrees that the patient is a procrastinator may also say, "You are wasting your hour." And if the patient misses the appointment, then he is probably an evasive procrastinator and should be made aware of this quality and charged for it. I would rather say when the person is late or has missed an appointment, "You are living our assigned time together in this way and I am living it by waiting for you, dreaming about something, reading a book, writing a letter, or maybe even thinking why you might be late. How can I say to you that you are wasting your time when the hour we have arranged is ours?"

But if I cannot give my time away, can I sell my skills? I don't believe so. The argument that it is impossible to meter a service is useful but incomplete. I occasionally speak to a patient in some variation of the following comments:

"How I am with any person, a friend, a patient or my wife, depends on all the subleties and depths of feelings we subsume under the heading of qualities of relationship. These cannot be metered. Try it if you will. Try measuring your feelings as some people seem to do and see what happens. You might succeed for a period of time to control your vitality because the person you are with doesn't appear to want or deserve your investment of self. However, you'll have to let go somewhere, somehow, in a dream, in an outburst of irritation or exuberance after he and you part. Hopefully, letting go will not be in terms of a headache or depression. Come to think of it, you are here to see me because you have become a *measurer* of feelings.

"I go to a physician to cure my aching back or to remove my diseased gall bladder, and he charges me for services rendered. But I am making my body available to his attention, and the better his mechanical skill, the higher the fee, usually. Of course, his bedside manner is of considerable help, because my feelings are also hurting along with my back. But there is a relatively concrete measure of a successful outcome of his therapeutic skill, and so I can readily think of getting my money's worth in the reparation of my broken body. But in our relationship? What can we predict will happen, what do we define as successful psychotherapy for you, what concrete goals are you asking me to achieve? Do I set a price of five thousand dollars on your getting married? Do I get a slice of an increase in your wages because you become more energetic, less self-defeating, promoted to a more lucrative position and more adept in your stock investments?"

The alternative answers to the question, "What is the therapist selling, his time or his service?" are both correct and incorrect. He cannot give away time, and if we can say he is selling his services, he is also selling himself. The clearest recognition of the position of the therapist is that he sells nothing and everything. His whole person is there in time for the patient to use. The therapist only appears to sell what he can't give away, and yet he also profits from this ambiguity. He collects the fee and is generally enriched in his experiences with people in the depth of being together. It is the patient's immediate capital which is spent, and thus his income depreciates. Hopefully, the investment in money will be akin to a capital investment which will bring profit later on. But at any moment this is uncertain, even though he may feel relief as treatment proceeds. This way of stating the issue of the exchange of money, I think, helps the patient look outward and helps him get out of the inner sanctum. When a patient stops coming, he will have more money to take a trip or satisfy some delayed desire. If then he finds that he is wasting his time and money, he can return. We can again try to get him out of therapy into relations which are less expensive just because he feels reasonably satisfied in them and expends less money than he does when in psychotherapy.

RESISTANCE TO PAYING FOR IT

Occasionally, a patient, after we have worked together for a period of time, will balk at meeting his bills. The refusal to meet the financial aspect of our contract will in some instances represent a thinly disguised wish to stop coming. This is easily met. The patient and I can discuss his reasons for believing our relation is a waste of time, or, as he might put it, "not worth the price of admission," and then agree to part if the feeling persists.

Some others, however, have much more complex motives in refusing to pay, such as subtle bargaining for my affection or retaliation for my having unknowingly struck them very hard with an interpretation. The relation becomes quite sticky in such instances. I didn't wish to barter my skill or affection, which are for me synonymous terms anyway, and yet my vocation is that of being human. The patient in his own way is representing our culture by bartering money for friendship, which, to repeat, is reinforced by the opinion of most therapists that they are selling their services. I wish to be paid, and yet I wish to convey that the exchange of money is essentially extrinsic to our effort. I do want him to register my understanding and consideration. He may in turn respond to my consideration in not pressing for payment as an indulgence and a sign that I am weak and give in to his demands for love unencumbered by money. For a time it may be unclear to both of us that no relation can exist, including that between husband and wife or between lovers, which does not involve some sacrifice and some payment. The exchange of goods and many kinds of services is represented by wages and salaries. And as much as the patient and I may want our relation to be ideal, it cannot be a pure one.

But how can we proceed so that he becomes aware of his demand on me and I convey that love is not for sale and that I am not a verbal gigolo? I try not to settle the matter on the basis that unless he meets the bills we will stop. Though it is useful to voice this point by reminding him that he did agree to pay, and that our efforts are dispersed when either one of us unilaterally changes our agreement, I like myself better when I do not retaliate in kind. As much as I wish to be paid, I do not wish to lose patience and have the patient finally prove that all I am interested in is his money. Another reason for not being arbitrary is that in many instances it is always difficult to assess how much the patient's economic problems are entangled with his manipulations of personal feelings. I would rather run the risk of having a debt defaulted than set up an arbitrary across-the-board rule. Sooner or later the underlying disturbance in our relation will ripen, the fruit will fall into our hands or will rot on the ground.

As any businessman must, I also capitalize the business part of my affairs and am ready to take a capital loss. Every year I estimate that about 2 or 3 percent of my bills are defaulted. I don't know what proportion of loss the experts on such matters would say is economically acceptable, but I do know that asking a patient to leave for nonpayment of bills is a bigger strain than losing some money. In a few instances, I have finally refused to go on because of nonpayment, usually when I discovered the patient had been actually deceiving me about his financial resources. But still I remained with the thought, was there another way to stop or continue? And I know that my preoccupations also belong to my conflicts over money and my dreams of living an easy life so readily prompted by the daily residues of the affluent society.

SOME GAMES WITH TIME THE EQUALIZER AND MONEY AS BALM

A new day which is the same old day, day after day, hopefully will make us cry for help. When one's pace in life becomes as regular as measured time, he suffers from the worst of mental aberrations, boredom, and should see a therapist or anyone else whose actions with him will be different enough to cause his heart to skip a beat. The therapist gives the person many a lift and many a jolt. But I know of no better way to define his effectiveness than to say that the patient finds the therapist intriguing, his thoughts different and his person entertaining. Treasuring this resource is the therapist's first responsibility to the patient. Killing it with therapeutic routine and ritual is doing unto the patient what others have done unto him before he became a patient. Interactions involving the clock, the time of the session and the length of the hour can become just such debilitating rituals.

Who really knows how the fifty-minute hour began? The only sensible thing about it is that a fifty-minute hour is different from a sixty-minute hour, but really not by much. It does have the virtue of making the therapist's schedule tidy. He can also have a ten-minute rest before the next one, but some successful therapists get so busy they eliminate the ten-minute rest. I realize that a time-limited structure is supposed to help the patient work harder, stop procrastinating and learn about the value of life. I still think this is a neat rationalization, after the fact of the requirements of the doctor's schedule. I do, by and large, have such a schedule, but I don't try to fool myself that imposing a set structure helps anyone learn the value of freedom, compassion, respect and the other values I like to talk about. I find that the majority of patients are likely to use a set time awkwardly. Many are relieved when the session is up. When the patient accepts the limited fifty minutes and we get on well from there, I appreciate his accommodation.[7]

When the patient frequently arrives late, I generally interpret this as a wish that he also could have something to say about the length of time we meet or even the time of day. Some people get moving fast and others are night owls. I, of course, am as steady as the clock and give my best at all hours, night and day. I tell the patient who comes late that I was concerned about him or that I used his tardiness to catch up on some journal article or that I took a little nap. But I try not to badger him with recriminations about his resistance to therapy, his fear of some emerging complex and his hatred for his father who arranged the schedules for professional baseball teams. If he asks me straight out, we can try to alter our typical routine. Even if he asks me right on the spot, I don't dismiss it with a reminder about the next patient, but think about what it might mean to the person who will be kept waiting or whom I may have to ask to come another time.

One advantage of my readiness in revealing that the schedule is arbitrary and for my convenience because I have more of them than the patient has of me is that it changes the battleground between us. Instead of saying to him, "I have power over your time, or even our time," I say, "What do we do to make you an equal with me in the matter of the length of time we are together? You may think it is limited by your pocketbook, and that is a difficulty. But what if we could both feel that each of us can say at any time, we've had it for the day, a week, or year? Why shouldn't I place the clock in the office where you as well as I can see it?"

I think the placement of the clock is one of those items which symbolizes the culture of the society of therapists. The clock is usually where only the doctor can see it. The patient is given the added burden of guessing when the time is about up by observing the therapist's furtive glance at his desk, or, if he is lying on the couch, by the change in pace of the doctor's breathing or the squeak of his chair. Not permitting the patient to see the time is supposed to facilitate letting go and dropping into the timeless unconscious. This is an important technique within the psychoanalytic tradition, but it doesn't explain to the patient how at a moment's notice he is supposed to become time-bound again when the analyst begins his interpretation. We are always listening to and looking at each other. Why not both look at our shared time?

Of those who miss appointments for one reason or another, it is only the rare fellow who doesn't call me in advance or shortly after he awakens to the fact that he "stood me up." The excuse for not calling me is "I was going to see you soon anyway." In these few instances the test of my concern is quickly revealed. Whether or not the forgetfulness was motivated by hostility, the patient may follow up his arbitrary cancellation of our time by telling me in effect that it should not matter to me where or how he was. "If I met with a tragedy, you'd know soon enough, Doc, so relax."

But again, such infidelities are rare among middle-class patients, though by the standards of middle-class doctors very frequent among other cultural groups. In fact, setting regular appointments with some types of patients is a big joke and the sign of a square rather than a regular guy. Yet even with middle-class individuals the culture of therapists partakes of the view that a missed appointment is a violation of a sacred trust. The therapist, of course, can on occasion miss one because he is called to a special meeting or delayed at a conference or at the emergency room. The patient, on the other hand, is always suspect. Especially if he breaks his leg skiing.

The correlation between body and soul can be invoked, of course, as a hypothesis. The admonition nonetheless gets across. "You miss an appointment; for whatever reasons, the pattern of your resistance begins to emerge." And so quick are some patients to turn around for a spanking that they themselves volunteer, "You can put it in on my bill." Freud counseled charging the patient for the time because he found that patients missed fewer appointments that way.[8]

Occasionally the patient will be a little more independent and dare to protest against his disturbance, if that was what caused him not to come, being turned into a gain for the doctor. "But I haven't filled the time and I have lost income," the doctor will retort, though in less gross language. "You mean, Doctor, that you never have anything to do while waiting for me that is productive? Why not just relax? You'll live longer. By the way, do you know of any profession that charges the patient for missing an hour? Some physicians and dentists will ask for a fee if the cancellation occurs less than twenty-four hours before. Will that be all right with you?"

Any move the patient makes which forces the therapist to individuate his response to any situation is a boon to the therapist and a sign the patient is getting out of there. When I have been tempted to charge for an hour during which I wasn't working, it is simply because I resented the patient for doing something over which I had nothing to say. I could tell him that I'll bill him to assuage my annoyance. But I console myself with an analysis of the circumstances of our time together. Tat is for tit. The whole setup is an imposition. I chose my vacation time to suit my convenience and not his, etc., etc., etc.

My policy on these matters, as on others, is that we make an agreement and unilateral cancellations of the agreement corrupt our relation. But unilateral actions on my part to reassert the original agreement are just as corrupting. If, before the contract is made, the therapist informs the patient that every missed hour will be billed, there is no arbitrariness of course. The buyer can beware.

So I try to get him to discuss his arbitrary arrangements. He comes in and tells me that he will not be in on Friday. He has made another appointment. "But why didn't you discuss the matter in advance with me? You could have called on the telephone. In effect you contracted to be in two places at the same time."

Patients, being what they are, are often too in awe to speak directly and argue with me. But I hope that some patients do think as follows even if they don't speak. "Well, you have a point. I could have called you. But you also 'require' me to act freely, take my life into my own hands, be grown up and not have to check out every wish I have with an authority figure. Last week when I was telling you how my mother would insist I tell her everywhere I go, you pointed to this as a factor in the development of what you have labeled passive-dependency and a cover-up for anger. Now I act independently, and you tell me I should have checked with you. Dear Doctor, I think you may be sore because you may have conflicts about charging me. You say nothing which suggests you will miss me or whether you hope I enjoy the other engagement."

There is one aspect of the therapeutic contract itself which militates against any charge for missed appointments or any recriminations about the manipulations of time. The contract, it is true, is on a per hour basis, but the total amount which the patient will pay is indeterminate. If the contract was set for a specified period, then a missed hour is a loss of income for me and a saving of money for him. This is rarely the case. Perhaps therapists and patients should experiment with a contract for a fixed amount of money for a fixed length of time. Time-limited treatment has been used as an approach by the Rankian school, and in an experiment at the Counseling Center at Chicago, which is Rogerian in orientation.[9] However, as long as there is not a fixed total fee, the doctor can't say he is losing money.

"Oh, yes, I can say that," a voice in me protests. "My monthly income drops." Then my other side answers, "How do you know? If you are budgeting on an estimated monthly income, as you must in private work, then your estimate must include some variability, and it is based on all sources of income and not on that particular patient alone. Doesn't it happen that a new patient calls for a consultation, or another patient asks to see you more frequently? Or, in a larger sense, that hour which doesn't seem income-producing can be used to see a colleague, write a paper or read a book, which will improve your professional work and professional standing, and thus is in a sense income-producing."

I do not see how I can justifiably ask the particular patient to take more responsibility for my income level than I do. In fact, I should not require him to do so at all. At any particular time his right to break an appointment should be equal to mine. If he's running away, let us find it out, in a spirit of freedom and equality. This becomes impossible when issues of money, in which I am directly culpable, are involved as a means of coercing the patient to discussing his "avoidances." What a game I have played! I prefer the present one much better. Give the patient the right to come and go freely, and he will learn more quickly to do this fairly with me and with others.

14

ARE THERAPISTS SUCCESSFUL?

When I tell a patient that I can't guarantee success, the patient usually understands, since he is aware that even miracle drugs don't work with everybody. He also knows somehow that his wish for a magical cure is unrealistic since he has lived with his suffering for a very long time and has tried numerous other poultices before coming to see me. On the other hand, he is also encouraged by the words we use to equate psychotherapy with medical treatment and thus may expect a cure. After all, the very word "psychotherapy" suggests that I, the doctor, am administering something to the patient. In offering this treatment, this something, I am suggesting that the consumer will benefit when he takes it in the proper way. The state, always an interested party in the welfare of its citizens, has established some minimal regulations and standards of safe and ethical practice to guide the offering of professional services to the public. Thus the patient can logically ask: "How successful is psychotherapy and is the risk worth taking?"

Research psychologists have been trying over the decades to provide an answer to these questions. The practitioner, whether or not he thinks systematic research can actually determine the usefulness of psychotherapy, is obligated to the patient to come to terms with the results of research on the outcome of treatment. And it also helps to remind the patient that success in our endeavor doesn't mean a cure in the sense of a return to normality. We must confess, as Marie Jahoda has done in her book *Current Concepts of Positive Mental Health*, that we are as much in disagreement over what constitutes this prized state as are ministers, philosophers, educators and common citizens.[1] However, what can I say to a patient who quotes the following from the widely circulated book by Bernard Berelson and Gary A. Steiner, *Human Behavior: An Inventory of Scientific Findings?*

There is no conclusive evidence that psychotherapy is more effective than general medical counselling or advice in treating neurosis or psychosis. Strictly speaking, it cannot even be considered established that psychotherapy, on the average, improves a patient's chances of recovery beyond what they would be without any formal therapy whatsoever.[2]

As a therapist, educated and imbued with the values of the scientific attitude and the usefulness of its methods, my conscience calls on me to doubt seriously the efficacy of my help and to examine the results from which this conclusion stems. If this conclusion is a reasonable one to derive from the data, I should seriously consider shutting up shop. Or, at least, I should warn the patient that what we will be doing together is highly experimental. Increasingly, my professional colleagues are saying publicly what they had for a long time said among themselves and in professional journals: psychotherapy is always experimental. However, there are no indications that the rapid increase of psychotherapeutics since the last great war is slowing down, let alone being reversed. The clinical testimony of practitioners leads them not to give up any "ghost."

My personal experience also leads me not to accept the above conclusion. Not only do I derive deep satisfaction from my work, but I believe that I help most of those who seek me out. Enough of my patients tell me this to warrant my believing it. Many who despaired of their marital prospects do get married, marital discord is reduced in many instances, and so forth. Of course, there are a number of patients with whom I have struggled who have gotten worse, or have left therapy dissatisfied with the returns on their investment in time and money. Memories of these patients introduce a note of caution about the outcome of any particular case, but they never lead me to think that I am wasting most of my patients' time as I collect their payments. I recognize that I do have a vested economic interest in maintaining my practice, and this interest must always be considered as a possible factor in continuing with any particular patient who is unrewarding, i.e., not improving. Yet I do not think that making a fair income in private practice is the significant reason why my own experience as a practitioner leads me to doubt the conclusion reached by Drs. Berelson and Steiner. My scientific values, however, require me to meet the challenge of their statement.

Obviously, had I reached the conclusion that what I was doing was offering the patient potluck, I wouldn't be writing this book. So I should state the conclusion I have reached after examining the data and reading the opinions of many experts pro and con over the usefulness of psychotherapy.

The discussion and clarification of the results of systematic outcome research, whether of good, bad or indifferent design, and the issues raised by these studies demand a revision of the model on which the practice of psychotherapy is based. The published testimony should do for the profession what the experience with his own patients should do for the individual practitioner. As the therapist's experiences with different people over a period of time inevitably lead to a revision of his approach in the office, the published data must lead to a change in our general theory of the nature of the psychotherapy which we offer to the public. We should revise the usual definition of that therapy toward an emphasis on its highly personal nature and the significance of the relationship between the therapist and patient in the process of healing.

Let us turn to the research data and the arguments which have encouraged Dr. Berelson to reach the conclusion that psychotherapy is not efficacious. These arguments against psychotherapy can be organized under three headings.

The Relative Success of Different Brands

The rate of success of any one brand of therapy has not been shown to be superior to that of any other brand despite the claims of the protagonists of different cures of the human condition. As previously mentioned in Chapter 8, Dr. Werner Wolff found that about 70 percent of Freudian, Jungian and Adlerian analysts believed their form of therapy best without any evidence for this claim. The fact that no school is better than another does raise a serious problem concerning the concepts and methods of psychotherapy.[3]

In 1951 Miles, Barrabee and Finesinger published a paper in which they summarized in a table the results of twenty-four studies on outcome, which included over eight thousand cases.[4] When the ratings of cured, much improved and improved were combined, it was found that the average rate of improvement was 64 percent. Dr. Hans Eysenck, the best-known critic of psychotherapy, also published a table summarizing eighteen studies on psychotherapy with children in which almost 3,500 cases were involved.[5] The average percentage of improvement was 67. It should be noted that the ratings are those made by therapists and are not based on independent criteria. We do not know, then, whether therapists underestimated or exaggerated the degree of improvement of their patients. It might be that the therapists' hopes for their patients' welfare led them to overestimate how much therapy had helped, and it might be that modesty or scientific caution tended to reduce the ratings. This is one important reason why researchers recommend studies based on such other criteria as work performance and social adjustment.

These studies were carried out in different settings, with different kinds of patients and under different types of therapy. No study showed a significantly better rate of improvement than any other which could not be explained by the kinds of patients treated. The most severely disturbed people showed the lowest rates. If we do not question the research design of the studies, we may wonder about psychotherapy as a useful approach. Does the apparent two-thirds success rate warrant the investment of the time and money which is usually required by a psychotherapeutic relationship? Classical psychoanalysis, for example, which involves the biggest investment in money and time and thus implicitly promises greater returns, did not produce better results than other types of psychotherapy. In fact, the few studies available seem to suggest that psychoanalysis may yield a lower rate of success.

Is Some Psychotherapy Better Than None?

Even if we accept this approximately 70 percent rate of improvement as a reliable figure, it still has to be shown that suffering people who do not have formal therapy recover at a significantly lower rate than do patients who come to professional healers. What would have happened to the patients in psychotherapy if they had been un- treated?

Dr. Eysenck martials a number of researches on patients diag- nosed as neurotic who did not receive psychotherapy but did receive another type of treatment, or in some instances no treatment at all, though it should be noted that these conditions were defined by the researcher and not by the patients. For example, in one study about two-thirds of the patients who went to their general practitioners and were given the time-honored attention good physicians have always given their patients—i.e., a combination of encouragement, tonics, suggestions and probably placebos—were rated as recovered within two years. In another study two-thirds of the patients diagnosed as neurotic and hospitalized in New York State between 1917 and 1934 were discharged annually. Since it is quite unlikely that these patients received any kind of help besides the custodial care custo- marily given to all hospitalized patients, Dr. Eysenck concluded that these data support the interpretations that neurosis is "self-limiting" and that as many neurotics "spontaneously" recover as get help from a psychotherapist.

Another study Dr. Eysenck cited was of neurotic soldiers, some of whom received psychotherapy and others not. The average changes in the two groups returning to duty were approximately equal. And still another involved delinquent children who received special case work. When their posttreatment records were compared with the records of delinquent children who had been exposed to the same living situation except for special psychotherapy, the rate of recidiv- ism of both groups was approximately the same.

Do Patients Actually Change?

Researchers also have tried to demonstrate the usefulness of a method of psychotherapy by using measures of change independent of therapist ratings. Carl Rogers and his students have led the way in setting up such rigorously designed research. They have collected tape recordings, developed rating scales and coding systems for mea- suring change and administered questionnaires and projective tech- niques such as the Ink Blot Test before and after psychotherapy.

These studies have demonstrated that clients of nondirective coun-
selors do change significantly.[6]

Still, a hard-nosed critic would point out that the percentage of
cases showing such improvement is not much higher than the usual
70 percent. And furthermore the tough critic would analyze the
design of these rigorous studies and find them deficient. On the other
hand, as I will discuss in the chapter on psychological science, the
defects of any study on human behavior is an endemic problem. An
interesting example of this problem of "bias" in designing studies
and interpreting results can be found at the doorstep of Dr. Eysenck
himself, the chief advocate of those bedeviling psychotherapy. In his
animus toward psychoanalytic types of treatment he had claimed
that so-called conditioning therapy is much better and cited improvement rates of 90 percent or higher. Then along came Drs. Louis
Breger and James McGaugh, who clearly demonstrated the inadequacy of the researches on which Dr. Eysenck based his claim that
behavior-type therapy was the wave of the future.[7]

How can these arguments pro and con be reinterpreted and understood as requiring a different conception of healing rather than
the abandonment of any kind of professional help? A variety of
counterarguments have been offered, and I think they can be
grouped into two classes. The first group refers to the assumption
that research can be designed to demonstrate the *objective* usefulness of psychotherapy. I will argue in detail in the following chapter
why I think this is impossible. At this point, a brief summary of the
problems of such research is also useful in support of the interpretation that healing lies in the concrete reality of a particular relation.
After this summary, I will discuss the definition of the ends and
means of therapy, which requires an emphasis on the concrete relation.

SOME PROBLEMS IN RESEARCH ON PSYCHOTHERAPY

An attempt to design a comprehensive study controlling the complex variables in therapy would have to account for the following:

1. Such variables within the patient as age, sex, type of disturbance, severity, age of onset, education, marital status, social class
and motivation.

2. Therapist variables, such as age, sex, theoretical orientation, personality disposition, therapeutic optimism and so on.

3. Variables in the treatment situation, such as frequency, clinic or private treatment and so on.

4. Environmental variables, such as range of relations, work situation, urban-rural differences and so on.

5. All these processes (or variables), of course, function through time, which in psychotherapy is often months or years in duration. Changes occur "naturally," that is, because of forces besides those unleashed in psychotherapy. How can this be controlled?

6. The variable of treatment goals. What are the criteria for good mental health?

When we "recover" from the complexity of the task of designing an adequate study *with proper controls*, we come to realize that the very way we define adequately controlled research may itself be the problem. We may have asked the wrong question. If we remember that the psychotherapist begins by assuming a noncontrolling attitude while the experimenter assumes the opposite, the appropriateness of applying one method of investigation to both settings is thrown into question. Put another way, by "experimental" design the psychotherapist does not treat each patient alike, even patients with the same diagnosis. One obsessive-compulsive neurotic is older, prettier, a little more intelligent than the next.

However, research based on the control group method requires the therapist to treat a specified group in a similar manner. And this argument assumes that, in principle, two groups could be set up equivalent in all respects except the type of treatment. In other words, the very conditions of psychotherapy as traditionally defined call for a nonrestricted, i.e., noncontrolled, "experiment." This requirement stands in opposition to the requirements of "pure" systematic research, whose aim is to set an experiment in motion under a particular set of conditions and not to change direction until the data are in and have been analyzed. Those psychotherapists who insist that an objective demonstration of the superiority of one system over another is possible are vulnerable to criticism based on scientific methods.

However, when we recognize that research in psychotherapy cannot be controlled by standards of objectivity derived from the natural sciences, we can "relax" and apply other criteria. We could use the kinds of standards employed in evaluating the usefulness of education or of marriage. We would do our best to make public our approaches and open up our methods to the continuous give and take of public discussion. This is actually what is often done in our field, though not often enough nor publicly enough. The evaluation process, when it is carried on by honest people who suspend their vested interests by acknowledging them, takes many forms, including systematic research. These colloquia should lead to a revision of the question, "Does psychotherapy work?" Instead, we should ask, "How do certain kinds of therapy work in certain kinds of situations in which certain kinds of patients meet with certain kinds of psychotherapists?" Or ask, "How do any two people in a relation get on together?"

I can present this argument in another way. As far as I know, there have been no qualitative, let alone quantitative, studies on what brings about changes in a therapist's ways of working with a patient. It is simple to suggest a list of factors, such as age, educational opportunities and personal experiences. I think being a patient oneself has a profound effect on being a therapist. A trusted friend or a beloved spouse could very much influence the practice of therapy. A few tragedies with patients, which shocked me and occasionally still haunt me, have undoubtedly changed my outlook. The social characteristics of the patients one sees, as I've discussed in the chapter on patient-therapist equality, bring about gradual alterations in attitudes as well as procedures. In my case, the number of patients I have encountered with commitments to theological study has given me a much more open-minded appreciation that every person is struggling to harmonize the Ground of Being and being on the ground.

When we recognize the nature of our discipline, its limits and its aspirations, the naïveté of Drs. Berelson's and Steiner's conclusions is exposed. Psychotherapy is not and cannot be a thing dispensed by a well-organized phalanx of psychotherapists according to formulae established in the laboratory. It is not even a loose federation of denominations. Psychotherapy, in the scientific mode and in a democratic society, is rather any relation in which any two persons experience growth in a form which is consonant with their common values of open-minded evaluation of the evidence.

PSYCHOTHERAPY AS A CONCRETE FORM OF A GENERAL RELATION

A few references and quotations can serve to make the point that it is a relationship which matters and that there are no such things as "spontaneous" cures in living. In 1904 Freud wrote:

All physicians, therefore, yourselves included, are continually practicing psychotherapy, even when you have no intention of doing so. . . . It is not a modern dictum but an old saying of physicians that these diseases are not cured by the drug but by the physician, that is by the personality of the physician, inasmuch as through it he exerts a mental influence.[8]

And in 1965 Dr. Jerome Frank referred to a study on the question whether neuroses are self-limiting processes, like the common cold. "In one five-year-followup study of treated outpatient neurotics we found that most reported having consulted medical practitioners or other healers at least once in the interval, suggesting that this type of patient may seek out favorable regimes."[9]

When some people feel distress, they don't just sit there and wait until it goes away. The feeling of distress is not only a sign of disequilibrium. Its explicit acknowledgment and confession signal an effort to restore a balance. The person will turn to some relation, be it a person, a book or something else. Dr. Frank also summarized several studies of outpatients who experienced a significant diminution of symptoms during the initial clinic interview. Is this a spontaneous or accidental occurrence?

There are many happenings outside our offices which do lead to changes. I have repeatedly made this point. And it has been made by the South American woman who, at the end of treatment, told the psychiatrist treating her for a severe depression, "Doctor, you helped me much, but I want to tell you also, all the time I was seeing you I was going to my priest and also going to the head man of my secret society." Some people just don't wish to take any chances.

The notion, proposed by Dr. Eysenck, that suffering of a neurotic kind is self-limiting and that patients should sit it out for two years, more or less, is rather belied by a host of evidence. For example, Dr. Srole and his colleagues found that about 80 percent of the people residing in "Midtown," a section of Manhattan, have symptoms of disturbance, while about 20 percent are severely incapacitated.[10]

Unless these investigators were mad themselves, the notion of spontaneous recovery is quite wild since the neuroses would disappear if 67 percent of the patients always recovered in two years.

Clinicians have the opposite experience. I have never seen a patient, in any of the settings in which I've served, or ever heard any doctor tell of a patient in whom the duration of the complaints for which he finally sought help could be measured in anything but years. Most patients are desperate when they come for help and most have tried a half-dozen or more ways to break out of their distorted lives. Most clinicians decry the procrastination of people who put off getting help until the complaints or symptoms have become a way of life. How often a patient says to the therapist, "If only I had come to see you years ago, as soon as I first became aware that I had these disturbed feelings."

For the sake of my arguments, let me turn the question around and state that the crucial issue is not the number who get better under any regime but the number who do not. It is, after all, a moot question whether those who recovered after a stay in a hospital would also have been helped by psychotherapy, as it is a moot question whether those who were helped by some relation conventionally called psychotherapy would have changed more if they had gone to a swami or taken sulphur baths. By analogy, it would also be ridiculous to assert that because only approximately 70 percent of married couples rate their marriages as moderately or very happy, this suggests that marriage is not a very well-established way of finding contentment.[11] Should we abolish the institution if, for example, studies in other countries indicated that many more than 70 percent of Italians or Israelis or Pakistanis think they are happily married?

What could happen to the 30 percent of patients who do not improve? I would speculate as follows: A small number, perhaps a third, are the so-called intractable cases, unsuitable for any kind of known treatment because of constitutional factors, organic damage or personal tragedy which has embittered the individual to such an extent that his only wish is for a lingering life this side of the grave.

My therapeutic optimism in estimating that about 10 percent of all those seeking help from psychotherapists cannot be helped was revealed to me by the estimate of Dr. Paul Meehl, a past president of the American Psychological Association. He said that only about 25 percent of patients are appropriate for psychotherapy as practiced currently.[12] This difference in the concepts he and I have about the goals of psychotherapy would account for the discrepancy. I would accept Dr. Meehl's figure if I could accept the concept that psychotherapy should only be offered to the kind of people Freud originally believed were best suited for psychoanalysis, that is, the intellectually and emotionally well-endowed. However, I begin with the assumption that anyone can be helped to some degree and that it is a matter of time and resources as well as knowledge which limits our usefulness. Dr. Meehl suggests this, too, when he introduces the note that because of the shortage of trained personnel it isn't socially justified to give help to everyone seeking it. Dr. Meehl believes we should be more selective, i.e., that we treat only the elite.

So, setting aside the 10 or so percent "incurables," I would say that the largest proportion of the unsuccessful 30 percent were unlucky. They just got involved with the wrong helper. The Baptist, so to speak, got hung up in a Methodist church. The patient with an Adlerian complex went by chance to a Jungian. In sum, our difficulties as helpers may be to a large degree due to the fact that we don't do the right kind of matching or we just don't know enough or we just don't think it important enough.

The proper matching of patient and doctor occurs more often in private practice than it does in clinics or other outpatient facilities. This is rarely acknowledged by the profession. Dr. Paul Meehl is an exception when, after estimating that at least 40 percent of patients are untreatable by psychotherapy, he confesses that he rejects the large majority of cases who seek him out. We may not like his tough-mindedness, but we cannot question his candor. He wants to be successful, and he states what every successful private practitioner knows and does. Dr. Meehl also exposes the well-known secret that all therapists have a black book of their favorite colleagues. To them, they refer people they feel involved with. The stranger just takes a bigger risk because he is sent to someone else. No wonder some people get better and others get pushed about. The key to success, as amplified by Dr. Meehl, is to have good connections and make a good match.

My own total clinical experience leads me to the assertion that the private practitioner is not deluding himself or others when he claims a higher rate of success than 70 percent. At this time I estimate that about 80 to 90 percent of the patients with whom I make a contract improve and testify to the help they have received. Five years ago I estimated about a 70 percent rate of improvement and ten years ago even less. When I worked at a clinic, I think I helped 50 percent of the patients. We also must assert the obvious point that private patients are usually the most highly motivated and most similar to those described by Freud as suitable for psychoanalysis.

Another aspect of success should also be highlighted. The more experienced and older a therapist, the better and wiser he is. Research confirms this common observation. However, my experience has not only increased my sensitivity and tact with patients with whom I've already made a contract. Increasing experience and a relatively adequate load of patient hours help me be more discreet in selecting those whom I believe I can help. I can afford to turn away those I believe are less likely to respond to my ways of healing. When I calculate success rates, I do not count those I've seen for only a few times or those with whom the agreement was for a specified "trial" period. Also, private practice is based to an extent on referral by ex-patients and colleagues, and one's reputation is of very critical importance in the outcome. New patients often have quite a good deal of accurate knowledge about me. Most of them are not so self-destructive as to choose me and then have as their major goal the reduction of my average.

Returning to the comparison between marriage and psychotherapy, I suggest that in the present phase of our understanding of how to get married and our values about marriage 70 percent is about the best people do on first trials. Now, the latest figures on the over-all divorce rate are about 20 to 25 percent. Let us make the reasonable assumption that the divorced are composed mainly of the 30 percent unhappily married people. Of this group of once divorced, a very large portion remarry, and their satisfaction in second marriages is about as high as those of first marriages.[13] After a few go-rounds, the general level of satisfaction with the mate approaches 90 percent, with a hard core of 10 percent or so who find wedlock an unholy state. Perhaps psychotherapists should encourage their patients to try "divorce" from the therapist if they feel they are not being helped, and we should do so without suggesting the patient is intractable or resistant, i.e., a failure. There is such a thing as incompatibility, and the therapist is as responsible as the patient when the healing partnership doesn't work. In one sense, he is even more responsible since he should be more in touch with his feelings toward the patient than is the patient in touch with his feelings toward the therapist. Psychotherapists could improve their rate of success if they would attend more to compatibility between the patient and themselves than they attend to diagnoses and prognoses.

Psychotherapists also should emphasize compatibility between patient and therapist in the light of the research evidence. A closer examination of the results reveals the inadequacy of any across-the-board conclusion regarding the usefulness of psychotherapy. Though the average amount of change between a treated group and an untreated group may not differ, the variability of change is often enough higher among the people in therapy. In other words, in some psychotherapy relations people become considerably better and in others, considerably worse. Attention to this evidence requires that I inform each patient that I can hurt him as well as help him.[14]

Again and again, throughout this discussion, I am saying that it is the qualities of the relationship that count, and when I speak about a patient, I speak about myself. If we were consistently to see ourselves in the transaction, we would become as much interested in the applicant's first impression of us, that is, his tentative "prognosis" regarding the doctor, as we are usually concerned with our diagnostic impression of the applicant. And if the client or patient or help-seeker expressed some qualms about talking with us, we could respond with "Well, why not speak with Dr. So-and-So?" What choice do we give patients who come to clinics? And though the private patient is presumably in a better financial position to select a doctor, what choice do we give him when he says, "I am afraid of you"? More often, we assume that the patient's initial uneasiness is due to his condition, his resistance and his transference reaction rather than to his realistic assessment of us and the relationship. What our educated common sense tells us are the ways of love should be the ways of psychotherapy.

15

PSYCHOLOGICAL AND SOCIAL

RESEARCH: SCIENCE OR

HUMANISTIC STUDY

The mantle of scientist is an honored one, and the practitioner with a degree indicating scientific training is respected by most patients. The person seeking help usually does have faith in the empirical testing of hypotheses and often enough has studied in the social sciences. He thus expects that the therapist is an applied scientist, like a physician who adapts the information developed by such "pure" sciences as biochemistry, physics, and anatomy to the practical problem of curing an illness. The patient usually also understands that there is an art in the practice of medicine or psychotherapy. However, he assumes that, more or less, scientific knowledge, and not capricious intuition, is the basis of the art.

There are, of course, different opinions and a great deal of debate on the nature of science, the relation between scientific methods and the scientific attitude, the differences among the physical, biological and social sciences, and the relation between research data coolly amassed in the laboratory and the sweaty thoughts emerging in the consulting room. An understanding of these issues is burdensome enough, but the therapist is not aided in this undertaking by his proclivity to be impatient with nonpractical matters. In the office the anguished face of the patient also demands of the therapist that the two of them "get down to what works." Speculations regarding the relation between his art and the science which he also represents appear superfluous and an indulgence at the patient's expense.

Nevertheless, I think it is incumbent on the therapist to have as clear a point of view· on these issues as he possibly can if he does advance himself to the patient as a scientifically trained professional. In New York as in many other states, a psychologist cannot practice therapy and call himself a psychologist unless he has been certified by the State Education Department. To be certified, the psychologist must demonstrate his competence through credentials describing his training and experience and then must pass a test. All these require study in psychological science.

However, this is not the only or even the major reason for keeping up with the philosophy of science. I shall try to show that an understanding of the problems of social science and its differences from natural science is actually helpful in the practice of a therapy based on democratic values. I will try to show that it is almost as useful for the patient to understand the nature of psychological study as it is for him to understand the intricacies of parent-child relations. The quicker he gets over his awe of science, the quicker he will get out of the clinic room.

The notion that science can solve everything if given enough time is not based only on the person's unresolved infantile and magical wishes for the key to the secret of life. Much in what the physical and natural sciences have achieved fosters this idea, and much in the attitudes of social scientists suggests an identity between the physical and social sciences. It thus should be quite therapeutic to some patients, especially educated ones, for the doctor to discuss with them the magical notions derived from science which often buttress a childish longing for a life stripped of painful ambiguities. If the therapist were to make plain to the patient that his knowledge is highly relative, he would aid the growth of the patient's self-confidence and increase the very quality which is the hallmark of science: open-mindedness.

My claim is unproved and, I confess, unusual. I have never read a case report which included a discussion between the therapist and the patient on, for example, psychological science as a social system in which they are both involved. I doubt if any therapist maintains that his work is based on solid scientific knowledge, and I'm sure almost everyone would agree with Dr. Jerome Frank when he wrote: "There is no independent, objective criterion for the truth of any interpretation in psychotherapy."[1] But how many of us tell this to our patients and discuss the implications of this evaluation for the very demands the patient makes on us? Such discussions are ruled out as intellectualizing with the patient and as issues not relevant to the deep problems for which the patient needs help.[2]

The consequence of this omission degrades the patient's intelligence, the superiority of the doctor as the knowledgeable scientist is maintained, and both avoid considering the possibility that the patient's goal of achieving a reasonably good life does not require special scientific knowledge of himself obtained from a professional psychotherapist. As I will try to show, much of what we consider psychological knowledge is a translation, in special "jargon," of common sense. The special language helps the doctor maintain a control over the patient. In some therapeutic encounters this control has taken the form of discouraging, even prohibiting, the patient from reading in the psychological literature. The rationalization for this is that the patient will become too intellectual about his problems.

My encounter with the literature on the philosophy of science and the research literature composed by behavioral scientists has led me to the following six related propositions:

1. The data psychologists develop with their scientific experiments, methods and tests are always in large measure a product of the kind of relationship which is established between the researcher and subject. The relationship depends not only on the particular problem under investigation and the methods used, but on a number of variables which can be only partially controlled. These include such factors as the experimenter's attitudes and character, the dispositions of the subjects and the hidden as well as known meanings the experiment has for both parties to the laboratory contract. The experimenter is a participant observer in the very same sense as is the clinician who is enmeshed in the therapeutic encounter.

2. The interpretations of whatever data are developed are in principle always an expression of the interpreter's values as to what ought to be.

3. The predictive power of an interpretation or generalization

derived from systematic research is not any higher than the predictive power derived from the common agreement reached by a therapist and his patient as to what is likely to happen next in the life of the patient. Statistically significant results of an experiment are essentially an outcome of a consensus reached between experimenter and subject. The subject, in other words, behaves like the experimenter thought he would under the controlled conditions of the experiment. The subject, in this sense, had been programmed by the experimenter to give the correct responses.

4. An experimenter's hypothesis which is proved to be valid by statistical tests of significance is often itself a shrewd insight into the learned modes of behavior of his subjects. The hypothesis is in this sense proved before it is tested. The researcher's ingenuity in demonstrating his hunch is manifest in the particular methods he uses to test his idea. Since he has set up the procedure, his chances are great that the collected data will validate the hypothesis.

The classic research of Ivan Pavlov on the conditioned reflex is an example of the care a researcher must take when he designs an experimental setting to demonstrate his hypothesis. Pavlov's method involved placing his dogs in a very elaborate rig so that he could carefully measure stimulus-response sequences. Well, he had a time of it, selecting and training animals who would daily accept the laboratory situation. Some dogs, far from dogged followers, broke down and revealed signs of what animal researchers have called experimental neuroses. Pavlov got results and supplied a cornerstone for the behavioristic tradition in psychology. However, he accomplished this only by making sure that the dog and experimenter accepted the reasons for being together by playing their traditional roles of faithful domesticated pet and benevolent rewarding master.

Described this way it would seem that I am accusing researchers of unethically rigging their results. I suppose a few do, but most, I maintain, do so in following the canons of adequate research design. If a person wants to test a hypothesis, he should give it the fairest trial possible. He should anticipate, that is, deduce, as many of the possible determinates as he can and account for them in the design of his study which will yield data into which he can induce a generalization. This is what the clinician also does. In the laboratory and the clinic both deductive and inductive processes are so intertwined that they are often indistinguishable. Yet the notion persists that a laboratory study is less contaminated than clinical study because it is an empirical test of a hypothesis deduced from a general theory.[3] On the contrary, I am indicating that in social science the connection between general theory and a hypothesis is more often than not quite tenuous. This connection is often as close as that between a general theory about the nature of emotional disorders and the interpretation offered to a patient. Both involve an imaginative reordering of data which is essentially ambiguous.

5. Psychology as a separate science is very limited in its capacity to establish comprehensive and general laws from which predictions can be made. Its province of special investigation is at the crossroads of the body and mind, psyche and soma, spirit and corpus. Its data must always be in the process of becoming better understood as they are affected by biological processes on the one hand and social-cultural transactions on the other. What always remains after the investigations are over is the mystery of personal freedom in the face of social and biological determinants. Research psychologists are thus always discovering the unmeasurable range of nonpredictability, i.e., the limits of regularities. Psychologists try to understand and explain human behavior rather than foretell it. This is essentially what the psychotherapist is about with his patient.

6. The concept that science discovers fixed natural laws is also an erroneous one. Though the physicist can predict concrete events with an extraordinary degree of accuracy, physical theories are always in a process of revision. The natural sciences are always discovering indeterminacy. All science is now conceived as involving unknown and known assumptions and as partaking in a faith that meaning is discernible but never fully revealed. The rigid dichotomy between the process of faith and reason, between subjective and objective ways of knowing, is giving way to the idea that these distinctions refer more to the subject matter under investigation than they do to the logical structure of science itself.

Some Illustrations from Psychological Study

Though I have chosen a very few illustrations of these six propositions from the psychological literature, I think they are also in the main stream of up-to-date discourses on psychology as a scientific discipline.

Richard Solomon is an outstanding leader in the field of the experimental study of animal behavior. He has prepared a thorough review of the laboratory work in a special problem which itself originated at the end of the last century. Dr. Solomon discusses the laboratory evidence on the effect of reward and punishment on the problem-solving behavior of, in the main, rats, monkeys and cats. In his introductory remarks he warns us: "If there is one idea I would have you retain it is this: Our laboratory knowledge of the effects of punishment on instrumental and emotional behavior is still rudimentary—much too rudimentary to make an intelligent choice among conflicting ideas about it."[4]

The conflicting ideas Dr. Solomon refers to are essentially the old dispute over the best way to discipline a person: "Spare the rod and spoil the child" versus kindness and love. Dr. Solomon is moved in his review to caution those who hold to the view, or legend as he would have it, that punishment often results in undesirable effects. He tells us this isn't necessarily so, which shouldn't surprise us. What would have left us flabbergasted would be a review of research on animals, whose patterns of behavior are much less complicated than those of humans, in which precise laws about reward and punishment were articulated. A longer quote from the summary of Dr. Solomon's paper is instructive, and again I maintain that it is typical of every summary of a large body of psychological literature:

The major points I have made are as follows:

First, the effectiveness of punishment as a controller of instrumental behavior varies with a wide variety of known parameters . . . [author's italics]. *Some* [my italics] of these are: (a) intensity of the punishment stimulus, (b) whether the response being punished is an instrumental one or a consummatory one, (c) whether the response is instinctive or reflexive, (d) whether it was established originally by reward or punishment, (e) whether or not the punishment is closely associated in time with the punished response, (f) the temporal arrangements of reward and punishment, (g) the strength of the response to be punished, (h) the familiarity of the subject with the punishment being used, (i) whether or not a reward alternative is offered during the behavior-suppression period induced by punishment, (j) whether a distinctive, incompatible avoidance response is strengthened by omission of punishment, (k) the age of the subject, and (l) the strain and species of the subject.[5]

My first reaction when I read this was to wonder what happened to the sex of the subject and if there is a real distinction between instinctive and reflexive responses. I am also sure animal psychologists could add to the list of Dr. Solomon's distinctions. But what Dr. Solomon's scientific language boils down to is: *it all depends*. We must remember that the studies he reviews almost always found some significant results reflecting some regularities among the variables. Yet, when they are all put together, the exceptions prove the rule. The more we know regarding the behavior of living forms, the more we have to specify the particular conditions under which the knowledge emerges, and the more we have to circumscribe any generalization we make. It would seem that, carried to its ultimate logical conclusion, lawfulness and predictability are fully definable only in a relationship of two.

The next example is a review by Natalie Chapanis and her husband of the research studies which have mushroomed in the last years from the soil of Leon Festinger's theory of cognitive dissonance. Dr. Festinger's theory is an attempt to predict the conditions under which attitudes and opinions change. It is a simple theory, and if parsimony is a virtue, this theory has it. Dr. Festinger assumes that you can reduce the meaning of a complex social situation to a series of simple ideas or cognitions describing personal beliefs, opinions and attitudes. When there is inconsistency among the cognitions, then the person, it is assumed, will strive to reduce the noise or the "dissonance."

This is a far from novel or startling idea. Perhaps consistency is the hobgoblin of little minds, but whenever we speak of adjustment, adaptation or landing feet first, we are describing an amoeba-like attempt to spit out or absorb an irritant. In physiology, Claude Bernard in the late nineteenth century, and Walter Cannon in the 1920's and 1930's, talked of homeostasis. An organism or an aspect of an organism can be characterized as a system maintaining a steady state through change, very much like a thermostat. We see this concept of the feedback mechanism again in what Norbert Wiener called cybernetics. Prescott Lecky's self-consistency theory described personality development as a continuing attempt to maintain a consistent self-picture through the incorporation of whatever fits in with the artful design and through the rejection of incompatibilities. Karl Menninger's latest work calls this "The Vital Balance." And there are many others.

The Chapanis' in their review, "Cognitive Dissonance: Five Years Later," noted the array of outstanding social psychologists who have been impressed by Dr. Festinger's idea and the work of his students and himself. However, after a careful and critical analysis of the methods and results of the experimental work, they conclude:

Having now reviewed much of the experimental work supporting cognitive dissonance theory, we conclude that as a body of literature, it is downright disappointing. Too many studies have failed to stand up to close scrutiny. Yet, it is also obvious that the dissonance framework has a seductive allure for many social scientists, an allure not possesed by the rather similar interpretations by Heider, Osgood and Tannenbaum or Newcomb.[6]

The Chapanis' seemed to have stopped just short of accusing Dr. Festinger of being a Madison Avenue type. Since this critical attack, others have come to the support of Dr. Festinger and have provided erudite answers to the imputation that he is a good salesman and a poor researcher.[7] Such sharp exchanges do have the virtue of enlivening our journals, but they also bewilder even the sophisticated nonpartisan. Who is correct, or are all the results perhaps incorrect?

Dr. Solomon's review of the experimental work on punishment said in effect that all previous research provided only very partial explanations, which were in turn determined largely by the method of study used. You want to prove a rat learns by trial and error? Put it in a maze where it can't see anything but the opening in front of its nose. You want to prove insight as a feature of learning? Put the animal in a situation where it can look about and explore its environment. These controversies usually do not establish the superior truths of one system or theory, but they do have a useful function. The criticisms demonstrate that each system has its own measure of truth as it finds it, and that under the scrutiny of another disinterested or hypercritical observer the truth is incomplete.

The studies stimulated by L. Festinger's theory did produce significant results, but these are limited by the methods used. The methods may be called imprecise and the theory used to explain the results may be called simplistic, but an order .of meaning is established which doesn't violate common or uncommon sense. The work on cognitive dissonance is no better or worse than that produced by many other reputable scholars.

Indeed, the significance of a scholar's work in a social science is highly correlated with the interest and controversy it arouses. Through the process of critique and defense, alterations occur in the theories and in the research. Psychology in the laboratory and in the clinic is in this sense very much alike. Both emerge in a contest and a dialogue between the subject-patient and experimenter-therapist, and between the scientist-clinician and his colleagues. Polemics, an outstanding feature of humanistic study as well as political theory, is in as good supply in the social sciences as it is in short supply in the physical sciences.

The "establishment" in American psychology certainly has maintained that it is in the laboratory that basic knowledge will be discovered. The most to be expected in the clinic is that fruitful hypotheses may be generated as by-products of helping people. Though the statistical method which is always employed implies that there are limits to any generalization, i.e., that probabilities rather than certainties are assessed, it has been pounded into the head of every psychology student that the clinic is an inferior place in which to carry on scientific study.

This split, which I am suggesting was arbitrary and a matter of convenience rather than necessary as a matter of truth, contributed to a sort of contempt for consciousness and mentalistic categories. The subject's opinions and attitudes were epiphenomena. The elimination of consciousness as a variable in behavior was an axiom of the behavioristic approach formulated by John Watson, Clark Hull and B. F. Skinner. But, as Skinner himself noted, this view of consciousness also characterizes psychoanalysis. Apparently differing on every score, psychoanalysis and behaviorism for a long time were in agreement that the real truth required the elimination of conscious personal values.

Robert Holt took note of this in a paper on "Imagery: The Return of the Ostracized." He said that "ironically psychoanalysis has as little systematic interest in images as academic psychologists." Writers and artists and common folk always have reveled in the infinite variety of imagery, of pictures and word pictures and in closing one eye and then the other while looking at the sky or the forest. The rich flow of what William James called the stream of consciousness was banished to the limbo of madmen or intoxication. Dr. Holt observed:

> We live in an age of literalism, an era that distrusts the imagination. . . . It is little wonder that our children rapidly lose their eidetic capacity and that adults are made uneasy by the admission that they can experience things not factually present. . . .[8]

And then he asked, "But must we choose between abstract thought and the richness of fancy?" An image is peculiarly a meaningful mental picture of a particular relationship usually accompanied by the cascade of feelings which provided the ground for the dance of the figures in the recollection.

THE LIMITS OF PSYCHOLOGY

Psychology cut out its own heart in trying to emulate the natural sciences by restricting its laboratory studies to data manipulable by the methods of the natural sciences. The irony of this has been sharply exposed by Michael Scriven, a philosopher and historian of science. I think he has provided us with a useful map of the province of psychology. Dr. Scriven's comments could be taken as a blow to our prestige as scientists. But to those of us who see in the definition of our relative limits the opportunity to work with a scientific open-mindedness, his points are liberating. He departs from the question: is it possible for psychology to discover the kind of fundamental law which makes for unity among some branches of physical science, such as the law of gravitation which unites astronomy and mechanics? His answer is a firm no, and he presents three reasons for this.

"The first fact is that the territory of psychology is, in a curious way, sharply restricted by common sense."[9] Psychological science can describe something in a systematic way, but it often boils down to what the ordinary person has already observed or whatever all of us have learned from the accumulated record of thousands of years of human putterings or what every creative genius throughout history has sensed. Psychology begins and ends with what is observable without mechanical techniques.

In turn, the discoveries of psychology are quickly taken over by, at least, the educated man. These discoveries are old even before they have been verified in the laboratory according to the standards of scientific method. One outstanding example of this is Freud's discovery of the unconscious. Actually, as L. Whyte has shown, it wasn't a discovery at all but an application of a point of view to certain phenomena.[10] But even granting that it was a startling idea, the intellectual community seized hold of the notion and applied it to literature, politics, etc., "as if" it were true, long before experimental psychologists had been able to verify the existence of unconscious ideas.

The patients who first came to Freud were intelligent and educated people. They were certainly impressed by the novelty of his requests and his erudition. After Freud's ideas were popularized those who went to an analyst had already agreed with his system. They were onto it. New developments occurred and new patients read the new publications and the new ideas became common knowledge. And as intramural disputes became interparty squabbles, scholars reassessed the "discoveries" and found them reformulations of age-old ideas.

William James described the four phases of a theory. The first is the period in which it is ignored. The second is the period in which it is attacked. Then it is seen as meritorious and, finally, as a rehash of ancient wisdom. It is the language in which common wisdom is expressed that gives it its apparent novelty. The ethical psychologist, in this context, is one who tells the patient or the public that the order of correlation found in the laboratory or the clinic is so necessarily circumscribed by exceptions that the dawn of understanding brings with it the awakening of what was thought about all along.

Returning to Dr. Scriven, he writes of the second limitation as follows:

The second limitation on psychology, for which it cannot be blamed but which radically affects our assessment of its capacities, is that its territory is restricted and, indeed, constantly being annexed by other sciences: biochemistry, biology, genetics, biophysics, physiology, neurology, neurophysiology, and so on.[11]

Dr. Ernest Nagel, a leading philosopher of science, made essentially the same point in discussing the development of universal laws as requiring an extraordinary refinement of the discriminations among pertinent variables.

However, there are some grounds for doubting that the social sciences are likely to refine their current distinctions beyond a certain point—a point fixed by the general character of the problems they investigate and the level of analysis appropriate for dealing with those problems—unless indeed these disciplines as presently constituted are transformed almost beyond recognition. For suppose that in order to obtain universal social laws, it would be necessary to classify social phenomena in part by reference to minutely differentiated physical and physiological traits of human participants in these phenomena, and in part on the basis of detailed data concerning the culturally acquired habits and beliefs each participant possesses.[12]

Dr. Nagel reminded the social scientist that a universal law obtained in this way may not have any advantage over a limited statistical statement. A generalization covering all of humanity would be either a physicochemical law or one so broad when stated in the words of the social scientist that it would be obvious and already known.

Standing as it does at the juncture of the social and natural sciences, psychology is often befuddled as to its identity. The more a psychologist tries to refine his power of observation as a basis for prediction, the more he is pressed toward the materiality and manipulability of the somatic process. For example, the phenomenon of memory and our living with the awareness of time is a central, if not *the* central, problem of psychology. The literature on the variables or forces affecting our memories is almost *the* literature of psychology. Still an explanation of a high order of generalization hasn't been formulated. However, with the invention of precise techniques for probing and stimulating the brain, Wilder Penfield was able, under local anesthesia, to cause a patient to have a psychical experience, felt as in the present moment but recognized as a past event, and described as such by the patient. When Dr. Penfield stopped the electrical stimulation, the memory stopped. This may eventually be the psychotherapy we've been waiting for, but whether or not it will be so, neurophysiology is encroaching on the psychologist's ground.[13]

The more the psychologist examines his propositions, procedures and functions, as an experimenter or as a clinician, the more he turns to explanations provided by sociology, history, politics and economics. For example, mental symptoms are found to vary in type and in frequency with social class as August B. Hollingshead, Fritz Redlich and Leo Srole, among others, have demonstrated. To become an expert in systematic research, the psychologist must become either a part-time biologist or a part-time sociologist.

What is left to the psychologist in which he can be just himself? He can lavish his attention on the person, with all the ambiguity of his unique organization of biological and social forces. The psychologist can always have the faith and the reason that man's spirit and creative intelligence are an eternally satisfying subject for investigation with the tools of an open mind. The psychologist too often resorts to pale replications of creative interpretations of the personal world offered by novelists, philosophers and biographers. The psychologist may envy the artist and retreat to taxonomy with the justified rationale that classification is always an important phase of science. But if he is to preserve his identity as a student of individual behavior, he must return to the person, with whatever talent he can muster, and try to discern what has been overlooked in the name of scientific rigor.

The third and related limitation on psychological science noted by Dr. Scriven is that the outcomes it is asked to predict are largely of such a nature that the information required to make a prediction just cannot be obtained. Practical considerations prevent us from finding out all we conceivably would need to know in order to tell what kind of woman a man will marry. Let us suppose, however, that we could get all the information necessary about a man to make a very accurate profile of the traits he seeks in a woman. We would have to ask him many questions to gather this data. Of course, through this procedure he would get to have more information about himself and thus foil the whole business. This is what often happens in therapy and is sometimes labeled resistance if the therapist's question is rejected, and sometimes creativity if the probe leads to the unexpected.

A psychologist, be he a clinician or an experimentalist, can be quite good at providing explanations for what happens. We can make shrewd and imaginative inferences with the benefit of hindsight. But when we confuse an explanation based on retrospect with a prediction, we follow what Dr. Scriven said was "a classic myth of traditional philosophy of the first part of this century that explanation and prediction are logically similar." We expand like a blowfish to hide our very small power of prediction. Psychotherapeutic theory and practice have so often confused the two. Explaining the past does not necessarily increase the possibility of knowing the future, unless through a measure of control built up in the relationship itself the patient stops being a spoilsport and alters his behavior to that predicted by the doctor. A similar form of machination occurs in the laboratory.

When one becomes attentive to language and its meaning, the sharp divisions fade between faith and reason, between the psychology laboratory and the clinician's office, and between the man in the street and the man in the university. The acquisition of language occurs in communion, and specialized scientific languages grow out of natural languages. It takes only two people to evolve a "new" language community. The evolution giving rise to a new set of signs often appears to the noninitiated as gibberish. In time the new ways of communicating will be judged as a wild idea or the beginning of a revolution in thought leading to new interpretations and new data.

Physical scientists can decide whether the new language is a misstatement of reality through an experiment in the laboratory or by observing natural events as in astronomy. Psychologists, whose languages are much more like natural languages, cannot settle a dispute over the correct interpretation of reality by means of a crucial study.

THE CHANGING VIEW OF SCIENCE

Like a lower-class citizen striving to ape his betters, psychologists have emulated the scientific antics of men playing with things. And like the citizen who discovers that just when he has acquired the proper habits of dress the fashion has changed, the psychologists, clinical and experimental, look up and are told by their superiors, "You are old-fashioned. The kind of science you have been trying to make is no longer the kind we are making." Sigmund Koch has commented:

But for some years now, physicists and biologists, philosophers of science and historians of science, have been converging upon a view of science which emphasizes the extent to which the scientific process is, in principle and at all stages, *undetermined by rule* [author's italics] . . . [and] in acknowledging the dependency of theory construction and use at every phase on *individual sensibility, discrimination, insight, judgment, guess* [my italics].[14]

Logicians and physical scientists are telling us the lesson of biological evolution: change and unfolding are the reality underlying the emergence of identifiable and fixed structures. Axioms are only tentative positions which stimulate deductions, which in turn may help clarify some aspects of the questions we pose.

This is at the heart of the historical religious belief that God will fully reveal Himself only on the last day of judgment. It is the crucial concept in what has been called process philosophy. The central idea of process philosophy is that reality is defined in relational terms. All forms of life and nonlife, as different as they appear to be, are similar in that they are continuously in flux and are identifiable as structures only in a context of other structures. Neither the one extreme of rigid stasis, where the structure can be exactly defined and determined, nor the other extreme of complete freedom and ceaseless change can be grasped by the mind when we observe nature. However, these extremes define a continuum of social process, of levels of relative organization out of which emerge unpredictably new events which we in turn reorganize into new hierarchies, and on and on.

A process we call a thing is only a convenience of the moment, an abstraction serving the need to point, to simplify and thus to distort by ignoring the ground out of which the structure or thing was wrenched. A scientific rule is such a thing, and in psychotherapy an interpretation or a reference to the self is such a thing. God, in such a metaphysical analysis, is also such a thing. Dr. Hartshorne described the new concept of God, replacing the traditional one Western man has held:

Wisdom and goodness are essentially relationships, and the wholly nonrelative or pure absolute can in no intelligible sense, know or intend anything: more obviously, if possible, it cannot love anything. Moreover, if God were wholly absolute and immutable, he would be less, not more, rich in fullness of being than if he were relative and mutable; for modern analysis has shown, more and more clearly, that the relative includes the absolute and more besides, and that becoming includes being as well as something additional. We have come to see that by abstracting from relations and changes we can indeed conceive the absolute and the changeless, but only as something abstract and deficient in actuality or concreteness.[15]

The convergence in thinking between liberal theologians and modern philosophers of science need not be interpreted as a sign of sentimental ecumenicism. The theologian has always been concerned with the apparent duality between faith and reason. And scientists now see this issue as at the core of their efforts at comprehending the infinite reaches of the universe from atom to the distant galaxies. The psychotherapist is always directly involved in clarifying his and the patient's beliefs and faith as they stimulate or interfere with sensible reasoning on the basis of facts. The relation between the clinic room and psychological science can be further understood by taking up the problem of faith and reason.

16

REASONABLE FAITH AND

DEDICATED REASON

Faith and reason have been usually considered as opposites and incompatible. Very few of the authorities on scientific psychotherapy employ the word "faith" in their explanations of how their system of healing works. When they do, such as in describing so-called "faith cures," the word is used in an odious sense, implying an irrational and primitive force which turns the person away from facing his real difficulties. A state of faith must be unreasonable. It is what unthinking people fall back on when they avoid the evidence of reasonable men facing them with knowledge derived from research. Faith is supposed to be a state in which people adhere blindly to an authority whose power is sanctified by a divinity. However, some authorities are not abashed in using the term "faith" as an explanation of healing. Jerome Frank wrote: "The only point I would like to emphasize about them [patients] is that it is the state of faith, and not the object of faith that seems to release the healing force."[1]

Over sixty years ago Freud did say in a lecture to the College of Physicians of Vienna:

In the first place, let me remind you that psychotherapy is in no way a modern method of healing. On the contrary, it is the most ancient form of therapy in medicine. In Lowenfeld's instructive work, many of the methods of *primitive and ancient medical science* [my italics] are described. The majority of them must be classed under the head of psychotherapy; in order to effect a cure a condition of "expectant faith" was induced in such persons, the same condition which answers a similar purpose for us today.[2]

Words in psychology appear to be also subject to dictates of fashion. The concept of suggestion was banned because it was imprecise and appeared to beg the question it was to explain. The blind faith of a person in a powerful authority, the phenomena accompanying hypnosis, the fluctuations of the symptoms of hysterics and the buying habits of a public exposed to commercials seemed much too complex to be dealt with by the word "suggestion." This term was mentalistic and could not be operationally defined. But nowadays suggestion is back in other forms presumably available to empirical testing. We psychologists now speak of operant conditioning when it is found that a person's rate of using nouns can be increased as the experimenter, presumably without the person's awareness, says "uh-huh" every time the subject produces a noun. Or we speak of subliminal perception to explain such a phenomenon, again producible in a laboratory, when a word or picture not seen by the subject nevertheless influences his perception of another word or picture that he does see. Another word which has been in fashion a long time is conformity. This word conveys phenomena observed by social psychologists, such as a person's altering his attitude toward that held by the majority of a particular group. By whatever name it is called—suggestion, operant conditioning, conformity, persuasion —the faith and trust given by a person to another always become, for the psychologist, the gullibility of the child endowing his parents with omnipotence and omniscience.

There is much justification for this view. The historian's documents testify to the extent to which men who have placed their lives in the hands of others who promised them the true interpretation of the meaning of existence always have been betrayed. The clinician's documents often provide evidence of the devastating effects on children when parents assume the posture of all-wise beings who exploit the child's vital dependence on his nurturant parents.

I choose two illustrations from the psychologist's laboratory in which educated people manifest a blind faith in the goodwill and power of the experimenter himself. Ironically, the man in the white smock who designs the study to control nonrational factors and who is supposed to represent open-minded and critical reason himself has become the worshiped idol.

Martin Orne and his colleagues at Harvard have turned their attention to what they call the social psychology of the psychological experiment. Dr. Orne's group tried to develop a boring task which subjects would quickly abandon. In such a task the investigators believed they would have a standard for measuring the influence of hypnosis in changing the point in time at which nonsensical and meaningless work would be given up. For example, they asked their subjects, who were college students, to add adjacent numbers of sheets filled with rows of random digits. To the surprise of the experimenters, the subjects continued for hours until the experimenter himself gave up. On inquiry it turned out that the subjects did not perceive the task as meaningless at all. Why? Dr. Orne recognized that volunteers in psychological experiments have such motives as making money or fulfilling course requirements. But Dr. Orne and his co-workers were not content with these explanations and suggested:

Over and above these motives, however, college students tend to share (with the experimenter) the hope and expectation that the study in which they are participating will in some material way contribute to science and perhaps ultimately to human welfare in general. . . . The student volunteer is not merely a passive responder in an experimental situation but rather he has a very real stake in the successful outcome of the experiment.[3]

The experimental subject becomes in this view a brother of the help-seeking person, and the experimenter whose laboratory was supposed to be sterile finds himself guilty of associating with the profane clinician. So the modern researcher is catching up with the philosopher A. H. Pierce, who observed back in 1908: "It is to the highest degree probable that the subject's . . . general attitude of mind is that of ready complacency and cheerful willingness to assist the investigator in every possible way by reporting to him those very things which he is most eager to find."[4]

The second study painfully illustrates the effect of the subject's faith in science on the results of a scientific study. Stanley Milgram devised an intriguing experimental procedure by which he tested how a subject would act in a situation where a conflict occurred between, on the one hand, the cherished value of being humane and, on the other hand, the value of scientific inquiry.

Volunteers were ordered to administer increasingly severe shocks to a "victim." The volunteers were misled to believe the shocks were real and a necessary feature of an experiment purporting to study something about the laws of learning. The "shocks" were in thirty graded steps, from one labeled "slight shock (15 volts)" to one designated "Danger—severe shock (450 volts)." Of the forty subjects, twenty-six or 65 percent obeyed the experimenter and continued to administer these "shocks" to a person to the end of the series of thirty. The experimenter had no explicit power to enforce his request that the subject continue for the sake of the study. Many subjects revealed intense strain and expressed strong disapproval against "shocking" the "victim," who was instructed to pound heavily on the door of his cubicle after the 300-volt "shock" point was reached. There was much pounding, but the majority of subjects continued to obey the instructions. After the experiment ended many obedient subjects mopped their brows and showed other signs of nervousness. A few, of course, were cool throughout it all.

Dr. Milgram introduced his report with a brief reflection on the horrors of concentration camps, horrors rationalized by the perpetrators in the name of obedience to higher authority. Cruelty and sadism, we hardly need remind ourselves, are a bloody theme throughout history, so it may be that this segment of adult Americans has only a primer coating of civility and the grain of meanness can emerge under the proper encouragement. The most pessimistic of a group of Yale seniors, who were told of the experimental design and were asked to predict the results, quite naïvely guessed that only about 3 percent of the subjects would continue giving shocks to the end. This may be seen as evidence of the degree to which some young Americans deny latent hostility. However, an interpretation of the results must also take into account the auspices under which the experiment was done. In Dr. Milgram's words:

1) The experiment is sponsored by and takes place on the grounds of an institution of unimpeachable reputation, Yale University. It may be reasonably presumed that the personnel are competent and reputable. . .

2) The experiment is, on the face of it, designed to attain a worthy

purpose—advancement of knowledge about learning and memory. Obedience occurs not as an end in itself, but as an instrumental element in a
situation the subject construes as significant, and meaningful. He may
not be able to see its full significance, but he may properly assume the
experimenter does.[5]

Other explanations offered by Dr. Milgram referred to features of
the experimental method, such as the fact that the subject understood the "victim" to be a volunteer who became the "victim" only
because he drew the wrong lot.

Dr. Milgram did not discuss the ethics of lying to the subjects and
then making it possible to put them through an experience which for
many was extraordinarily upsetting. This fact itself underlines the
priestly authority of the scientist, who isn't inhibited from violating
the value of honesty in the name of the value: knowledge about obedience. From this point of view, Dr. Milgram and his colleagues are
not different from their subjects. All are found to be culpable in their
faith in the scientific laboratory as the source of truth.

It has been difficult to accept the fact that the laboratory is prone
to be infected by the mysteries of faith revealed in a wide variety of
beliefs not only in false gods but in the "true" ones of science. This
grows out of the erroneous notion that fact and value, belief and
reason, faith and empirical evidence are quite separable. The laboratory relation and the therapeutic relation are based to a considerable
extent on the development of a consensus between experimenter-
therapist and subject-patient. This consensus is now recognized to
reflect values and a basic faith in the meaningfulness of research-
clinical transactions. Open-minded clinicians are supposed to be critical of the hidden bias of the therapeutic relationship. And now
"pure" scientists must also account for their results in terms of
values and the hidden impacts, or demands, which the experimenter
makes on the subject. In a recent view of the laboratory experimenter's meaning to his subjects Dr. McGuigan could have been
writing a report of therapy cases when he concluded:

While it is not possible to adequately specify the experimenter's characteristics in the report of the experiment, it should be recognized that
this inability does not remove the problem—it persists and for a worker
in a particular area the question of generalization, from a single experiment, can assume nightmarish proportions.[6]

Dr. Milgram's subjects and Dr. Orne's students are like all our ancestors, who in a time of suffering turned in faith to the man in the community designated the medicine man. Arthur Shapiro reviewed the history of the so-called placebo effect in the practice of medicine. He recounted for us that up until very recent times most of the drugs in the physician's pharmacopoeia were noxious or inert and thus could not by themselves have had the physiological effects which for hundreds of years were ascribed to them. Medicine as a scientific discipline in Western society would have disappeared but for the prestige of the doctor and the faith placed in him. Many patients swore by the prescriptions and got well, though many also died. The placebo is now intentionally used in general medicine and often enough in psychotherapy.[7] Given with confidence, a placebo will work, while a potent drug may not when given by a physician who dispenses it to the patient as he dispenses a tranquilizer. This is the placebo effect in reverse. When the physician conveys a sense of the worthwhileness of the prescription, the medication works much better. The relationship makes the difference.

After the initial excitement over the hallucinogenic drugs such as mescaline, which are potent drugs indeed, the compiled reports add up to the same point. Sanford Unger reviewed the literature on the clinical and experimental use of these drugs and quoted a number of reports by the drug takers themselves. As potent as the drugs were in creating all sorts of ecstatic and terrifying experiences, the particular qualities of the drug session also depended on the attitude of the experimenter who administered the drug. The skeptical researcher found many more takers of the drugs reporting severe distress and nearly intolerable fright while enthusiasts claimed the drug session transported the imbiber on a magic carpet to the pleasure dome of Kubla Khan and back.[8]

In an attempt to correct for the distortions of an overtrusting attitude, the rationalist became himself a blind believer in his reasoning. Of course, a credulous person can become a victim of any popular philosophy, including those of scientific psychotherapists, and such a patient must be confronted with his gullibility. But who can adequately make a clear distinction between a gullible individual and an awe-struck person open to the wonders of others? Who is to be given the authority to distinguish between the articles of faith called blind and the articles of trust called confidence? I think these distinctions should be made only on the basis of as full as possible a disclosure of the qualities of the relations between any two persons and not be left to the decision of one. As I have stressed throughout, obedience and rebellion are twins. Where there is blind faith, there is likely to be passive resistance. It is thus not the terms by themselves which differentiate one relation from another, but the ways in which the twin processes of faith and reason are revealed between persons.

Through the wisdom of hindsight, the apparent conflict between faith and reason also may have been a semantic one. The leaders of the psychological revolution proclaimed the events in the nursery as the fateful ones. The more the life of the child with his parents was investigated, the more important seemed to be his earliest relation to his mother. Freud called the first year or so of existence the oral period. This label conveyed a tone of sober neutrality and medical objectivity. Melanie Klein was not content with this nomenclature, and she saw the child in the first year of life as in a depressive-paranoidal position. The infant was essentially possessed by the de-sire to swallow his mother and the fear that he would be devoured. Her tone was alarmist. Erich Fromm, who has been accused of being an optimist, emphasized the receptivity of the infant's orientation to his mother. All the authorities whose views derive from the psycho-analytic image of human nature commonly accented the negative aspects of early childhood.

This did serve as a useful corrective to the pre-twentieth-century notions of childhood innocence and plasticity. But the corrective tended to go too far. The infant's active cooperation with his mother was relatively overlooked. The mother's dependence on the child was underplayed. The child's capacity for saying no to his "omnipo-tent" parents was recognized but not given its proper value in de-scriptions of the earliest years of life.[9]

Among the reasons for Erikson's highly deserved acclaim is the way he has revised the psychoanalytic theory of libidinal develop-ment. He has correlated the concept of maturation, and its emphasis on an orderly sequence of inevitable stages, with the cultural and familial influences on our lives. Erikson distinguished eight stages and gave them the following headings: trust vs. basic mistrust, au-tonomy vs. shame and doubt, initiative vs. guilt, industry vs. inferiority, identity vs. role diffusion, intimacy vs. isolation, generativity vs. stagnation and, the last stage, ego integrity vs. despair. Erikson emphasized that growth from one stage to another *does not* mean that the developmental issues of the previous stage are left behind. Rather they are reworked and re-expressed in different forms in succeeding stages, whose unique developmental tasks call for this reworking. The transactional quality of all social relations through all periods of life makes it possible to redeem part of what has been sorely missed in the past. When he described the first stage of life and called it the period of trust vs. basic mistrust, he focused our attention on the essential equality of giving and receiving that marks even the earliest relation between child and parent.

Erikson emphasized, as did others, that the growth in the infant of a faith and trust that life makes sense depended on the quality of the care given to him by the mother. However, in turn, the mother can do this only if she feels herself to be trustworthy. She acquires this feeling not only through the experiences of her own infancy but also from the web of relations called the culture and its "life style." Faith is ever renewable through the pattern of relations which emerges and makes reasonable sense to both parties in the relation. When the reasonableness of experience is weakened, then faith in the harmony of life is eroded. When one's trust is met with articulated trust and with communicated but not necessarily spoken reasonableness, faith is not blind.

If we think of reason as referring only to verbalized experience and only to those data which scientific study can categorize and measure, then the infant's private experience of his particular relation to his mother is unreasonable. If reason is thought of as dealing only with the universal and the abstract, then faith, when expressed in a particular way, is not reasonable. But what if we began with a faith in the reasonableness of the heart? This is the faith which brings behavioral scientists to study the patterns of mothering and then communicate to us the reasonableness of such qualities as warmth, acceptance, grace, forgiveness and trust. The poets sing their songs and the scientists prosaically lecture, and they meet at the center of experience where an intuitive grasp of reality is as meaningful as a logical description of the recipe for the good life. It is a blind faith, too, which refuses to conclude that the evidence of a suffering and bestial world is reason enough to die. How often has the following story told me by Dr. Leo Srole been repeated in the lives of those who have survived the horrors of persecution?

"There is the testimony of a woman in a concentration camp. Having passed the limits of her endurance, she lapsed into the apathy of passive suicide that was certain to carry her to the gas chamber. A transport arrived with new prisoners and in it was a childhood girl friend. The restored friendship revived her energies, her will to live, and she survived!"

Insofar as any person's faith leads him to disparage the faith of others then he justifies the attacks leveled against men of faith by those who extol reason. He who appears righteously certain about his own position must condemn others for the errors in their ways. But men of reason know that this kind of faith is just the attitude of the fanatic answering his own nagging doubt rather than the reasonings of others. The intolerant have never themselves experienced adequate tolerance.

The proper blend between faith and doubt and between commitment and open-minded questioning is a lofty attainment. It is a first goal of any educational relationship. It is at the heart of the scientific outlook and in the "mind" of an ecumenical theology. Whether we approach an analysis of a situation from the side of naïve faith or from the perspective of coolheaded contemplation, we are soon thrust to the other side of reality if we are not to become sterile through cold abstraction or exhausted by incomprehensible bombast. Coolheaded men are faithfully committed men, unless they are faking it and unless they deny the necessity of maintaining a vigilance over the misuse of reason through the denial of skepticism. Gardner Murphy concluded his great work on *Personality* with a chapter on "The Skeptical Psychologist." The last lines of this chapter are:

But like our predecessors, we shall rectify mistakes not primarily by the minor readjustment of the lines of the argument but by recognition of the fundamental limitations of the whole present system of conceptions. It is preparation for this destruction and rebirth of knowledge to which serious research should be directed.[10]

All the work from the psychological laboratory and all the evidence from therapeutic relations require that faith be accompanied by a reasonable doubt and that reason be accompanied by a valued skepticism.

Faith in the present is realized and justified in the meaningful communion of mutual revelation. Faith in the past is the experience of trusting the feelings and giving life to a remembered relationship. Faith in the future is the security that, come what may, there will be further revelation. The difference between faith and reason is no longer that between rival ways to apprehend the truth. The difference is in the particular content of the relationship in which meaning is sought.

Relativity of judgment rests on the objective historical evidence that "truth" unfolds itself and that we are always limited in what we can know by our nature, our person and our time and place. Those with whom we choose to converse and who, whether we like it or not, confront us with our own being define for us our faith and our reason.

17

THE REALITY OF SELF

IS IN RELATIONS

The patient says, "I feel poorly and I want to do something about it." The therapist answers in effect, "I will try to help you change your image of yourself." The stress is on the I, the self, the ego, personal identity. The self has become the key concept in all theories of personality and is conceived of as the organizer of experience.

Throughout this volume I have repeatedly emphasized the interactional quality of therapy and all our involvements. It follows from this view that I would define the self in the following way. The self is a more or less fluid patterning of a diversity of relations at the core of which lies a relation to the unknown—sometimes called God, sometimes mystery, sometimes creativity, sometimes the future. Whether we can observe it or not, the self is always involved in some exchange with another identity, and thus the "only" reality is in relations. (I place the "only" in quotes to remind myself not to sound dogmatic at the very moment that I am criticizing other theoretical systems for suggesting their system is the best.)

We are brought up in a society with a democratic ideology. We are trained to speak of individual rights, responsibilities and personal freedom. We emphasize self-actualization and self-fulfillment, terms favored by the large majority of clinicians and psychologists stressing growth and change. If I question the reality of the self and stress that the I is real only when experienced as a part of a relation, does this reduce personal responsibility and lead toward communal control? Do I not befuddle the person when I say, "You need to learn to see how you go about making choices," and then question the reality of the "you" apart from the other?

The answer to these questions appears so obvious that it seems to make them ridiculous. Do not our senses affirm the reality of the discreet organism and does not an increased awareness also lead to the apparently inevitable conclusion reached by Descartes: "Thinking so, I am so"? The impressive creative experience seems so obviously a unique coming forth of a singular being that it seizes us by surprise and we stand for the moment in isolated awe of the other. Leadership, for instance, is the trait of an individual who has differentiated himself from others and can maintain his stance independently of those who attempt to divert him from his vision and his ideals.

Existential philosophies accent the individual standing alone, as do psychologists with a humanistic emphasis. A few quotations from Abraham Maslow illustrate the radical delineation of the lone ego. In discussing existential psychology he wrote: "To me it means essentially a radical stress on the concept of identity and the experience of identity as a sine qua non of human nature and of any philosophy or science of human nature." And by identity Dr. Maslow meant: "There is no place else to turn but inward, to the self as the locus of values."[1]

The language used by Dr. Maslow and other humanistic psychologists places the emphasis on the independent self. Psychologists first employed the term "self" as an alternative to the mystical and nonempirical soul. For the theologian, the soul was and still is in an ultimate relation to God. But long before God was pronounced dead by some theologians, the question of an ultimate relation to an Unknown was solved by psychologists in the simplest fashion. They ignored the matter. The self thus appeared to be in an ultimate relation to itself. The unknown and unknowable appeared to be denied.

This has been the essence of the critique leveled against Western systems of psychotherapy and psychology by students of Eastern modes of defining reality. Alan Watts in his forceful presentation of

Zen Buddhism as a way toward harmony centered his fire on the concept of the self or the ego as a reality.

In sum, then, the Buddhist discipline is to realize that anguish or conflict arises from the grasping of entities singled out from the world by ignorance—grasping in the sense of acting or feeling toward them as if they were actually independent of context. This sets in motion the samsara or vicious circle of trying to solve the false problem of wresting life from death, pleasure from pain, good from evil, and self from not self, in short, to get one's ego permanently "one-up" on life. But through meditation discipline the student finds out that he cannot stop this grasping so long as he thinks of himself as the ego which can either act or refrain from acting.[2]

The inextricable involvement of ego and cosmos as defined by Buddhism appears to lead to a passive acceptance of the status quo, which is, I think, a fair criticism of any de-emphasis of social progress. But the Zen views on the reality of relation can provide a corrective to the usual Western emphasis on man for himself.[3]

Unfortunately, we have not yet developed an adequate language which directly denotes qualities of relatedness.[4] Our vocabulary befits our concept that reality resides in singularity and individuality. Plural pronouns are insufficient because they do not contain the sense of bipolar tension between two identities, neither of which is an identity without the other. The word "marriage" is an interactional concept, but it is also an abstract category which is made a little more concrete by using the words "husband-wife." Hyphenations of nouns such as doctor-patient or helper-helpee are clumsy, though they accent the interdependence of the two parties. Our attention to the singularity of the terms "father," "mother," "soul," etc., can be used to embellish the experience of relation if we do not ignore that, in the terms of Gestalt theory, one is figure to the ground of another and no one can be a figure without a ground.

Among the possible interpretations of the relative absence from our language of words denoting relationships, I already have suggested two interrelated ones. I have stressed the difference between the experience of the observer as he contemplates an inanimate object and his experience as he tries to grasp his involvement with life. I have tried to show that the social scientist in effect has tried to suppress his participation in the very events he is studying by adopting the position of an inspector of matter toward which he can be cool and neutral.

However, I think the basic reason for the vocabulary gap is the fact that throughout human history social arrangements have been based on degradation and exploitation. In a hierarchical arrangement each unit in the pecking order tends to be perceived by the unit above or below as an object to be exploited and used or obeyed and feared. The ideal of equality has moved men to revolt against the use of men as machines. The slogans of the libertarians—"man for himself," "the rights of the individual," "man stands alone," etc.—are cries of protest expressing the utopian idea that we need not accept the tragedies of history as inevitable.

Today humanistic social scientists extend the democratic aspirations of the downtrodden by studying and extolling "the actualization of the individual," a phrase first used by Karl Marx in the 1850's. The protest against domination by overwhelming powers leading to a man's despair and alienation from other men has been grandly etched for us by Kafka in *The Trial*. The hero asserts his only and final choice in the face of the nameless blind forces who will destroy him: he refuses to commit suicide when he is given this option to avoid being executed.

Does this emphasis on personal freedom as the alternative to life as a dependent automaton lead to rank individualism? A patient once wrote: "As long as I feel the burden of comfort and support for my total life is almost totally on my shoulders, it is very easy for this individualism to be blind to anyone else." Is this what is happening to all of us? Simone de Beauvoir believes that personal freedom and self-transcendence are conditions which require each other. The existentialist stress on freedom is individualistic

. . . if one means by that that it accords to the individual an absolute value and that it recognizes in him alone the power of laying the foundations of his own existence. It is individualism in the sense in which the wisdom of the ancients, the Christian ethics of salvation, and the Kantian ideal of virtue also merit this name; it is opposed to the totalitarian doctrines which raise up beyond man the mirage of Mankind. But it is not solipsistic, since the individual is defined only by his relationship to the world and to other individuals; he exists only by transcending himself, and his freedom can be achieved only through the freedom of others. He justifies his existence by a movement which, like freedom, springs from his heart but which leads outside of him.[5]

Personal freedom cannot be experienced without a transcendence of the self. A creative act, whether it be a work of art, a love affair or a leap of the imagination that correlates the movement of planets and the fall of an apple, is the actualization of a capacity to differentiate that which is novel from the same old thing. The feeling of freedom arises when we suddenly experience that a differentiation has been made—a change which, wrought out of the morass of similarity, is celebrated in a relation.

Another principle of the humanistic tradition revived in present-day psychology is: "Discover your true nature!" This appeal to authenticity finds a receptive albeit anxious ear. The urge to shed our sham, I think, is never squashed. Tolstoy's Ivan Ilyitch can die peacefully only when he has honestly penetrated the lies about him and within him. I think the wish to be one's self precedes the wish to be by oneself since the latter largely arises when the former is blunted by another's domination. Yet recognition of this "eternal" longing, given its lyrical voice in the romantic tradition, should not obscure the fact that our personal history is a development in which potential is always in a process of actualization through interaction with others.

The lesson of human development is that from birth to death man is always becoming a complexity of relationships. The self is a more or less fluid patterning of relationships whose change or permanence depends on the stability of the relationship of which the person is a part. Before birth there are the parents. Behind them and backward through eternal time there is the mystery of creation, again experienced by the new organism growing through the mother-child pair. Without nurture death ensues or the lingering death of bland memory. At the other end of life there is the unknown, even if we have no belief in any kind of afterlife.

At the moment just preceding bodily death our relation to all others is infinitely complicated because we cannot know in the next moment anything more of what our remembrances mean. A person never dies alone unless he is stillborn, and then he is not yet a person. When he is alive, his experience is dependent not only on traits under his skin but upon the qualities of the field of transaction in which he is only a nodal point. The person who appears completely alone may be a hermit in the wilds of the woods, but he is in communion with memories, nature and his God. The person who feels completely alone and has lost hope of a relation will become a patient in the back wards of the mental hospital or a suicide.

There is no "nature" which is true apart from the social milieu in which the individual acts. When we speak of a secure person, an adult who is "self-actualizing" and relatively independent of the vast majority of other individuals, we are also speaking of a child whose parents accepted him as a separate individual. It was in relation to them that he learned the difference between separateness and rejection. The organismic will, the restless movement of a unique organism becoming a person, has been received by the parents as a treasured gift to .be returned. The person with a strong ego who actualizes his potential cannot become so without the affirmation of "significant others." And, furthermore, he cannot continue to affirm his creative possibilities unless he finds at least one other person who continues to affirm his being.

In my emphasis on a conception of the relatedness of the individual person, I am in agreement with theological criticism of the humanistic notion of man standing alone. If we get beneath the tendency of religious people who, in their denominationalism, equate the creative force in the universe with their particular image of God, we can recognize an "eternal truth." The borderline between what is already given and what is novel is a mystery through which we must pass at some considerable risk to previously attained harmony. When we successfully pass through this crisis of integrity, we feel in touch with something beyond ourselves. We are not alone then. Someone in the past or present is with us. Only when we fail to pass do we experience the despair of an isolated being. A successful integration is accompanied by a feeling of gratitude to whatever it was in the unknown that gave us life. Without gratitude, we become proud and arrogantly hide our despair. We proclaim that the movement onto a new level of reality is all an illusion, just a trick of the imagination.

18

RECITATIVE

The patient and I are up against the systems which have made us human. We are enmeshed in the biological and social heritages which have given us substance and form, and yet we hope to be free from them. We try to speak wisely of our limitations rather than ignore them. Through the knowledge and interpretation of revealed experience we hope to transcend those memories that have imprisoned us. Yet we also know, somehow, that the simple folklore printed in desk calendars and in almanacs often expresses the sense of life both of us labor so hard with our erudite language to infuse into the stories of our sufferings and achievements. And yet we go on. If we make a good compact, the patient's life becomes a surprise and a novelty. If we don't, the routine of systems grinds even more deeply into his every moment and makes him extol the rare inconsequential events which are bound to break the monotony of anyone's day and night.

Both of us know within our respective capacities for poetry that sensitivity to the tragic ways in life gives us the power to transform the inevitable into a lesson which somehow, through an act of faith, brings us into a new relationship. We know that what we might find is nothing so new that it cannot be categorized as the quest for love in mortal existence. The poets and the artists and the faithful believers have told us over and over again that each of us seeks a way back from being on the outside and from having fallen into our private purgatory. The divine comedy is in this life, and it is made our own only through the terribly powerful and exalted force of personal example. Nothing is new under the sun but that which comes from encounter and engagement between man and man.

Why is it, we ask each other, that until our suffering is shared we feel we haven't really, *really* met? We repeat "really" as if the word might produce the reality we are striving for. In the office the patient and I assume that if he feels I have met him, understood him, liked him and accepted him, he will take this as a believer takes grace, as something of divine inspiration, to be given in turn to others. Can that really happen in a situation which is itself beset by rituals and techniques, artificial limitations and separations, and those compromises which paradoxically make it possible for us to go on together? I always am surprised when I sense that the patient and I have deeply met, partly because his tears or laughter, as expected as they are, accompany a story I never heard before. And partly I am surprised that it occurs at all, even though it has occurred before with him and with others. I must be a visionary to believe there is more to this person than he has yet unfolded. I must be an idealist to believe in what he is doing to care for his lives by coming to see me. I must be a moralist in the prophetic tradition to assume the guise of the healer and presume I have something to say which will enlighten his life. And yet I must be concerned with his concern with the everyday concrete sensations of existence; indeed, I often must show him the celebration in everyday life.

Writ large, the words "brotherhood" and "universal love" are the hollowest of hypocrisies, which in the moment of their exposure cannot be ameliorated by the justifications of human imperfection, realistic aims and the slow march of progress. Yet the patient and I must believe in the possibility of making something better and reaching another in love even as our daily lives belie this ideal. A man immolates himself and wants us to believe that it is his protest against the violation of the commandment, "Thou shalt not kill." We who are singed daily cannot precipitously dismiss this suicide as evidently pathologic or patently inspired by revelation. We may see him as a deluded victim, but he is also an extreme instance of what we may risk when we try to give destiny a meaning different from what we are informed it has and should have.

The older I have become and the longer I have plied my trade and practiced my profession, the more I have become a believer in some kind of worship. I ask the patient if he is properly worshipful, and I think he is when he says, "I look forward to going to my friend," or when he says, "I look forward to meeting my brothers in church." It doesn't matter to me whether he calls himself a Christian, a humanist or a Jew as long as he can unreservedly tell me, "I look forward to what I have planned to do or what will happen." Not all the time, of course, but much of the time. To be able to look forward unreservedly and not turn away from the unexpected is much of what I hope for. And for those who say they can't, I have been taught to request of them to look back.

The thrust of social history has been described as the unfolding of the human species' capacity for increasing awareness. And in the last sixty-odd years this movement toward awareness has expressed itself in the examination of our own personal histories. Autobiography has become more than chronology of actions observed by others. It is today the confessions of our inner actions which no one can know, including the dreamer, until he has confessed. And our history is then mainly the history of our relation to our parents, our relatives, and then to all our friends, teachers and acquaintances. So to look forward I ask the person to look back and learn to do so with interest and not pain, with ease and not effort.

NOTES

Chapter 1: On Schools and Systems

1. M. I. Stein, *Contemporary Psychotherapies*, New York, Free Press, 1961.
2. R. A. Harper, *Psychoanalysis and Psychotherapy: 36 Systems*, Englewood Cliffs, New Jersey, Prentice-Hall, 1959.
3. D. Hammarskjöld, *Markings*, New York, Alfred A. Knopf, 1964, p. 155.

Chapter 2: Out of the Inner Sanctum

1. S. Freud, *The Future of an Illusion*, New York, Liveright, 1953.
2. S. Freud, "Analysis Terminable and Interminable," *Collected Papers*, Vol. V, London, Hogarth Press, 1953, p. 353.
3. C. Rogers, *Client-Centered Therapy*, Boston, Houghton Mifflin Co., 1951.
4. W. Schofield, *The Purchase of Friendship*, Englewood Cliffs, New Jersey, Prentice-Hall, 1964.
5. Some of the evidence for this will be discussed in Chapter 14, "Are Therapists Successful?"
6. M. Lorr, "Relation of Treatment Frequency and Duration to Psychotherapeutic Outcome," in H. H. Strupp, and L. Luborsky, eds., *Research in Psychotherapy*, Washington, American Psychological Association, 1962, pp. 134–141. Dr. Lorr's chapter is a review of studies on this question.
7. J. Shlein, "Toward What Level of Abstraction in Criteria?," in Strupp and Luborsky, *op. cit.*, pp. 142–154.
8. D. R. Stieper and D. N. Wiener, *Dimensions of Psychotherapy*, Chicago, Aldine Publishing Co., 1965.
9. G. W. Allport, "The Right to Be Believed," in S. J. Beck and H. G. Mollit, eds., *Reflexes to Intelligence*, New York, Free Press, 1959, p. 10.
10. The very rapid growth in the treatment of whole families is a recent and useful development. Interestingly enough, this approach has grown out of efforts to help people of low socioeconomic status. Its use in private practice lags far behind. Among others, see N. W. Ackerman, *The Psychodynamics of Family Life*, New York, Basic Books, 1958.

CHAPTER 3: KEEPING THE DOOR OPEN

1. Hardly a day goes by in which the New York Times does not carry an item on the legal problems of privacy. A recent discussion of this value in our society with particular reference to psychological and social research is to be found in The American Psychologist, May 1966.

2. See the discussion of this issue as it pertains to classical psychoanalysis in T. Szasz, "The Problem of Privacy in Training Analysis," Psychiatry, 25, 1962, 195–207.

3. The radical emphasis throughout on self-revelation as the therapist's responsibility as well as the patient's is implied by the work of, among others, S. M. Jourard, The Transparent Self, Princeton, New Jersey, D. Van Nostrand, 1964.

4. L. Binswanger, "The Case of Ellen West," in R. May et al., Existence, New York, Basic Books, pp., 308–309. I am puzzled when I read such proponents of the existentialist approach as Dr. Binswanger and Dr. Rollo May. They describe the dilemmas of their patients in existential terminology but at the same time omit their own struggles with "being and nothingness." An outstanding exception to this generalization is Viktor Frankl. In his Man's Search for Meaning, New York, Washington Square Press, 1965, his own three years in the hell of concentration camps became a basis for his approach to despair this side of death.

5. Some other illegal acts about which therapists learn and on which they take a position, implicitly or explicitly, are collusion in divorce cases, the taking and selling of marijuana and abortion.

6. O. H. Mowrer, "Payment or Repayment? The Problem of Private Practice," American Psychologist, 18, 1963, 519.

7. P. Tillich, The Shaking of the Foundations, New York, Charles Scribner's Sons, 1948; also The Courage To Be, New Haven, Yale University Press, 1952.

8. C. A. Whittaker and T. P. Malone, The Roots of Psychotherapy, New York, Blakiston, 1953.

CHAPTER 4: INTO THE WORLD AT LARGE

1. M. R. Stein, The Eclipse of Community, Princeton, New Jersey, Princeton University Press, 1960.

2. T. Szasz, and R. A. Nemiroff, "A Questionnaire Study of Psychoanalytic Practices and Opinions," Journal of Nervous and Mental Diseases, 137, 1963, 209–221.

3. The evidence that even the therapist's gestures and physiological activity are correlated with the patient's is accumulating. See, among others, J. I. Lacey, "Psychophysiological Approaches to the Evaluation of Psychotherapeutic Process and Outcome," in E. Rubinstein and M. B. Parloff, Research in Psychotherapy, Washington, American Psychological Association, 1959, pp. 169–179. See also A. E. Sheflen, "Communication and Regulation in Psychotherapy," Psychiatry, 26, 1963, 126–135.

4. W. Bonime, The Clinical Use of Dreams, New York, Basic Books, 1962.

5. C. Hall, The Meaning of Dreams, New York, Harper & Bros., 1953.

6. W. Bonime, op. cit., pp. 237–238.

7. See, among others, G. Zilboorg, Psychoanalysis and Religion, New York, Farrar, Straus & Cudahy, 1962.

8. H. D. Lasswell, *Psychopathology and Politics*, Chicago, University of Chicago Press, 1930. Of the many others, T. W. Adorno *et al.*, *The Authoritarian Personality*, New York, Harper & Bros., 1950, is the most comprehensive and seminal.

9. E. Erikson, *Young Man Luther*, New York, W. W. Norton, 1958.

10. See, for example, F. Riesman, *et al.*, *Mental Health of the Poor*, New York, Free Press, 1964.

CHAPTER 5: SUFFERING: REMEDIABLE AND NOT

1. P. Goodman, *Growing Up Absurd*, New York, Random House, 1960.

2. I. Bieber *et al.*, *Homosexuals and Their World*, New York, Basic Books, 1962. See also J. Marmor, ed., *Sexual Inversion*, New York, Basic Books, 1965.

3. D. Thomas, *Collected Poems*, New York, New Directions, 1957, p. 128.

4. See *Daedalus: Journal of the American Academy of Arts and Sciences*, Summer 1965.

5. Josephine Hilgard *et al.*, "Strength of Adult Ego Following Childhood Bereavement," *American Journal of Orthopsychiatry*, 30, 1960, 788–798.

6. B. Steinzor, "On Faith, Doubt and Suffering," *Journal of Religion and Mental Health*, 4, 1965, 119–145.

7. R. W. White, "Motivation Reconsidered: The Concept of Competence," *Psychological Review*, 66, 1959, 297–333. Dr. White reviews the theories of human drives and the research on them, and makes an excellent argument for stressing the significance of the need to be effective.

8. N. L. Farberow, and E. S. Schneidman, eds., *The Cry for Help*, New York, McGraw-Hill, 1961; also E. S. Schneidman and N. L. Farberow, eds., *Clues to Suicide*, New York, McGraw-Hill, 1957.

9. K. Eissler, *The Psychiatrist and the Dying Patient*, New York, International University Press, 1955.

CHAPTER 6: JOY, CELEBRATION AND PLAYFULNESS

1. See J. R. Warren, "Birth Order and Social Behavior," *Psychological Bulletin*, 65, 1966, 38–49. This fine review also discusses the evidence tending to support the hypothesis that oldest children are more conforming than siblings.

2. S. Potter, *Lifemanship*, New York, Henry Holt & Co., 1950.

CHAPTER 7: EQUALITY BETWEEN PATIENT AND THERAPIST

1. T. Szasz, *The Myth of Mental Illness*, New York, Harper & Bros., 1962, pp. 296, 251. Among others writing in a similar vein, see P. London, *The Modes and Morals of Psychotherapy*, New York, Holt, Rinehart & Winston, 1964.

2. J. H. Masserman, "Comments on Kiev's 'The Study of Folk Psychiatry,'" *International Journal of Psychiatry*, 1, 1965, 552.

3. Euripides, *The Phoenician Maidens*. Translated by A. S. Way, Loeb Classical Library Edition. Reprinted by permission of Harvard University Press. See the interesting book by G. C. Abernathy, *Equality: An Anthology*, Richmond, Virginia, John Knox, 1959. A. de Tocqueville had much to say about equality in his classic study, *Democracy in America*. Among other points, he linked the ideal of equality with the idea of infinite perfectibility.

4. E. Erikson, *Childhood and Society*, New York, W. W. Norton, 1950.

5. P. Aries, *Centuries of Childhood*, New York, Alfred A. Knopf, 1962. This

is a fascinating and startling book. Aries shows us that the idea of the child as a person in his own terms is a modern idea.

6. U. G. Foa, "Convergences in the Analysis of the Structure of Interpersonal Behavior," *Psychological Review*, 68, 1961, 341–353.

7. M. Jones, *The Therapeutic Community*, New York, Basic Books, 1953.

8. C. C. Jung, *The Practice of Psychotherapy*, New York, Pantheon Books, 1954, pp. 5 and 18.

9. P. Tournier, *The Meaning of Persons*, New York, Harper & Bros., 1957, p. 135.

10. D. Hammarskjöld, op. cit., p. 174.

11. J. P. Spiegel, "Some Cultural Aspects of Transference and Counter-transference," in F. Riesman et al., op. cit., p. 318.

12. R. M. Williams, *Strangers Next Door*, Englewood Cliffs, New Jersey, Prentice-Hall, 1964

CHAPTER 8: SELF-KNOWLEDGE OR REVELATION OF SELVES

1. W. Wolff, "Fact and Value in Psychotherapy," *American Journal of Psychotherapy*, 8, 1954, 466–486.

2. S. Freud, "Sexuality in the Aetiology of the Neuroses" (1898), in *Collected Papers*, Vol. I, London, Hogarth Press, 1953, p. 228.

3. C. Rogers, op. cit., p. 29.

4. See C. B. Truax, "Reinforcement and Nonreinforcement in Rogerian Psychotherapy," *Journal of Abnormal Psychology*, 71, 1966, 1–9. The research demonstrates the directiveness in nondirective treatment.

5. A. N. Whitehead, *Religion in the Making*, New York, Meridian Books, 1960, p. 127.

CHAPTER 9: HOW THE THERAPIST'S SYSTEM CORNERS THE PATIENT

1. G. Bateson et al., "Towards a Theory of Schizophrenia," *Behavioral Science*, 1, 1956, 251–264.

2. See J. Haley, *Strategies of Psychotherapy*, New York, Grune & Stratton, 1963, for another account of cornering in therapy.

3. E. J. Shoben, "A Clinical View of the Tragic," *Journal of Social Issues*, 20, 1964, 29.

4. H. Strupp, "The Therapist's Contribution to the Treatment Process," in H. Strupp and L. Luborsky, eds., op. cit., p. 31.

5. See D. Bakan, "The Mystery-Mastery Complex in Contemporary Psychology," *American Psychologist*, 20, 1965, 186–191.

6. A. Watts, *Psychotherapy East and West*, New York, Mentor Books, 1963, pp. 124 and 126.

CHAPTER 10: THE DEFACEMENT OF PERSONS: TRANSFERENCES AND FIGURES

1. R. Grinker, "A Transactional Model for Psychotherapy," in M. Stein, op. cit., p. 192.

2. See Ernest Jones's three-volume biography, *The Life and Work of Sigmund Freud*, Vol. II, Chapter 6, "The Committee," New York, Basic Books, 1953. The man I'm referring to is Dr. Max Eitigon. My own analyst's name is available on request, as is the length of time I lay on the couch.

3. E. Erikson, *Young Man Luther*, op. cit., p. 19.

4. I will in a later chapter refer to a paper by Richard Solomon on "Punishment" which deals with the literature on animal studies. He points out the many exceptions to the idea that only reward facilitates learning. See also the review by W. A. Kennedy and H. C. Willcut, "Praise and Blame as Incentives," *Psychological Bulletin*, 62, 1964, 323-332. This paper concerns itself with humans.

5. See the two very fine papers by Isidor Chein and Henry A. Murray on "Man and Satan," *Journal of Social Issues*, 18, 1962, No. 4.

6. S. E. Hyman's thesis in his *The Tangled Bank* is that the influence of Darwin, Marx, Frager and Freud was their power as imaginative writers.

7. H. Meng and E. Freud, eds., *The Letters of Sigmund Freud and Oskar Pfister*, New York, Basic Books, 1963, p. 35, June 1910. There are a number of interesting analytic studies of Freud. Maryse Choisy maintains, in her *Sigmund Freud: A New Appraisal*, New York, Citadel Press, 1963, that Freud had a lifelong anxiety about dying and correlates this with his theories.

8. T. Szasz, "The Concept of Transference," *International Journal of Psychoanalysis*, 44, 1963, 442.

9. T. Szasz, *Pain and Pleasure: A Study of Bodily Feelings*, New York, Basic Books, 1957.

10. In his *The Problem of Lay Analysis*, New York, Brentano, 1927, Freud argued against the idea that analysis was a medical treatment and therefore must be done by an M.D. However, the notion of the therapist as the expert judge of the complaints and the condition was taken over from medicine.

11. K. Menninger, *Theory of Psychoanalytic Technique*, New York, Basic Books, 1958, p. 86.

12. "The Concept of Transference," op. cit., p. 442.

13. L. Wolberg, *The Technique of Psychotherapy*, New York, Grune & Stratton, 1954, p. 399.

14. F. Redlich and A. Hollingshead, *Social Class and Mental Health*, New York, John Wiley & Sons, 1958.

15. R. Holt, "Ego Autonomy Re-evaluated," *International Journal of Psychoanalysis*," 46, 1965, 164.

16. S. Freud, "Analysis, Terminable and Interminable," *Collected Papers*, Vol. V, London, Hogarth Press, 1953, pp. 351-352.

17. *Young Man Luther*, op. cit., p. 125.

18. M. Buber, *I-Thou*, New York, Charles Scribner's Sons, 1958, p. 3.

CHAPTER 11: ON DREAMS

1. This was first reported in a brief piece in *Science*, 118, 1953, 273-274.

2. Books describing what we know and don't know about dreams are multiplying. See E. Diamond, *The Science of Dreams*, New York, Doubleday, 1962. See also the review by D. Foulkes, "Theories of Dream Formation and Recent Studies of Sleep Consciousness," *Psychological Bulletin*, 62, 1964, 236-247.

3. E. L. Hartmann, "The D-State," *International Journal of Psychiatry*, 2, 1966, 11-30.

4. E. Fromm, *The Forgotten Language*, New York, Grove Press, 1951, p. 33. See also T. M. French and Erika Fromm, *Dream Interpretation: A New Approach*, New York, Basic Books, 1964. They stress the integrative and problem-solving aspects of dreaming rather than the disorganized aspects.

5. See A. Siirala, *The Voice of Illness*, Philadelphia, Fortress Press, 1964.
6. E. Fromm, *op. cit.*, pp. 167–168.

CHAPTER 12: DREAMS TOLD AND UNTOLD IN THE OFFICE

1. W. Bonime, *op. cit.*, p. 10.
2. *Ibid.*, p. 124
3. E. Fromm, *op. cit.*, pp. 165 and 166.

CHAPTER 13: THE FEE AND PAYING FOR "IT"

1. "Analysis Appeals to the Educated," *New York Times*, May 2, 1964.
2. "Medicare Rules Issued to Guard Traditional Ties," *New York Times*, May 31, 1966.
3. D. N. Wiener and O. N. Raths, "Cultural Factors in Payment for Psychotherapy," *American Journal of Psychoanalysis*, 20, 1960, 66–72.
4. E. Goffman, *Asylums*, Chicago, Aldine Publishing Co., 1962, p. 327.
5. K. Menninger, *Theory of Psychoanalytic Technique*, New York, Basic Books, 1958, p. 32.
6. Frieda Fromm-Reichman, *Principles of Intensive Psychotherapy*, Chicago, University of Chicago Press, 1950, p. 67.
7. E. Glover, *The Technique of Psychoanalysis*, New York, International Universities Press, 1955. Though an orthodox analyst, Dr. Glover is refreshingly candid with patients and tells them that the time and fee setting are for the convenience of the therapist.
8. S. Freud, "Further Recommendations in the Technique of Psychoanalysis," in *Collected Papers*, Vol. II, London, Hogarth Press, 1953, pp. 342–365. In this paper Freud's views were, in retrospect, more liberal than those of a number of his followers, as was often the case.
9. J. Shlein, *op. cit.*

CHAPTER 14: ARE THERAPISTS SUCCESSFUL?

1. Marie Jahoda, *Current Concepts of Positive Mental Health*, New York, Basic Books, 1958. See also I. I. Rinder, "New Directions and an Old Problem: The Definition of Normality," *Psychiatry*, May 1964, 107–115. Of course, Thomas Szasz is at it all the time.
2. B. Berelson and G. A. Steiner, *Human Behavior: An Inventory of Scientific Findings*, New York, Harcourt, Brace & World, 1964, p. 287.
3. W. Wolff, *op. cit.*
4. H. H. W. Miles et al., "Evaluation of Psychotherapy," *Psychosomatic Medicine*, 13, 1951, 83–105. See also Chapter I of Jerome Frank's *Persuasion and Healing*, Baltimore, Johns Hopkins University Press, 1961.
5. H. J. Eysenck, "The Effects of Psychotherapy," *International Journal of Psychiatry*, 1, 1965, 97–142. All further references to Dr. Eysenck are taken from this *Journal* issue, which is largely devoted to a discussion of his paper.
6. C. Rogers and Rosalind Dymond, *Research in Psychotherapy*, Chicago, University of Chicago Press, 1954.
7. L. Breger and J. L. McGaugh, "Critique and Reformulation of 'Learning-Theory' Approaches to Psychotherapy and Neuroses," *Psychological Bulletin*, 63, 1965, 338–358. A number of discussants in the *International Journal of*

Psychiatry also expose Dr. Eysenck's bias.

8. S. Freud, "On Psychotherapy," *Collected Papers*, Vol. I, London, Hogarth Press, 1953, p. 251. Unfortunately this statement of Freud's was shoved into limbo. It took decades to bring it back into focus.

9. J. Frank, "Evaluation of Eysenck's Paper," *International Journal of Psychiatry*, 1, 1965, p. 150.

10. L. Srole *et al.*, *Mental Health in the Metropolis*, New York, McGraw-Hill, 1962.

11. G. Gurin *et al.*, *Americans View Their Mental Health*, New York, Basic Books, 1958.

12. See Dr. Meehl's discussion of Dr. Eysenck's paper in the *International Journal of Psychiatry* cited above.

13. P. H. Jacobson, *American Marriage and Divorce*, New York, Rinehart, 1959.

14. A. E. Bergin, "Some Implications of Psychotherapy Research for Therapeutic Practice," *Journal of Abnormal Psychology*, 71, 1966, 235–246.

CHAPTER 15: PSYCHOLOGICAL AND SOCIAL RESEARCH:
SCIENCE OR HUMANISTIC STUDY

1. J. Frank, *Persuasion and Healing, op. cit.*, p. 9.

2. As I was "proofing" these pages, I came across Abraham Maslow's latest work, *The Psychology of Science*, New York, Harper & Row, 1966. Here is a book which can be excellent "bibliotherapy." See, also, K. Fisher, "The Assumptions in Scientific Therapy," *Psychoanalytic Review*, 51, 1964, 85–105.

3. Clinicians also believe this. See D. McK. Rioch, "Communication in the Laboratory and Communication in the Clinic," *Psychiatry*, 26, 1963, 209–221.

4. R. L. Solomon, "Punishment," *American Psychologist*, 19, 1964, 252.

5. *Ibid.*

6. Natalie P. Chapanis and A. Chapanis, "Cognitive Dissonance: Five Years Later," *Psychological Bulletin*, 61, 1964, 20.

7. I. Silverman, "In Defense of Dissonance Theory: A Reply to Chapanis and Chapanis," *Psychological Bulletin*, 62, 1964, 205–209.

8. R. Holt, "Imagery: The Return of the Ostracized," *American Psychologist*, 19, 1964, 262.

9. M. Scriven, "Views of Human Nature," in T. W. Wann, ed., *Behaviorism and Phenomenology*, Chicago, University of Chicago Press, 1964, p. 167. This is an excellent symposium, bringing together, among others, Skinner and Rogers.

10. L. L. Whyte, *The Unconscious Before Freud*, New York, Basic Books, 1960.

11. M. Scriven, *op. cit.*, p. 168.

12. E. Nagel, *The Structure of Science*, New York, Harcourt, Brace & World, 1961. This is a worthy book, though mainly for the initiated.

13. W. Penfield and T. Rasmussen, *The Cerebral Cortex of Man*, New York, Macmillan, 1950. I sometimes say to a patient, "Why not stop our wandering in the dark and wait for some development that can unhook your short circuits?"

14. S. Koch, "Psychology and Emerging Conceptions of Knowledge as Unitary," in T. W. Wann, *op. cit.*, pp. 21–22.

15. C. Hartshorne, *Reality as Social Process*, Free Press, Glencoe, Illinois, 1953, p. 168. See also J. Huxley, "Knowledge, Morality and Destiny," *Psychiatry*, 14, 1951, 127–151.

CHAPTER 16: REASONABLE FAITH AND DEDICATED REASON

1. J. Frank, in M. Stein, *op. cit.*, p. 35. Dr. Frank led the way. But now others are following. See for example, A. Kiev, ed., *Magic, Faith and Healing*, New York, Free Press, 1964.
2. S. Freud, "On Psychotherapy," *op. cit.*, p. 250.
3. M. Orne *et al.*, "On the Social Psychology of the Psychological Experiment," *American Psychologist*, 17, 1962, 778.
4. Quoted by M. Orne, *op. cit.*, p. 776.
5. S. Milgram, "Behavioral Study of Obedience," *Journal of Abnormal and Social Psychology*, 67, 1963, 377. Diana Baumrind in the June 1964 issue of *The American Psychologist* does take Dr. Milgram to task on the issue of ethics.
6. F. J. McGuigan, "The Experimenter: A Neglected Stimulus Object," *Psychological Bulletin*, 60, 1963, 427. See also B. C. Kintz *et al.*, "The Experimenter Effect," *Psychological Bulletin*, 63, 1965, 223–232. These authors remind us of the famous case of Klüger Hans, the talking horse. He did do his sums. He picked up subtle cues from his master, who was not faking, but was unaware that he was sending signals.
7. A. K. Shapiro, "A Contribution to a History of the Placebo Effect," *Behavioral Science*, 5, 1960, 109–135.
8. S. M. Unger, "Mescalin, L.S.D., Pscilocybin and Personality Change," *Psychiatry*, 26, 1963, 111–125.
9. See Katherine Banham, "The Development of Affectionate Behavior in Infancy," *Journal of Genetic Psychology*, 76, 1950, 283–289.
10. G. Murphy, *Personality: A Biosocial Approach*, New York, Harper & Bros., 1947, p. 927.

CHAPTER 17: THE REALITY OF SELF IS IN RELATIONS

1. A. Maslow, "Existential Psychology: What's in It for Us?," in R. May, ed., *Existential Psychology*, New York, Random House, 1961, pp. 53–54.
2. A. Watts, *op. cit.*, p. 60
3. The documentation of this point is very easy. Menninger wrote *Man Against Himself*. So Fromm answered with *Man for Himself*. Even those who adhere to an interactional theory lose sight of it because of our common view of the lone ego.
4. This point is at the center of B. L. Whorf's work. See his "Language, Thought and Reality," in J. B. Carrol, ed., *Selected Writings of B. L. Whorf*, New York, John Wiley & Sons, 1956.
5. Simone De Beauvoir, *The Ethics of Ambiguity*, New York, Citadel Press, 1962, p. 156.

INDEX

[257]

ABOUT THE AUTHOR

Dr. Bernard Steinzor currently practices in New York City. A graduate of the College of the City of New York, he received his doctorate at the University of Chicago in 1947. In 1948 he became Staff Clinical Psychologist at the Menninger Clinic, and in 1950 he joined the psychology staff at Sarah Lawrence College, where he worked until 1959. During that time he held posts as Chief Clinical Psychologist at Montefiore Hospital, Consulting School Psychologist for the Westchester County Public Schools and Clinical Psychologist at the Morningside Mental Hygiene Clinic. He has also engaged in private practice since 1951. His teaching assignments have included positions at CCNY and the National Training Laboratory in Group Development. He is currently a lecturer in the Program of Psychiatry and Religion at the Union Theological Seminary. Dr. Steinzor has published several articles on various aspects of psychology.

He lives in New York City with his wife, Luciana, and their two daughters.

Format by Mort Perry
Set in Linotype Electra
Composed, printed and bound by The Haddon Craftsmen, Inc.
HARPER & ROW, PUBLISHERS, INCORPORATED